SUFFOLK RECORDS SOCIETY

SUFFOLK CHARTERS

Founding Editor
the late R. Allen Brown

XXI

THE CARTULARY AND
CHARTERS OF THE PRIORY OF
SAINTS PETER AND PAUL, IPSWICH

SUFFOLK RECORDS SOCIETY

SUFFOLK CHARTERS

ISSN 0261-9938

General Editor
Nicholas Karn

THE CARTULARY AND CHARTERS OF THE PRIORY OF SAINTS PETER AND PAUL, IPSWICH

PART II: THE CHARTERS

Edited by David Allen

The Boydell Press

Suffolk Records Society

First published 2020

Published for the Suffolk Records Society
by The Boydell Press
an imprint of Boydell & Brewer Ltd
PO Box 9, Woodbridge, Suffolk IP12 3DF, UK
and of Boydell & Brewer Inc.
668 Mt Hope Avenue, Rochester, NY 14620–2731, USA
website: www.boydellandbrewer.com

ISBN 978 1 78327 494 9

A catalogue record for this book is available
from the British Library

The publisher has no responsibility for the continued existence
or accuracy of URLs for external or third-party internet websites
referred to in this book, and does not guarantee that any content
on such websites is, or will remain, accurate or appropriate

This publication is printed on acid-free paper

Typeset by BBR Design, Sheffield
Printed and bound in Great Britain by TJ International Ltd, Padstow, Cornwall

CONTENTS

ILLUSTRATIONS

FIGURES

NOTE ON REFERENCES

Full references to works cited in Part II are to be found under Abbreviations and Bibliography in Part I, pp. viii–xiv.

ACKNOWLEDGEMENTS

The charter texts are published by kind permission of the Suffolk Record Office, Ipswich; the British Library Board; the University Librarian, the John Rylands University Library, Manchester; the National Archives, Kew; and the Bodleian Library, University of Oxford. Figure 1 is reproduced by kind permission of the Suffolk Record Office, Ipswich, and Figures 2–4 by kind permission of the National Archives. The editor wishes particularly to thank Dr Leanna Brinkley for her meticulous work in converting the indexes to electronic format.

Fig. 1 The square Romanesque font bowl of the priory church, of black Tournai marble, with a frieze of monumental lions *statant guardant*. The Perpendicular base with four standing figures is a replacement from the time of Wolsey's College. Drawn and engraved by T. Higham for the *Antiquarian Itinerary*, published by W. Clarke, 1817. Reproduced with kind permission from Suffolk Record Office, Ipswich Branch.

THE CHARTERS

Royal Grants in Favour of the Canons

339. Letters Patent of inspeximus and confirmation by King Edward III of writs of King Henry I and King Stephen, both couched in similar terms, ordering that the King's canons of Ipswich of his alms should hold their churches, lands, tithes and other possessions in peace.

(Henry I's writ May × July 1133;[1] Stephen's writ [1135 × 1139];[2] inspeximus 24 July 1337)

Patent Roll, 11 Edward III, pt 2; TNA, C66/190, mem. 17 (*CPR*, Edward III vol. 3 (1334–38), 476).

[Margin:] Pro priore et canonicis de Gippewico de confirmacione.

Rex omnibus ad quos etc. salutem. Inspeximus cartam quam dominus H[enricus] quondam Rex Anglorum progenitor noster fecit in hec verba.

[**339A**]. H[enricus] rex Anglorum episcopo de Norwicha et Ricardo archidiacono et Ricardo Bass[et] et Alberico de Ver et ministris eorum salutem. Precipio quod canonici mei de elemosina mea de Gipeswicha habeant et teneant ecclesias suas et omnes terras et decimas et omnia sua quocunque teneant bene et honorifice et in pace ne super hoc breve meum aliquis faciat eis inde iniuriam vel contumeliam. Et si quis versus eos quicquam clamaverit quod ecclesie sue datum sit in elemosinam, non placitent inde nisi coram episcopo de Norwicha et Ricardo Basset et A[lberico] de Ver, desicut canonici mei sunt et de me clamant tenendum. Teste Ricardo Bass[et] apud Burnam.

Inspeximus etiam quandam aliam cartam quam dominus S[tephanus] quondam rex Anglorum progenitor noster fecit in hec verba.

[**339B**]. S[tephanus] rex Anglorum episcopo Norwichensi et archidiaconis suis et H[ugoni] Bigot et ministris suis salutem. Precipio quod canonici mei de elemosina mea de Gipeswica habeant et teneant ecclesias suas et omnes terras suas, decimas et omnia sua de quocunque teneant, ita bene et honorifice et in pace sicut melius et liberius tenuerunt tempore regis Henrici et die qua fuit vivus et mortuus. Et prohibeo ne aliquis eis inde faciant iniuriam neque contumeliam super hoc meum breve. Et si quis versus eos quicquam clamaverit quod ecclesie sue datum sit in elemosinam non placitent inde nisi coram Episcopo de Norwicha et coram mea iusticia dominica, desicut canonici mei sunt et de me clamant ad tenendum. Testibus R[ogero][3] Cancellario et Hugone Bigot.

  Nos autem donationes et concessiones predictas ratas habentes et gratas eas pro nobis et heredibus nostris quantum in nobis est dilectis nobis in Christo nunc priori et canonicis loci predicti tenore presentium concedimus et confirmamus sicut carte predicte rationabiliter testatur et prout iidem prior et canonici ecclesias

1

terras et decimas modo tenent, ipsique et eorum predecessores easdem ecclesias terras et decimas a tempore confectionis cartarum predictarum semper hactenus rationabiliter tenere consueverunt. In cuius etc. Teste Rege apud Westmonasterium xxiiii die Iulii.

1 Place date from royal itinerary.
2 Roger le Poer was Chancellor 1135–39.
3 Roger le Poer.

Private Grants in Favour of the Canons

The arrangement of the charters deals first with the core estates of the priory in Ipswich and its environs (mostly in Samford Hundred), followed by outlying holdings elsewhere in Suffolk.

CORE ESTATES

BELSTEAD

(N.B. Great Belstead is known in modern times as Washbrook, and Little Belstead as Belstead).

340. Grant in free, pure and perpetual alms by William of Goldingham to the canons, for the salvation of his soul and those of his ancestors, of 3 acres of land in Belstead which Richard Ballard held in 'Haresfeld', to hold free of all secular demands save the king's service.   [1180s – early thirteenth century]

TNA, E40/3405. 132 × 78mm, 13mm turnup, 92mm tag with shreds of brown wax. Endorsed: de ii acris in ?feld de Belsted/Belsted de ? (16c., in different hands).

Universis Sancte Matris Ecclesie filiis, Willelmus de Goldingham salutem. Sciatis me concessisse et dedisse et hac presenti carta mea confirmasse Deo et ecclesie apostolorum Petri et Pauli de Gipeswico et canonicis ibidem Deo servientibus, tres acras terre in villa de Belstede, quas Ricardus Ballard tenuit, que iacent in campo qui dicitur Haresfeld, in liberam et puram et perpetuam elemosinam, pro salute anime mee et antecessorum meorum, tenendas in perpetuum, libere et quiete ab omnibus secularibus serviciis et consuetudinibus, salvo servicio Domini Regis. His testibus: Roberto decano de Gipeswico, Roberto capellano de Beri, Hanfrido capellano, Iohanne capellano, Ada de Ulmo, Hugone filio Alani, Mansero de Guthelesford, Mansero de Ponte, Willelmo Angod, Henrico de Sureun, Hamone Wicher, Osberto le Marescal, Osberto filio Odonis, Ricardo de Tivile, et multis aliis.

Date: Robert the dean of Ipswich attests Dodnash Priory charters between 25 September 1188 and the early thirteenth century (*Dodnash Charters*, nos. 4, 6, 9, 87), and occurs as an adjacent landholder in 1204 or 1206–09 (*Leiston Cart.*, no. 30). Adam of the Elm attests Geoffrey II of Badley's confirmation of his uncle

William's grants to SS Peter and Paul *c.* 1180 (no. 44), and other charters relating to the priory including no. 48 in the 1190s and no. 76, 1190s – early thirteenth century. Richard de Tivile and Cecilia his mother quitclaimed Pannington in Wherstead to SS Peter and Paul on 12 May 1196 (no. 309).

341. Grant in perpetuity by Thomas of Rougham (*Rugham*) to the prior and canons, of all his lands and tenements in Great Belstead (*Belstede Magna*), Little Belstead (*Belstede Parva*), Chattisham (*Chatesham*), Sproughton (*Sproutone*), Copdock (*Coppedok'*) and Washbrook (*Wasebrok'*), without any retention. Also he grants that two messuages, 100 acres of land, 2½ acres of meadow, 5 acres of pasture, 2 acres of wood, 2 shillings' worth of rent and the rent of 4 hens which Laurence le Free and John his brother hold of Thomas for life in Stoke by Ipswich (*Stok' iuxta Gippewycum*), Wherstead (*Whersted*) and Greenwich (*Grenewich*), and which after their death ought to revert to Thomas and his heirs, shall wholly revert, after the death of Laurence and John, to the prior and canons and their successors in perpetuity; to have and to hold all the aforesaid lands and tenements to the prior and canons and their successors in perpetuity of the chief lords of those fees by the services by right due and accustomed in respect thereof. Warranty by the grantor and his heirs against all people in perpetuity. Sealed in testimony.

Hiis testibus: Rogero de Godelisforde, Iohanne Horold, Roberto de Bordeshowe, Iohanne Andreu, Roberto de Coppedok', Willelmo de Kenebrok', Willelmo Seman, Roberto Scot', Thoma le Maystir, Iohanne dil Pond, Ada de Sohedd clerico. Given at Ipswich, 12 June 3 Edward III. 12 June 1329

TNA, E40/3291. 254 × 130mm, 18mm turnup. Only the seal in red wax is attached through a slit, tag 118mm long. Design of quadruped beast with three-pronged tail, legend illegible, 15mm round in wax blob 22mm wide. The seal in green wax is identical, though sewn to the turnup on a tag 120mm long, seal 15mm round in wax blob 32mm wide. Endorsed: Thom' de Rugham (14c.); par' sancti Petri (16c.). On tag for red seal, words are legible inside tag; one side: Et Iohannis frater/Feoffator'; and on the other: Pastur' duarum acrarum/ -onis tenent de.

342A. Writ of Edward III to the sheriff of Suffolk. Whereas Thomas atte Dene in the king's court before his justices at Westminster has recovered seisin against John of Whitfield (*Whyttefeld*) and John his son, of one messuage, 120 acres of land, 5 acres of meadow, 6 acres of pasture, 3 acres of wood and 30s rent in Great Belstead (*Magna Belsted*), Sproughton (*Sprouton'*), Copdock (*Coppedok'*), Washbrook (*Whassebrok'*) and Little Belstead (*Parva Belsted*), by the default of John and John, the sheriff is to cause Thomas to have full seisin without delay. Witness J. Travers at Westminster, 18 October 4 Edward III. 18 October 1330

TNA, E40/3819(A). 245 × 32mm, plus a wrapping tie 4mm in height, no tongue. On the wrapping tie is written in the same hand as that of the writ: seis' vic' Suf' pro Thoma atte Dene ro. lxxxxiii. No endorsement on writ, which is stitched to E40/3819(B).

342B. Notification by Thomas atte Dene that, whereas he has lately in the king's court before the justices at Westminster recovered seisin against John of Whitfield (Whitefeld) and John his son, of one messuage, 120 acres of land, 5 acres of meadow, 6 acres of pasture, 3 acres of wood and 30s rent in Great Belstead (*Magna Belstede*), Sproughton (*Sproutone*), Copdock (*Coppedok'*), Washbrook (*Whasshebrok'*) and Little Belstead (*Parva Belstede*), by the default of John and John, by the king's writ, which lands and tenements the prior and convent hold on the day of the making of this deed, he has granted, remitted and utterly in perpetuity quitclaimed, for himself and his heirs, to the prior and convent and their successors in perpetuity, for a certain sum of money which they have given him in cash, all right and claim which he had, or has, or might have had, or in any way might have in future, in all the said lands and tenements, so that neither he nor his heirs, nor anyone in his name, may henceforth be able to claim any right therein. Sealed in testimony.

Hiis testibus: Nicholaio Bonde, Rogero de Godelisford, Iohanne Horold, Roberto de Bordeshowe, Iohanne Andreu, Willelmo Seman, Roberto Scot, Willelmo de Kenbrok', Iohanne Lewere et aliis. Given at Ipswich, Sunday next after the feast of St Hilary, 4 Edward III.   20 January 1331

TNA, E40/3819(B). 275 × 98mm, 18mm turnup, tag 123mm long. Seal is a vesica, 20 × 15mm, damaged and unintelligible. Endorsed: Whitefeld per breve; Belsted m[a] (both 15c.). Stitched to writ, E40/3819(A).

343. Notification[1] by John of Whitfield (*Whytefeld*), first-born son of John of Whitfield, that he has granted, remitted and utterly and in perpetuity quitclaimed, for himself and his heirs, to Prior Henry of Kersey, the canons and their successors, all right and claim which he had, has, or in any way might have had or might have in future, in all those lands and tenements which were Laurence le Free's in the townships of Great Belstead (*Belstede Magna*), Little Belstead (*Belstede Parva*), Chattisham (*Chatesham*), Sproughton (*Sproutone*), Copdock (*Coppedok'*), Washbrook (*Waschebrok'*), and also in all those lands and tenements which Laurence le Fre and John his brother held for their life of the prior, as of the right of his church, in Stoke by Ipswich (*Stok' iuxta Gyppewycum*), Wherstead (*Wherstede*) and Greenwich (*Grenewyht*), so that neither he nor his heirs, nor anyone in their name may henceforth in future claim any right therein. Warranty by the grantor and his heirs against all people in perpetuity. Sealed in testimony.

Hiis testibus: Gilberto de Burgh, Edmundo Petygard tunc ballivis ville Gyppewyci, Rogero de Gothelesforde, Iohanne Horold, Roberto de Bordeshowe, Nicholao Bonde, Iohanne Halteby, Iohanne Irp, Willelmo de Kenebrok' et aliis. Given at Ipswich, Wednesday next after the feast of St Agatha the Virgin, 12 Edward III.
                                                        11 February 1338

TNA, E40/3633. 242 × 133mm, 20mm turnup, 94mm tag. Seal 27mm round, containing a triangle within a border, details lost so meaning unclear. No counterseal. Endorsed: Ioh' Whitefeld (16c.), by Bettsted (17c.).

1 See also nos. 517 and 518.

344. Duplicate of 343. (Nos. 343 and 344 are not part and counterpart of a pair of indentures; there is no indented edge, and no clause to indicate alternate sealing.)
11 February 1338

TNA, E40/3763. 267 × 103mm, 13mm turnup, tag 110mm. Seal 21mm round in a blob of wax 33mm round. Endorsed: Ioh'es de Witfeld de terris que fuerunt Laurenc' Fre; Belsted magna (both 17c.).

345. Grant in perpetuity by Thomas of Rougham (*Rugham*) to the prior and canons, for an unspecified sum of money paid in cash, of an annual rent of 12d-worth, one gallon of lamp oil and one rose, to be taken, namely, the 12d from Richard Ale', Rose his wife and John his son annually at the usual terms, for a certain cottage and 2 acres of land which they hold of Thomas for their lives in Great Belstead (*Magna Belstede*); the said oil from Roger Ython for a certain tenement which he holds of Thomas in Ipswich (*Gippewycc*) below his messuage; and the said rose at the feast of the Nativity of St John the Baptist from Laurence le Free and John his brother for 2 messuages, 100 acres of land, 2½ acres of meadow, 5 acres of pasture, 2 acres of wood and 2s rent in Stoke by Ipswich (*Stoke iuxta Gippewycum*), Wherstead (*Wherstede*) and Greenwich (*Grenewych*), which they hold of Thomas for the lives of both of them by the said service. Also he grants, for himself and his heirs, that the cottage and land which Richard, Rose and Richard's son John hold, and also the two messuages, 100 acres of land, 2½ acres of meadow, 5 acres of pasture, 2 acres of wood and 2s which Laurence and John hold, and which after the death of Richard, Rose, Richard's son John, Laurence and his brother John ought to revert to Thomas and his heirs, shall entirely after the death of the tenants remain to the prior and canons and their successors in perpetuity, to have and to hold of the capital lords of that fee, by the services rightly due and accustomed in respect thereof in perpetuity. Warranty by the grantor and his heirs against all people in perpetuity. Sealed in testimony.

Hiis testibus: Rogero de Godelesforde, Iohanne Horold, Willelmo Andreu, Costentino Halteby, Semanno Meriel, Paulo clerico et aliis. Given at Ipswich, 10 June, 21 Edward III.   10 June 1347

TNA, E40/3534. 259 × 172mm, 20mm turnup, 80mm tag. Seal 20mm round, device of a four-legged animal with a human face, legend gone. Endorsed: Bettsted magna (16c.), xiid' (16c.), Bettsted (16c.), Rugham (16c.) (different hands).

BRAMFORD

346. Quitclaim by Norman of the Tye (*de la Ty*) of Bramford, chaplain, to the prior and convent, of all right and claim in the tenement which Alan le Scocher sometime held of them. Sealed in testimony.

Hiis testibus: Domino Iohanne de Lovetot milite, Petro de la Ty, Alano filio eius, Baldewino de Pesenhale, Mansero de Bordeshowe, Roberto et Hamone de

Bordeshowe fratribus, Galfrido filio Normanni de Bramford, Petro Mori, Simone le Vinter, Willelmo Warin, Willelmo del Hay et aliis. [?1270s]

TNA, E40/3945. 173 × 45mm, 13mm turnup, 85mm tag. Seal in green wax, 25mm round, much deformed and now unintelligible. On inside of tag: domine dominus omnibus. Nonsensical and meaning not obvious, but clearly reused. Endorsed: Bra … but rubbed and now illegible (?16c.).

Date: Baldwin of Peasenhall attests between the 1230s (no. 458) and 1277 (no. 470); Sir John de Lovetot attests no. 520, 23 April 1270, and no. 359, 4 April 1290. Alan le Scocher, who as a *former* landholder is presumably now dead, was alive on 23 April 1270 (no. 520).

BROOKS

347. Grant in perpetual alms by Geoffrey, lord of Brooks, to the canons, of one acre of land which was Alfred the Old's, half an acre which Ordmar Huchel held, and one piece of land at Horsewade which yields 4d *per annum* and two days' work in autumn, quit of all customs and secular services, for the salvation of his soul and those of his wife, his ancestors, and all the faithful. For this the canons have given him a palfrey worth 20s. [Later twelfth century]

TNA, E40/3826. 200 × 62mm, plus step for tongue at left, where total height is 89mm. Endorsed: Galfrid' de Broches (13c.); S (uncertain).

Gaufridus dominus de Broches omnibus hominibus suis Francis et Anglicis salutem. Sciatis me concessisse et dedisse ecclesie apostolorum Petri et Pauli de Gipeswico et canonicis eiusdem ecclesie, unam acram terre que fuit Alfredi Senis et iacet infra terram eorum que est in Broces, et dimidiam acram que Ordmarius Huchel tenuit, et unam terram ad Horsewade que reddit iiii denarios annuatim et ii operationes in autumpno, in perpetua elemosina, libere et quiete a cunctis consuetudinibus, et ab omnibus secularibus serviciis, pro salute anime mee et uxoris mee, et omnium parentum meorum, et pro animabus omnium fidelium. Et pro hac concessione et donacione dederunt michi predicti canonici unum palefridum de precio xx solidis. Testes: Ionas Decanus, Dionisius sacerdos, Radulfus sacerdos, Benyaminus sacerdos, Clemens sacerdos, Alfredus Senex, Lefwinus Godhand, Godricus Tureil, Ordmarius le Gar', Hugo [*blank*].

Date: For Geoffrey [of Badley] and his family, lords of Brooks, see Introduction, pp. 59–61. The grantor, Geoffrey lord of Brooks, as Geoffrey son of Robert, is the donor of no. 27, which dates between 1146 and January 1174, but probably not later than the 1160s. Both charters are attested by Jonas the Dean. The address to 'Francis et Anglicis' is most common in the decade 1150–60, remains common until 1200, and is rare thereafter (Gervers, 'DEEDS Project', fig. 1, p. 17). The description of witnesses as 'sacerdos' rather than 'clericus' also suggests a twelfth-century date.

348. Grant in perpetual alms by Robert son of Geoffrey of Badley, Beatrice his wife, and Geoffrey of Brooks their son and heir, to the canons, for their salvation and that of their parents and all their ancestors, of the land which Gerard of Gretford

held of them for 14d *per annum*, for which the canons have given to Beatrice one
hanging worth 16s. [Late twelfth century]

TNA, E40/3967. 183 × 64mm, but this includes a turnup which has been folded
out. Two slits for tags, but none survives. Endorsed: Rodbertus filius Galf' de
Badel (13c.).

Omnibus sancte matris ecclesie filiis Robertus filius Gaufridi de Badelea et uxor
Biatricia, et eorum filius et heres Gaufridus de Broches, salutem. Notum sit presentibus et futuris nos concessisse et dedisse ecclesie apostolorum Petri et Pauli de
Gipeswico et canonicis eiusdem loci, terram quam Gerardus de Gretford¹ tenuit de
nobis, silicet [*lost*] terras et [*lost*]diam pro quibus idem Gerardus reddidit annuatim
xiiii denarios, in perpetuam elemosinam, libere et quiete ab omnibus serviciis
nobis pertinentibus, et hoc pro salute nostra et patrum et matrum et omnium
parentum nostrorum. Et pro hac concessione et donatione dederunt predicti
canonici unam curtinam michi Biatricie precii sexdecim solidorum. His testibus:
Iona decano de Gipeswico, B[*illegible*] presbitero, et predicto Gerardo qui terram
tunc tenuit, Iordano filio Roberti, Anneis² domina de Broches.

   1 'Gretford' is probably 'Crakeford' near Thurleston (no. 185).
   2 Anneis, lady of Broches (Brooks), is the widow of Geoffrey I of Badley, the father of
     Robert the donor (see Introduction, pp. 59–60).

Date: Robert son of Geoffrey occurs at least as early as the 1170s (see Introduction,
p. 59). His son Geoffrey II occurs *c.* 1180–1212. Jonas the Dean attests no. 27, before
the death of Bishop William Turbe of Norwich on 16 January 1174 and probably
not after the 1160s.

349. Grant in pure and perpetual alms by Adam of the Elm to the canons, for his
salvation and that of his wife Juliana and his ancestors, of one acre of land in the
field of 'Wivelesdune' near the chapel of Brooks. Warranty is granted.
[Late twelfth or early thirteenth century]

TNA, E40/3851. 150 × 63mm, 16mm turnup, 80mm tag, seal missing. Endorsed:
Brok; Adam de Ulmo (two hands, both 15c.).

Adam de Ulmo omnibus hominibus suis et amicis Francis et Anglicis presentibus
et futuris salutem. Sciatis me concessisse et dedisse et hac presenti carta mea confirmasse Deo et ecclesie apostolorum Petri et Pauli de Gipeswico et canonicis ibidem
Deo servientibus, unam acram terre que iacet iuxta terram predictorum canonicorum in campo de Wivelesdune apud capellam de Brokes, in puram et perpetuam
elemosinam pro salute anime mee et Iuliane uxoris mee et antecessorum meorum,
libere et quiete ab omnibus serviciis et exactionibus secularibus. Et ego et heredes
mei debemus warantizare predictam terram predictis canonicis contra omnes
homines. His testibus: Galfrido de Brokes, Roberto filio eius, Rogero fratre suo,
Mansero de Bordeshowe, Mansero de Guthelesforde, Elya filio Turstun, Alexandro
de Sancto Edmundo, Mansero de Ponte, Rogero filio Normanni, Willelmo filio
Angod, Willelmo de Derneford, et multis aliis.

Date: Adam of the Elm attests no. 43, shortly after 1180; Elias son of Turstan (Elias
of Ipswich) occurs in a final concord concerning land in Dunwich in 1199, and

died in 1213, when his widow Alice claimed that he had been murdered in Ipswich market (*Sibton Cartularies*, I, introduction pp. 65–66). Geoffrey I of Brooks occurs before 1174 and was probably dead before 1200; his son Robert occurs from at least the 1170s (see Introduction, pp. 59–60). The formula 'Francis et Anglicis' is rare after 1200 (loss of Normandy, 1204).

350. Grant in free and perpetual alms by John de Beumes to the canons, of two acres of land in Brooks which Matthew de Luveys gave to him for his homage and service; to hold of John and his heirs for 18d *per annum* for all services etc. Warranty is granted. [1239 × 1241]

TNA, E40/3458. 166 × 80mm, 14mm turnup, 78mm tag. Fragment of seal 20mm round, dark wax but unintelligible. Endorsed: terr' in Brokys (15c.); Brokes (17c.).

Sciant presentes et futuri quod ego Iohannes de Beumes concessi, dedi, et hac presenti carta mea confirmavi, Deo et ecclesie apostolorum Petri et Pauli de Gypewico et canonicis ibidem Deo servientibus, in liberam et perpetuam elemosinam, duas acras terre cum pertinentiis in villa de Brokes, quas Mattheus de Luveys michi dedit pro homagio et servicio meo, que iacent inter terram domini prioris Sancti Petri de Gypewico et terram Rogeri Prikehert; tenendas et habendas illis et eorum successoribus de me et heredibus meis, libere, quiete, bene et in pace; reddendo inde annuatim michi et heredibus meis decem et octo denarios ad duos terminos anni, videlicet ad Pascha novem denarios et ad festum Sancti Michaelis novem denarios, pro omnibus serviciis, consuetudinibus, et demandis. Et ego dictus Iohannes et heredes mei warantizabimus dictam terram cum pertinentiis dictis canonicis et eorum successoribus per predictum servicium contra omnes inperpetuum. Hiis testibus: Domino Iohanne de Dulkote tunc vicecomite, Willelmo de Hakeford, Galfrido de Beumes, Waltero de Leyestune, Sylvestro filio Normanni, Constantino Fader, Willelmo Godeschalc, Baldewyno de Pesenhale, Augustino de Westerfeld, Vincente de Rubroc, Iustino de Nestun', et aliis.

Date: John de Dulkote/de Ulcote, sheriff.

351. Grant in perpetuity by John Testepin, son of William Testepin of Hintlesham, to the canons, for the salvation of his soul and the souls of his ancestors and successors, and for a fine of 40s of sterlings, of 15 acres of land in the field called 'Aldgate' in Brooks, 6d annual rent and 4 hens at the Nativity from Robert Coc and his heirs, and 8d annual rent from John Coc; on payment of 3s *per annum* to the chief lord of the fee and 6d to a church in Ipswich (the name of which has been deleted), and 1d *per annum* to the grantor and his heirs, for all services etc. saving the king's service of 5½d in 20s scutage. Warranty is granted. [1230s – 1240s]

TNA E40/3398. 213 × 90mm, 19mm turnup, 100mm tag. Seal 38mm round, legend … GILLV … H'NIS … Design unclear. Writing on inside of tag: 'in quindecim' on one side, 'tenuit de domino' on the other. No endorsements.

Sciant presentes et futuri quod ego Iohannes Testepin, filius Willelmi Testepin de Hintlesham, concessi, dedi, et hac presenti carta mea confirmavi, Deo et ecclesie Sancti Petri de Gypewico et canonicis ibidem Deo servientibus, pro salute anime mee et pro animabus antecessorum et successorum meorum, et pro quadraginta solidis sterlingorum quos michi dederunt in gersumium, quindecim acras terre cum pertinentiis iacentes in Brokes, in campo qui vocatur Aldegate, et sex denarios annui redditus percipiendos de Roberto Coc et de heredibus suis ad duos terminos anni, scilicet ad Pascha tres denarios, et ad festum Sancti Michaelis tres denarios, et quatuor gallinas ad Natale Domini percipiendas; et de Iohanne Coc octo denarios annui redditus ad dictos terminos percipiendos. Reddendo inde annuatim domino capitali eiusdem feodi et heredibus suis vel suis assignatis tres solidos ad duos terminos anni, scilicet ad festum Sancti Michaelis octodecim denarios, et ad Pascha octodecim denarios. Et ad ecclesiam [*deleted*] de Gipewico sex denarios ad dictos terminos solvendos, michi autem et heredibus meis unum denarium, scilicet ad Nativitatem Sancti Iohannis Baptiste, pro omnibus serviciis, consue-tudinibus et demandis, salvo servicio domini regis, scilicet quando scutagium super illud feodum evenerit, ad viginti solidos quinque denarios et obolum, et ad plus, plus et ad minus, minus. Et ego predictus Iohannes et heredes mei warantizabimus predictas quindecim acras terre cum pertinenciis, et predictum redditum, et predictas quatuor gallinas, dictis canonicis et eorum successoribus, per servicium prenominatum, contra omnes in perpetuum. In huius autem rei testimonium huic presenti scripto sigillum meum apposui. Hiis testibus: Willelmo Godeskalc, Matheo de Porta tunc temporis ballivis de Gipewico, Willelmo de Holebroc, Willelmo Testepin, Baldewino de Pesehale, Silvestro filio Waukelini, Roberto Wlfoun, Osberto de Foro, Osberto de Belinges, Iohanne Bolle, Stephano Strich, et aliis.

Date: In the same Ipswich borough administrative year (the same bailiffs are in office and there are seven other witnesses in common) as no. 45 which confirms this charter. The borough administrative year ran from 29 September to 28 September.

352. Grant in perpetuity by William son of William Testepyn of Hintlesham to the canons, for the salvation of his soul and the souls of his ancestors and successors, and for a fine of 40s of sterlings, of 10 acres of land in the field called 'Aldegate' in Brooks and 5d annual rent from Robert Coch and his heirs; to hold of the grantor and his heirs, paying 26d *per annum* for all services etc. saving the king's service of 3¾d in 20s scutage. Warranty is granted. [1230s – 1240s]

TNA, E40/3397. 199 × 79mm, 14mm turnup, 114mm tag. Seal 17 × 25mm and in poor condition. The hand differs from that of no. 351, but similarities in wording suggest that both were written within the priory, though no. 351 has no habendum clause. Endorsed: Brok (17c.).

Sciant presentes et futuri quod ego Willelmus filius Willelmi Testepyn de Hyntlesham concessi, dedi et hac presenti carta mea confirmavi Deo et ecclesie apostolorum Petri et Pauli de Gypewyco et canonicis ibidem Deo servientibus, pro salute anime mee et pro animabus antecessorum et successorum meorum, et pro quadraginta solidis sterlingorum quos michi dederunt in gersumam, decem acras terre iacentes in Brokes in campo qui vocatur Aldegate, et quinque denarios annui redditus percipiendos de Roberto Coch et heredibus suis. Tenendas et habendas de me et de heredibus meis, libere, quiete, bene et in pace, illis et eorum successoribus. Reddendo inde annuatim michi et heredibus meis viginti et sex denarios ad duos terminos anni, scilicet ad festum Sancti Michaelis tresdecim denarios, et ad Pascha tresdecim denarios, pro omnibus serviciis, consuetudinibus et demandis, salvo servicio domini regis, scilicet scutagio ad viginti solidos tres denarios et tres quadrantes, et ad plus, plus et ad minus, minus. Et ego Willelmus et heredes mei warentizabimus [*sic*] predictas decem acras terre cum pertinenciis et predictos quinque denarios annui redditus dictis canonicis et eorum successoribus per servicium prenominatum contra omnes imperpetuum. In huius autem rei testimonium, presenti scripto sigillum meum apposui. Hiis testibus: Domino Galfrido de Badele milite, Willelmo Godeskalch et Matheo de Porta tunc temporis ballivis de Gypewico, Willelmo de Holebroch, Baldewyno de Pesehale, Silvestro filio Wakelini, Roberto Wlfun, Hugone Lyu, Osberto de Foro, Osberto de Belinges, Stephano Stric, Petro Peper, et aliis.

Date: In the same Ipswich borough administrative year as no. 45 and no. 351: William Godeskalch and Matthew de Porta, bailiffs, and seven witnesses in common with each of those charters.

353. Quitclaim by Alice the widow of Nigel Cole to the prior and convent, of all her right of dower in four acres of land in Brooks, between the land of the canons of St Peter and that of the canons of Holy Trinity, Ipswich, which Nigel formerly held of the canons of St Peter. For this quitclaim the canons have given her half a mark. Sealed in testimony. [1240s – 1260s]

TNA, E40/3278. 164 × 52mm, 15mm turnup, 89mm tag, seal missing. Endorsed: Brokes (16c.).

Sciant presentes et futuri quod ego Alicia relicta Nigelli Cole resignavi et quietum clamavi priori et conventui Sancti Petri de Gypewico totam partem et totum ius quod michi contingebat nomine dotis de quatuor acris terre cum pertinenciis iacentibus in villa de Brokes inter terram dictorum canonicorum Sancti Petri et terram canonicorum Sancte Trinitatis de Gypewico, quas dictus Nigellus quondam tenuit de dictis canonicis Sancti Petri. Pro hac vero resignacione et quieta clamacione dederunt michi dicti canonici dimidiam marcam argenti. In huius rei testimonium huic scripto sigillum meum apposui. Hiis testibus: Silvestro, Matheo de Porta tunc ballivis de Gypewico, Willelmo de Holebroc, Willelmo Godeskalc, Rogero de Langestune, Waltero de Leystune, Roberto de Stanbrigg', Gerardo Richoud, Iohanne Provost, et aliis.

Date: Silvester [son of Wakelin] served as bailiff of Ipswich with John de Beaumes for a term sometime between 1227 and 1232. Matthew de Porta is known to have held the office in 1255–56, 1270–71 and 1278–79; the term he served in conjunction with Silvester is unknown, since the record is incomplete, but could well have been in the 1240s. By 1270 Silvester's son Vivian was bailiff, and his father does not occur in office thereafter. William of Holbrook attests no. 539, perhaps in the 1230s but certainly before May 1248.

354. Quitclaim by Thomas de Porta, for himself and his heirs, to John son of Hugh of Badley and his heirs, of all right and claim in an annual rent of one mark of sterlings out of 'Haveneford' (Handford) Mill, which he sometime purchased from John, to be taken from the same mill; to have and to hold to John and his heirs without any protest or challenge from Thomas or his heirs in perpetuity. For this grant and quitclaim John has paid 11 marks of silver. If John sells the rent, Thomas shall have first claim over any other. Sealed in testimony.

Hiis testibus: Matheo de Porta et Hugone Lyu tunc balivis Gypp', Roberto Wlfun, Oseberto de Foro, Iohanne de Sancto Georgio, Thorstun' del Cley', Andrea de Lond', Iohanne Bolle, Petro Peper, Ricardo de Stanham, Iacobo Crabbe, Iohanne de Ressemere et aliis. Anno regni regis Henrici tercii xl° mense Augusti.

August 1256

TNA, E40/3442. 219 × 78mm, 12mm turnup, 86mm tag. Seal is a vesica, 32 × 44mm, design of one big and one small sunburst, legend S' THOME DE PORTA. Endorsed: xx (late medieval); de molendino de Hanford (14c.).

355. Notification by Osbert of the Market (*de Foro*) of Ipswich (*Gypewico*) that he has quitclaimed, for him and his heirs, to Prior Nicholas and the canons now serving and those serving in future, in perpetuity, all that part of the mill of 'Hagneford' (Handford) which he held of them by the annual service of 40s and 40d, with its site, family, ways, paths, meadows, grazing lands and everything pertaining to that part of the mill; to have and to hold to the canons and their successors or assigns freely, quietly, well and in peace, without any opposition from Osbert or his heirs in perpetuity. Sealed in testimony.

Testibus: Matheo de Porta, Hugone Lyu tunc ballivis de Gypewico, Roberto Wlfun, Ricardo Fader, Roberto de Orford, Semanno Tophole, Thoma de Porta, Galfrido Baldewyn', Iohanne Martin, Galfrido Horold, Hugone Golding et aliis.

[Probably 29 September 1255 x 28 September 1256]

TNA, E40/3410. 173 × 70mm, 12mm turnup, 87mm tag, seal missing. Endorsed: molend' de Hant' (16c.).

Date: Matthew de Porta and Hugh Lyu are known to have served together as bailiffs in 1255–56 (no. 354); the record is incomplete and they may have served together previously, but this charter must post-date the election of Prior Nicholas of Ipswich in January 1253 (*Heads of Houses*, II, 396).

356. ?An unexecuted draft of no. 42, the acknowledgement by Osbert son of Saer of Littellund that he has received at perpetual farm from the prior and convent a half-part of Handford Mill and 6d annual rent; reciting the full text of the priory's grant.

[January 1267]

TNA, E40/3925. The text is defective; the charter is in poor condition, with a hole 50mm in diameter which has destroyed parts of the text in the middle of eight lines. There is no date, and no witnesses are named. 245 × 128mm, no turnup or evidence of sealing. Endorsed: Hanford (?16c.).

Date: The date must be similar to no. 42.

357. Notification by Robert the chaplain, son of the late John Nel of Brooks (*Broc'*), and Thomas his brother, that whereas they had requested from the prior and convent of St Peter right of entry to a messuage with buildings and land which John their father and Alveva their mother held of the prior and convent in Brooks at the will of the prior by the custom of villeinage, and the prior had various suits against them which he had remitted to them at the instance and petition of their friends, Robert and Thomas for them and all the family of their parents and themselves have quitclaimed to the prior and convent and their successors in perpetuity all right in the messuage and land by this present charter, and it is permitted according to the law of England that they cannot contest it. For the salvation of his soul the prior has given them 20s. Sealed in testimony.

Hiis testibus: Domino Galfrido de Badele capitali domino feodi, Ricardo de Holebroc, Matheo de Porta, Osberto de Foro tunc ballivis, Hugone de Langestun, Hugone Luy, Ricardo Fader, Baldewino de Pesshal, Semanno Tophol et aliis.

[1250s – 1270s]

TNA, E40/3276. 173 × 84mm, 11mm turnup, 2 tags. Right tag 88mm; on its inner sides are written: Osb'tus alic' fam' and xii kl' Aug' Ioh' cam' et sac'... Seal in red wax, 33mm round, fleur-de-lys device. Legend: ... THOMA ... Left tag 122mm, no seal. Across length of tag inside can be read: kl' Ian' Luc' can' et sac' sancte Marie de Mal{a}o; Rannulph' can ad succ{a}; Rog' de Neusu' miles; Ioh's, Will, Galfr', Gileb', Matildis, Cecilia, Sibilla, Eva, fam'. Hole 17 × 20mm at centre right. Endorsed: P.N. pro tribus acris terre in Brokes xx sol' (14c.); Brok (16c.).

Date: Matthew de Porta served as bailiff of Ipswich with Hugh Luy in 1255–56, and with Vivian son of Silvester in 1270–71 and 1278–79. The dates of his service with Osbert de Foro are unknown. Richard Fader and Seman Tophol served as bailiffs in 1266–67, and Fader served again in 1269–70, 1272–73 and 1279–80.

358. Notification by William Testepin of Hintlesham (*Hintelesham*) that he has granted, remised, quitclaimed and by the present charter confirmed to the church and canons and their successors in perpetuity, for the salvation of his soul and for those of his ancestors and successors, in free, pure and perpetual alms, an annual rent of 1d in which the canons were bound to him for 15 acres of land in Brooks (*Brokes*), in the field called 'Aldegate', with all right and claim which he or his heirs had or could have in the land or the rent. Sealed in testimony and in warranty.

Hiis testibus: Iohanne del Hel, Ricardo del Hel, Thoma del Hel, fratribus, Iohanne de Floketone, Ricardo Fader, Iohanne Clement, Willelmo Bule de Combes, et multis aliis.

[1260s – 1280s]

TNA, E40/3639. 195 × 65mm, 12mm turnup, 105mm tag. Seal 35mm round, design of a flower or sunburst, legend S' WILL' TESTEPIN. Endorsed: Brok (16c.).

Date: Richard Fader is known to have served as bailiff of Ipswich in 1266–67, 1269–70, 1272–73 and 1279–80.

359. Grant by Prior John [of St Nicholas] and the convent[1] to Matilda the widow of Wolfric of 'Brademere', of half an acre of land in Brooks (*Brokes*) lying in the field called 'Scocherslond', one headland abutting south on the highway from Ipswich (*Gipp'*) to Bramford, next to the messuage of Roger the cobbler (*sutor*); to have and to hold to Matilda and her heirs freely, quietly, well and in peace, in fee and by inheritance, of the prior and convent and their successors in perpetuity, paying 6d annually, that is, 3d at the feast of St Michael and 3d at Easter, for all the services, customs and demands. Warranty by the grantors against all people in perpetuity. Matilda's seal is appended for perpetual cognizance.

Testibus: Domino Iohanne de Lovetot, Domino Roberto de Bosco militibus, Willelmo Suylard, Philippo Harneys, Thoma Aylred, Roberto de Bordeshowe, Iohanne de la Dale, Martino Just' et aliis. Capp' [?Copdock], the feast of St Ambrose, 18 Edward. 4 April 1290

TNA, E40/5484. 190 × 84mm, 10mm turnup, 95mm tag. Seal: S' MATILD … ADERNE. Green wax, image of ear of corn with leaves, 25 × 35mm. Endorsed: I' prior (13c.); Brok' (17c.).

> 1 Though this is a grant *by* the priory, it is printed in this position because of its obvious relationship to nos. 360–63.

360. Notification by Matilda who was the wife of Wulfric of 'Brademere' of Brooks (*Brokes extra Gypewicum*), in the legal status of her widowhood, that she has granted, remised and utterly quitclaimed to the prior and convent, for her and her heirs in perpetuity, all right and claim which she had or could have in one piece of land which she held of the same religious in Brooks, next to her messuage which she has by their grant and gift; so that neither she nor her heirs may henceforth make any claim therein. For this quitclaim the prior and convent have given her 5s in cash. Sealed in testimony.

Hiis testibus: Domino Roberto de Bosco milite, Willelmo Suyllard, Iohanne de la Dale, Philippo Harneys, Thoma Aylred, Iohanne Rodlond, Roberto Cok', Iohanne de Stok' clerico, et multis aliis. At Ipswich, Saturday next after the feast of St Hilary, 23 Edward I. 15 January 1295

TNA, E40/3446. 197 × 84mm, 8mm turnup, 85mm tag. Seal 27mm round, but face mostly gone; it is merely white wax. Endorsed: Brok (16c.).

361. Notification by Matilda who was the wife of W'lfric of 'Brademere' of Brooks (*Brokes*), in the legal status of her widowhood, that she has granted, remised and utterly quitclaimed, for her and her heirs in perpetuity, to the prior and convent, the whole of her courtyard on the north of her house which she has and holds of them in Brooks, saving ten feet lineally from the traverse of the courtyard to the wall of the house against the courtyard on the north, as it is divided by the boundaries between them and her; to have and to hold to the prior and convent and their successors, so that neither she, her heirs, nor anyone in her name may henceforth make any claim in perpetuity. For this quitclaim the prior and convent have given to Matilda 2s of silver in cash. Sealed in testimony.

Hiis testibus: Thoma le Mayster et Thoma Stace tunc ballivis de Gypewico, Philippo Harneys, Iohanne filio suo, Thoma Aylred, Thoma Clement, Amisio et Roberto fratribus suis, Alexandro Margarete, Iohanne fratre suo, Ada de Holebrok', Iohanne de Stok', et multis aliis. [29 September 1295 x 28 September 1297; or 29 September 1299 x 28 September 1301]

TNA, E40/3634. 183 × 83mm, including folded-out turnup of 13mm. 73mm tag. Endorsed: [*smudged*] in brokis (17c.).

Date: Thomas le Mayster and Thomas Stace served together as bailiffs for these terms.

362. Notification by Augustine the son of W'lfric of 'Brademere' of Brooks by Ipswich (*Brokys iuxta Gippewycum*) that he has granted, remised and utterly quitclaimed to the prior and convent, for him and his heirs in perpetuity, all right and claim which he had, or in any way might have, in all the lands and tenements which the prior and convent have and hold by the demise of Matilda his mother in Brooks by Ipswich; so that neither he, his heirs, nor anyone in his or their names may henceforth make any claim therein. Sealed in testimony.

Hiis testibus: Willelmo Soillard, Iohanne de Freston', Petro dil Ty, Alano Garlond, Roberto Cok', Willelmo dil Cley, Roberto Fynch et aliis. At Ipswich, Wednesday next after the feast of the Lord's Epiphany, 6 Edward II.

10 January 1313

TNA, E40/3839. 270 × 87mm, 13mm turnup, 75mm tag; seal missing. Endorsed: vis' viiid' (14c.); Bradm'e; parochia sancti Petri (both 15c.).

363. Notification by Jacob the son of W'lfric of 'Brademere' of Brooks by Ipswich (*Brokes iuxta Gippewycum*) that he has granted, remised and utterly quitclaimed, for him and his heirs in perpetuity, to the prior and convent, all right and claim which he has, had, or in any way might have, in all the lands and tenements which the prior and convent have and hold in accordance with the demise of Matilda his mother in the hamlet of Brooks by Ipswich; so that neither he, his heirs, nor anyone in his or their names may henceforth make any claim therein. Sealed in testimony.

Hiis testibus: Petro dil Ty, Roberto de Bordeshoue, Iohanne Andrew, Iohanne Waryn, Roberto Cok' et aliis. At Ipswich, Sunday next before the feast of St Peter in Chains, 3 Edward III. 30 July 1329

TNA, E40/3838. 213 × 90mm, 20mm turnup, 120mm tag; seal missing. Endorsed: Iacob' de Brademor' dimidiam marcam (14/15c.); Heppe ii (?15c.).

364. Notification by John of Coddenham (*Codinham*) of Ipswich (*Gippewyco*) that he has granted, remised and utterly quitclaimed, for him and his heirs in perpetuity, to Prior Henry of Kersey (*Kerseye*), the canons, and their successors, all right and claim which he had or in any way could have had, or henceforth will be able to have, in one piece of land which the prior and canons have and hold in the hamlet of Brooks (*Brokis*), and which was formerly John Lorkin's, lying between John of Coddenham's land and the land of Robert Fynch, abutting at one headland upon the highway from Ipswich to Bramford (*Braunforde*), and at the other headland on the land of the prior and canons in 'Brademere'; so that neither he nor his heirs, nor anyone through him or in his name, may henceforth claim any right or make any claim therein in perpetuity.

Hiis testibus: Galfrido Stace, Willelmo Ringgyld tunc ballivis ville Gippewyci, Iohanne Haltebe, Iohanne Irp, Willelmo de Caustone clerico,[1] Gilberto Waleys, Willelmo de Neuthone, Semanno Mirihel, Milone le Smyth et aliis. At Ipswich, Sunday next after the feast of St Gregory the Pope, 8 Edward III.   13 March 1334

TNA, E40/3394. 242 × 87mm, indented at top and maximum measurement given here; parts of CYROGRAFUM visible over indentation, 13mm turnup, 127mm tag. Seal 26 × 28mm wax blob, 17 × 19mm impression, image of a woman's head with a prominent ponytail (?), legend: + EST … CAMOR. Endorsed: Brokys Brokys (16c.).

1 Although not mentioned here, John Irp and William Caustone were coroners for Ipswich in this year.

BURSTALL

365. Grant by Osbert le Neuman of Flowton to the church of the Apostles Peter and Paul and to the venerable fragment of the Holy Cross which may be seen there, for the salvation of his soul and those of his ancestors and successors, of 4½d annual rent which Alan son of [*illegible*] of Burstall was accustomed to pay to him for a piece of land called 'Thedulvesmere' in Burstall, to be taken at two terms of the year; with Alan's homage. Sealed in testimony.   [1220s – mid-thirteenth century]

TNA, E40/3880. 137 × 75mm, 14mm turnup, tag 110mm with a blade of grass tied around it; there are some stains of wax. Endorsed: Bustale (17c.).

Sciant presentes et futuri quod ego Osbertus le Neuman de Floketun' concessi, dedi et hac presenti carta mea confirmavi Deo et ecclesie apostolorum Petri et Pauli de Gipewico et venerabili particule sancte crucis que ibidem videtur, pro salute anime mee et pro animabus antecessorum et successorum meorum, quatuor denarios et obolum annui redditus quos Alanus filius [*illegible*] de Burstalle michi solebat reddere de una pecia terre que vocatur Thedulvesmere in parochia de Burstalle, ad duos terminos anni percipiendos, scilicet ad festum Sancti Michaelis duos denarios, et ad Pascha duos denarios et obolum, cum homagio dicti Alani, et omnibus ad dictum redditum pertinentibus. Habendos et tenendos libere et quiete, absque omni clamio vel contradictione mei vel heredum meorum. Et in huius rei testimonium presens scriptum sigilli mei appositione corroboravi. Hiis testibus: Willelmo Testepin, Roberto del Hel, Galfrido de Brokes, Radulfo filio Godwyni, Willelmo de Ry, Hugone Sprot, Normanno filio Petri de Bramford, Petro filio Alani de la Tye, Thoma filio Alani et multis aliis.

Date: Robert del Hel attests no. 436 (1220s – 1250s); William de Ry attests no. 286 (1230s – mid-thirteenth century).

366. Notification by Payne Tiptot, knight, that he has granted and given licence to William Andrew of Stoke by Ipswich (*Stoke iuxta Gippewicum*) that the reversion of all the lands and tenements which Isabella who was the wife of Thomas Horold holds for life in the townships of Burstall (*Burstalle*), Bramford (*Braunforde*) and Sproughton (*Sprowton*'), which are of Payne's fee and which after Isabella's death should revert to William and his heirs, may remain to Prior John and the convent; to have and to hold to the prior and convent and their successors in perpetuity, of Payne and his heirs, by the services previously due to him in respect thereof and of right accustomed; and that the prior and convent may accept the reversion of all those lands and tenements from William, and may after the death of Isabella enter and hold to them and their successors in perpetuity, notwithstanding the Statute of Mortmain, and rendering to Payne and his heirs [*amount left blank*] by name of a relief at each resignation, deprivation, cession or other vacancy, whether of John the now prior or of his successors in perpetuity. If the [*blank*] by name of relief when it falls due should be in arrears, either in whole or in part, then it may be lawful for Payne and his heirs to distrain upon all the lands and tenements and retain the things distrained until they are fully satisfied in respect of the relief. In witness whereof the parties have sealed each other's copy of this indenture. Ipswich, 5 September, 16 Richard II.   5 September 1392

TNA, E40/3877. 231 × 124mm maximum, 26mm turnup, 113mm tag, parts of CYROGRAPHUM visible at indented top edge. Seal missing. Endorsed: Pagan Tiptot miles Burstall' Bramforth et Spruton (?17c.).

367. Notification that, whereas Richard now King of England by his letters patent has given licence to William Andrew of Stoke by Ipswich (*Stoke iuxta Gippewicum*) to grant that one messuage, 200 acres of land, 12 acres of meadow, 15 acres of pasture, 5½ acres of wood and 13s rent in Burstall, Bramford (*Braunforde*) and Sproughton (*Sprouton*'), which Isabella who was the wife of Thomas Horold holds for life, and which after her death should revert to William, may revert after her death to the prior and convent and their successors, to have and to hold to them and their successors notwithstanding the Statute of Mortmain, by virtue of the letters patent, William has granted by these presents that the lands and tenements are to remain, after Isabella's death, to the prior and convent, to have and to hold to them and their successors of the capital lords of those fees by the services due in respect thereof and by right accustomed, performing all the burdens and services contained in the king's letters patent, as more fully appears therein. Sealed in testimony.

Hiis testibus: Georgio Fylbrygg', Iohanne Fastulf, Iohanne de Braham, militibus, Rogero de Wolferston', Gilberto Debynham [*one name illegible*], Waltero atte Hel, Rogero Mascal et aliis. Burstall, 23 September 16 Richard II.   23 September 1392

TNA, E40/3875. 273 × 117mm, 22mm turnup, tag and seal missing. Endorsed: Burstall et Sprouton' (16/17c.).

HINTLESHAM

368. Quitclaim in perpetuity by Baldwin the physician of Hintlesham to the canons, of all right and claim which he had or may have had in one acre of land of the fee of Simon Mauchael in Knapton [*in Hintlesham*], namely that which he gave to Thomas of Knapton in marriage with his sister Alice; paying annually to Simon as lord of the fee 3d in two instalments for all services, customs and exactions. For this the canons have given to Baldwin 6s of sterlings.   [1220s – 1230s]

TNA, E40/3900. 205 × 160mm, 18mm turnup, 167mm tag. Seal missing. Endorsed: Simon' Makel' iiid' de una acra (?15c.).

Sciant presentes et futuri quod ego Baldewinus medicus de Hintlesham concessi et hac presenti carta mea quetum [*sic*] clamavi Deo et ecclesie Sancti Petri de Gypeswico et canonicis ibidem Deo servientibus, unam acram terre cum pertinenciis que est de feodo Simonis Mauchael in Cnapetune, scilicet illam quam dedi Thome de Cnapetune in maritagium cum Alicia sorore mea. Et omne ius et clamium quod in eadem terra habui vel habere potui predicte ecclesie et dictis canonicis omnino quietum clamavi in perpetuum, de me et de heredibus meis habendam et tenendam libere et quiete, solvendo inde Simoni Mauchael domino feodi illius tres denarios per annum ad duos terminos, scilicet ad Pascha tres obulos, et ad festum Sancti Michaelis tres obulos, pro omnibus serviciis et consuetudinibus et exactionibus. Pro hac autem concessione et quieta clamatione dederunt michi predicti canonici sex solidos sterlingorum. His testibus: Willelmo Talebot, Simone Mauchael, Willelmo Testepin, Willelmo filio eius, Huberto preposito, Rogero Gocelin, Iohanne filio Andree, Galfrido Mauchael, Iohanne filio eius, Hugone Mauchael, Roberto de Norwude, Iohanne Mauchael.

Date: The names of several witnesses indicate a date similar to no. 83, 29 April 1227 x June 1232 (Sir Herbert de Alencun sheriff).

369. Notification by Robert Maukel the elder that he has granted, remitted and utterly in perpetuity released and quitclaimed, for himself and his heirs, to the prior and canons, 2s annual rent which they were accustomed to pay him for the tenements which they held of him in the township of Hintlesham (*Hyntlesham*), so that the prior and canons may have and hold all those tenements of Robert and his heirs by the service of 1d *per annum* only, to be paid at the feast of St Michael for all services in perpetuity. Sealed in testimony.

Hiis testibus: Fulcone Baroun, Nicholao de Aldham, Iohanne dil Hul, Roberto dil Hul, Ricardo de Coppedok', Nicholao Bonde et aliis. Hintlesham, 20 May 9 Edward II.   20 May 1316

TNA, E40/3535. 187 × 65mm, 12mm turnup, 90mm tag with string wrapped around it. Seal 23mm round, with device of two crossed gloves, legend illegible. Endorsed: Maukel id' (16c.).

370. Indenture whereby Thomas Maukel of Hintlesham (*Hyntlesham*), chaplain, has granted, given up and demised to the prior and canons, two shillings and one pennyworth of annual rent which he was accustomed to take from them for the lands and tenements which they held of him in Hintlesham; to have and to hold to them and their successors for the term of Thomas's life, for a certain sum of money which they have paid him in hand. Thomas will warrant, acquit and defend the rent to them against all people for the whole of his life; after his death the rent is to revert entirely to his heirs without any hindrance by the prior or canons. In testimony whereof the parties have alternately applied their seals.

Hiis testibus: Radulfo de Reydon', Iohanne de Cleydon', Iohanne dil Hul, Iohanne le Mareschal, Waltero dil Hul et aliis. Hintlesham, Sunday next after the feast of St Gregory, 1 Edward III. 15 March 1327

TNA, E40/3536. 213 × 71mm maximum, top edge indented and part of CYROGRAFUM legible, 11mm turnup, 82mm tag, some scrawl inside but not readily legible. Seal missing. Endorsed: Hi'tlesham (16c.); Maukel (17c.).

HINTLESHAM AND CAPEL

371. Confirmation in perpetuity by Robert of Hadleigh, son of Nicholas of Hadleigh, to the canons, of the gift which Nicholas his brother made to them of all which he had in Hintlesham, namely 6½ acres of land between 'Gosecroft' and the land which was John son of Adam of Hadleigh's; his part of the wood called 'Merweneswode' and 2 acres at the head of it; 2 acres of 'Pikeslond'; all his meadow with the wood of 'Ruges'; 3 acres of arable land extending upon the meadow; the homage of Thomas Germund with the annual rent of 6d, 22 days' customary work and 2 hens at Christmas with food; from William Piterich 13d *per annum* and 2 days' customary work in autumn with food and 2 hens at Christmas with food; 1d *per annum* from Roger Sparehurs; and 6d which the canons were accustomed to pay him annually for 'Wuluardeslond'. Also all the annual rent which he had in Capel, namely 12d from Gilbert son of Claricia, 8d from Robert the clerk, 2d from the widow of Sampson Bolle; and the whole fee from which the rent is taken. Warranty is granted. [29 April 1227 x June 1232]

TNA, E40/3321. 145 × 119mm, 20mm turnup, 115mm tag. Seal 35mm round, in green wax. Legend: + SIGILL' ROB'TI FIL' NICOL'; design of a sunburst or head of grain. No counterseal, no endorsement. Tag has writing on the inside, apparently musical notation; 'Vestimenta' legible at bottom.

Sciant presentes et futuri quod ego Robertus de Hadleg' filius Nicholai de Hadleg' concessi et hac mea carta confirmavi Deo et ecclesie beatorum apostolorum Petri et Pauli de Gypewico et canonicis ibidem Deo servientibus, totum donum quod Nicholaus frater meus eis fecit in terris et redditibus, in pratis et pasturis, in bosco et plano, et in omnibus que habebat in parochia de Hintlesham, scilicet sex acras terre et dimidiam inter Gosecroft et terram que fuit Iohannis filii Ade de Hadleg', et totam partem suam de bosco qui vocatur Merweneswode, et duas acras ad capud eiusdem bosci, et duas acras de Pikeslond, et totum pratum suum cum bosco de Ruges, et tres acras terre arabilis extendentes super pratum, et homagium

Thome Germund cum redditu, scilicet sex denarios per annum et viginti duo opera, et ad Natale duas gallinas cum cibo, et de Willelmo Piterich tresdecim denarios per annum et duo opera in autumpno cum cibo et duas gallinas at Natale cum cibo, et unum denarium de Rogero Sparehurs, et sex denarios quos dicti canonici solebant eidem annuatim reddere de Wuluardeslond. Et preterea totum redditum quem habuit in parochia de Capeles, scilicet de Gileberto filio Claricie duodecim denarios per annum, et de Roberto clerico octo denarios per annum, et de relicta Sampsonis Bolle duos denarios per annum, et totum feodum unde predictus redditus provenit. Habendum et tenendum libere et quiete in perpetuum. Et ego et heredes mei warantizabimus dictis canonicis predictum donum contra omnes homines. Hiis testibus: Domino Herberto de Alicun tunc vicecomite Suffolcie, Willelmo Danbli, Galfrido de Badele, Sewallo de Nuetun', Thome del Pond, Iohanne de Gloucestr', Waltero filio Edrici, Rogero de Aldham, Willelmo Testepin, Rogero Gocelin', Ricardo del Hel, Symone Malkael et multis aliis.

Date: Sir Herbert de Alicun sheriff.

IPSWICH, ST AUGUSTINE IN STOKE

372. Grant in free and perpetual alms by Thomas Sicht, son of William Thuri of Ipswich, to the canons, for the salvation of his soul and those of his wife Joice and their ancestors and successors, of 14d annual rent which Osbert of Bealings used to pay him out of a piece of land lying in the suburb of Ipswich, namely Stoke, upon the turbary before the gate of Thomas son of Roger Palmer; rendering to the grantor and his heirs 2d *per annum* at the Lord's Nativity for all services. Warranty is granted.   [Mid-thirteenth century]

TNA, E40/3301. 159 × 77mm, 13mm turnup, 79mm tag, seal missing. Endorsed: paroch' Augustini xiiiid' (?16c.).

Sciant presentes et futuri quod ego Thomas Sicht filius Willelmi Thuri de Gipewico concessi, dedi, et hac presenti carta mea confirmavi Deo et ecclesie beatorum apostolorum Petri et Pauli de Gypewico et canonicis ibidem Deo servientibus, pro salute anime mee et Ioece uxoris mee et antecessorum et successorum nostrorum, quatuordecim denarios annui redditus quos Osbertus de Belinges michi solebat reddere de una pecia terre iacente in suburbio de Gypewico, scilicet Stok', super torverium ante portam Thome fili Rogeri Palmeri. Habendos et tenendos dicte ecclesie et dictis canonicis et eorum successoribus de me et heredibus meis in liberam et perpetuam elemosinam. Reddendo inde annuatim michi et heredibus meis duos denarios ad unum terminum, scilicet ad Natale Domini, pro omnibus serviciis, consuetudinibus et demandis. Et ego Thomas et heredes mei waran-tizabimus dictis ecclesie et canonicis dictum redditum per dictum servicium contra omnes inperpetuum. In huius rei testimonium presenti scripto sigillum meum appossui. Hiis testibus: Roberto Wulfun, Matheo de Porta tunc ballivis de Gypewico, Domino Odone decano de Gypewico, Silvestro filio Walkelini, Iohanne de Sancto Georgio, Nicholao Godescalc, Nicholao de Foro, Clemente le Paumer, Iohanne Pecoc, Semanno de Cruce, Iohanne de Plat, Ricardo Sired, et aliis.

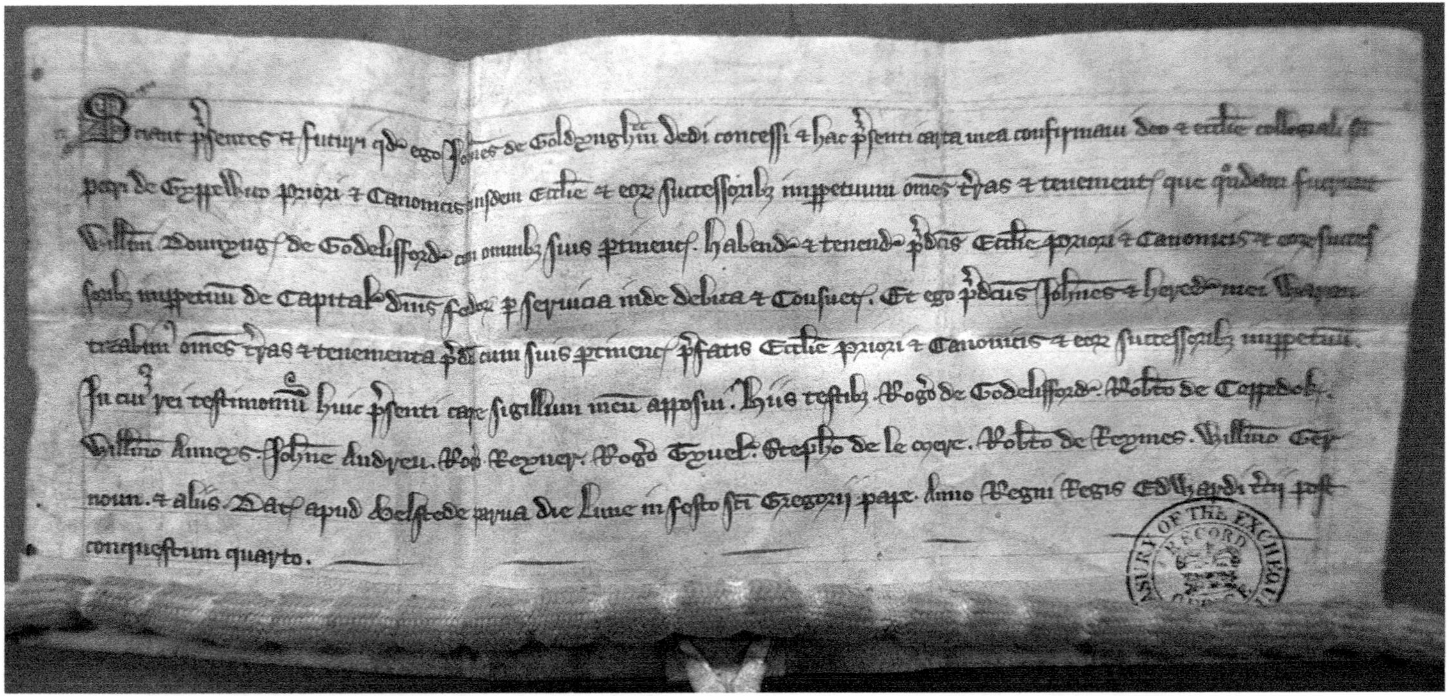

Fig. 2 Grant in perpetuity by John of Goldingham to St Peter's, of lands and tenements formerly William Dounyng's of Gusford, in Stoke-by-Ipswich, 12 March 1330 (no. 374). London, The National Archives, E40/3600.

Date: Odo the Dean, Silvester son of Wakelin and Clement le Paumer all participated in the inquiry into the right of presentation to the living of St Clement's, Ipswich, on 24 October 1251 (no. 315). Matthew de Porta's first known tenure of the office of bailiff was in 1255, though he may have served earlier. Robert Wulfun's term as bailiff is unknown.

373. Grant by Joan the daughter of Thomas le Maister of Ipswich (*Gyppewyco*) to the prior and canons, of all that tenement called 'Palmeres lond' which she held of them and had by the gift of Joan who was the wife of Thomas Aylred, in the parish of St Augustine next to the way called 'Lonsgate Weye' in the suburb of Ipswich; to have and to hold the tenement with its ways, profits and all its other appurtenances, to the prior and convent and their successors in perpetuity, of the capital lords of the fee by the services by right due and accustomed in respect thereof. Warranty by the grantor and her heirs against all people in perpetuity. Sealed in testimony.

Hiis testibus: Gilberto de Borugh', Edmundo de Castelacr' tunc ballivis Gippewyci, Iohanne de Watefelde, Henrico le Rotoun, Thoma Stace, Iohanne le Maister, Henrico Steyl et aliis. At Ipswich, Sunday next before the feast of St Bartholomew the Apostle, 18 Edward II.   19 August 1324

TNA, E40/3407. 192 × 108mm, 14mm turnup, 93mm tag. Seal 38mm round, dark wax, design of five oak leaves, legend rubbed. Illegible words on inner faces of tag. Endorsed: Ioh'a le meister vis. viiid. (?15c.); par' sancti Augustini (16/17c.).

374. Grant in perpetuity by John of Goldingham (*Goldyngham*) to the collegiate church of St Peter of Ipswich (*Gyppewico*), the prior and canons and their successors, of all the lands and tenements which were formerly of William Dounyng of Gusford (*Godelisford*), with all their appurtenances, to have and to hold to the prior and canons and their successors in perpetuity, of the capital lords of the fees, by the due and accustomed services in respect thereof. Warranty by the grantor and his heirs in perpetuity. Sealed in testimony.

Hiis testibus: Rogero de Godelisford, Roberto de Coppedok', Willelmo Anneys, Iohanne Andreu, Rogero Reyner, Rogero Tyvel, Stephano de le Mere, Roberto de Reymes, Willelmo Gernoun, et aliis. At Little Belstead (*Belstede Parva*), Monday the feast of St Gregory the Pope, 4 Edward III.   12 March 1330

TNA, E40/3600. 237 × 108mm, 15mm turnup, 103mm tag, seal missing. Endorsed: Dwning' de Godelisforth (?16c.); H. Prior … viii … Douning (?15c.).

IPSWICH, ST MARGARET

375. Letter of attorney by John Clement, burgess of Ipswich, in consideration of charity and for the salvation of his soul, constituting the prior and convent and their successors his attorneys in perpetuity to claim and recover in his name 6d annual rent towards the maintenance of the light before the altar of the Blessed

Mary in their church, to be received annually from John son of Alan Perminhed of Ipswich and his heirs or assigns whosever [*missing*]

Hiis testibus: Thoma le Maistre et Thoma [Stace][1] tunc ballivis de Gypewico, Alexandro [*missing*], Roberto Davy, Nicholao le clerk, Ada Verdam, Ada de Holebrok, Iohanne le Meistre, [*missing*], Amisio fratre suo, Alexandro Margarde, et aliis. Thursday after the Commemoration of Souls, 23 Edward I.

3 November 1295

Bodl., ms. charters Suffolk 214. 204 × 93mm, 13mm turnup. One slit for tag only. Endorsed: par' Margarete; de tenemento quod Ioh' de Waterfeld perquisivit de Will'o [*missing*] iuxta Michelisdowne in manerium Ioh's le [*missing*] (two different hands, both late medieval).

    1 The charter is in poor condition and a few lines, including the names of some witnesses, are lost. The surname of the second-named bailiff of Ipswich is illegible, and has been supplied from the borough archive (*IBAC*, p. 47).

IPSWICH, ST MARY AT ELMS

376. Grant in free, pure and perpetual alms by Thomas Testepin to the canons, for the salvation of his soul and those of his ancestors, of 4d annual rent in the town of Ipswich, which Thomas Chop used to pay him for a messuage in Elm Street, lying between the messuage of William Tolle and the house of Galiena Wrid. Warranty is granted. [Early – mid-thirteenth century]

TNA, E40/3949. 171 × 76mm, 13mm turnup, 70mm tag, seal missing. Endorsed: Th' Testepin & Th' Chop (?14c.).

Sciant presentes et futuri quod ego Thomas Testepin concessi, dedi, et hac presenti carta mea confirmavi Deo et ecclesie beatorum apostolorum Petri et Pauli de Gypewico et canonicis ibidem servientibus, in liberam, puram et perpetuam elemosinam, pro salute anime mee et antecessorum meorum, quatuor denarios annui redditus in villa de Gypewico, quos Thomas Chop michi solebat reddere de uno mesuagio in vico qui vocatur Ellstrete, quod iacet inter mesuagium Willelmi Tolle ex una parte et domum Galiene Wrid ex altera parte; tenendos et habendos illis et eorum successoribus, libere, quiete, bene et in pace inperpetuum, absolute ab omni servicio seculari. Et ego predictus Thomas et heredes mei warantizabimus predictum redditum predictis canonicis et eorum successoribus contra omnes. In huius rei testimonium huic scripto sigillum meum apposui. Hiis testibus: Domino Galfrido de Badele milite, Silvestro filio Waukeli[ni *omitted*], Hugone de Langestun', Helya filio Iohanni Normani, Amisio le Wineter, Costantino Fader, Iohanne de Beumes, Roberto Wlfun, Willelmo Godeschalc, Oseberto de Beling', Waltero de Leystun' et aliis.

Date: Sir Geoffrey of Badley (Geoffrey III) was admitted a forinsec burgess of Ipswich in 1233 or 1234 (Introduction, p. 61). Amis the vintner attests no. 31, 1190s – early thirteenth century, and William Godeschalc was among the first capital burgesses to be chosen for the borough under the charter of 1200, making it unlikely that this charter dates after 1250. John de Beumes was bailiff sometime between 1227 and 1232, and again in 1233–34, and was a surety to prosecute in a suit at the eyre of 1240 (*CPSE*, no. 1046).

IPSWICH, ST MICHAEL

377. Grant in free, pure and perpetual alms by Humfrey Geldeneston of Ipswich to the canons, towards the maintenance of the lamp before the altar of St Mary in their church, of 13d annual rent with the fee out of which it issues, to be taken from the hand of William Horold and his heirs at two annual terms, namely 6½d at the feast of St Michael and Easter, which William was accustomed to pay to Humfrey from the messuage sometime Andrew Peper's, situated next to the corn market, between the messuages of Hugh Golding and Humfrey; to hold and to have free from all secular service. Warranty is granted.   [Mid-thirteenth century]

TNA, E40/3707. 179 × 80mm, 17mm turnup, not slit for tag. Endorsed: Umfrid' Geldeneston xiiid' (14c.); Umfrid' Geldeneston xiiid' (14c., different hand); par' sancti Michael'[1] xiiid' (15/16c.).

Sciant presentes et futuri quod ego Humfridus Geldeneston de Gypewico concessi, dedi, et hac presenti carta mea confirmavi Deo et ecclesie apostolorum Petri et Pauli de Gypewico et canonicis ibidem Deo servientibus, ad sustentacionem luminis coram altari Sancte Marie in dicta ecclesia, in liberam puram et perpetuam elemosinam, tresdecim denarios annui redditus cum pertinenciis et cum feodo unde dictus redditus provenit, percipiendos de manu Willelmi Horold et heredum suorum ad duos terminos anni, scilicet ad festum Sancti Michaelis sex denarios et obolum et ad Pascha sex denarios et obolum, quos idem Willelmus michi reddere consuevit de mesuagio quondam Andree Peper sito iuxta forum quo venditur bladum, inter mesuagium Hugonis Golding et mesuagium meum. Tenendos et habendos illis et eorum successoribus, libere, quiete, pure et absolute ab omni servicio seculari. Et ego Humfridus et heredes mei warantizabimus dictum redditum dictis canonicis contra omnes imperpetuum. Hiis testibus: Willelmo Godescalc, Matheo de Porta tunc balivis, Roberto Wlfun, Silvestro filio Wakelini, Hugone de Langestun', Rogero fratre eius, Hugone Leu, Iohanne de Sancto Georgio, Amisio Bolle, Iohanne filio eius, Waltero de Leystun', Osberto de Foro, Osberto de Belinges, et aliis.

1 The identification of the parish as St Michael rests only upon an endorsement, and the reference in the charter to the property from which the rent derives lying next to the Corn Market suggests that the endorsement was perhaps an error for St Mildred on the Cornhill. The Domesday church of St Michael has disappeared so completely that its site is now unknown. See Introduction, p. 31.

Date: Amis Bolle and Andrew Peper were elected capital portmen, William Godescalc a capital burgess and alderman, and John of St George a capital burgess of Ipswich in 1200 ('Black Domesday', fols 78r., 80v.); Peper as a *former* owner of the property is presumably dead, and the others are unlikely to have been active beyond 1250. Godescalc was accused at the 1240 eyre, along with Prior Gilbert of St Peter's and Richard, dean of Coddenham, of disseising Master Robert of Coddenham of his free tenement in Ipswich. Roger of Langestun participated in the inquiry into the right of presentation to the living of St Clement's, Ipswich on 24 October 1251 (no. 315).

IPSWICH, ST MILDRED

378. Grant by John son of Alexander of Ipswich to the canons, of his shop in the Shambles of Ipswich, namely that which Osbert Cook and Richard Pilche sometime held of him, and all the rent which may be able to issue from it, and 12d annually from Hugh of Langestun' and his heirs from the land which was of Langlin' de la Baile, in free and pure alms for the salvation of his soul and those of Alexander and Claricia his father and mother, and of all his ancestors and successors in perpetuity. To have and to hold free of all service except the king's service of 4d out of the shop and 2d to the canons of Dodnash. Sealed for perpetual stability.

[Late twelfth – first third of thirteenth century]

TNA, E40/3293. 198 × 72mm, 18mm turnup, 97mm tag. On inside of tag is – universis ma [*gap*] – Omnibus omnibus. Seal 24 × 29mm, green wax, legend illegible, design of pillar with a standing human figure adjacent. Endorsed: par' sancte Mildrede (16c.).

Universis sancte matris ecclesie filiis presentem cartam specturis et audituris Iohannes filius Alexandri de Gipewico salutem. Noveritis me concessisse et dedisse et hac carta mea confirmasse Deo et ecclesie beatorum apostolorum Petri et Pauli de Gipewico et canonicis ibidem Deo servientibus, scopam meam que est in macello de Gipewico quam scilicet Osebertus Cocus et Ricardus Pilche aliquando de me tenuerunt, et totum redditum qui ex eadem scopa poterit provenire, et duodecim denarios annuatim capiendos de Hugone de Langestun' et heredibus suis de terra que fuit Langline de la Baile, in liberam et perpetuam elemosinam pro salute anime mee et Alexandri patris mei et Claricie matris mee, et omnium parentum et antecessorum et successorum meorum inperpetuum. Habendum et tenendum libere et quiete et solute ab omni servicio salvo servicio domini regis, scilicet quatuor denarios de predicta scopa, et canonicis de Dodenes duos denarios de eadem scopa. Et ut hec mea concessio et donacio perpetuam optineat firmitatem presens scriptum eis contuli sigillo meo consignatum. His testibus: Domino Radulfo de Pesehaulle milite, Rogero de Horsahe, Iohanne filio Normanni, Willelmo de Beamis, Iohanne de Beamis, Petro filio Eborardi, Iohanne filio Constantini, Rogero Lyu, Amisio Bolle, Rogero de Langestun', Rogero de Bruntun', Willelmo Herode et multis aliis.

Date: The donor John son of Alexander attests a charter of John de Beaumes (no. 386), late twelfth – first third of thirteenth century; John de Beaumes himself was a bailiff of Ipswich at some time between 1227 and 1232, and again 1233–34; he was party to a plea of *Utrum*, and amerced in a plea of warranty, during the 1240 eyre (*CPSE*, nos. 275–82, 1046, 1657). Sir Ralph of Peasenhall is Ralph II (*Sibton Cartularies*, I, pp. 80–81), whose father Norman II last occurs in 1210, and whom

Ralph had succeeded by 1217. Roger de Horsahe/Horsehag' attests no. 43, after Easter 1180 but before October 1198, and no. 437, 1227–32. John son of Norman attests nos. 48 and 49, 1180s – 1190s, and occurs into the 1230s (nos. 440, 458). He was one of the first pair of bailiffs of Ipswich chosen in 1200. Roger Lyu was coroner in 1200, and with Amis Bolle attests the agreement between Woodbridge Priory and the burgesses of Ipswich concerning the tolls of Woodbridge market, 18 November 1233 (SROI, HD 1538/435/4).

379. Grant in perpetuity by Richard, dean of Coddenham, to the prior and convent, of 2s annual rent from the messuage which he holds of them for 3s *per annum* at *Cotessloh* where timber is sold in Ipswich, so that he and his assigns pay to the prior and convent 5s *per annum* for the messuage, in two instalments. In return the prior and canons have given and quitclaimed the messuage with appurtenances which Osbert and Hawis his wife held of them to Richard and other burgesses of Ipswich for the increase and enlargement of the house of the Friars Minor. Sealed in testimony. [?*c.* 1219–1236]

TNA, E40/3292. 173 × 84mm, 16mm turnup. Seal 1 in centre, 75mm tag, seal 27 × 30mm, natural wax. Design of Agnus Dei, legend … CCE AGN … TA. Seal 2 at left, sewn to turnup and not originally part of charter (there is no slit for a tag in the turnup), 40 × 44mm, green wax, tag 97mm, design of flower or sunburst, legend S. UMFRIDI GILDENSTON. Endorsed: par' sancti Petri o' sancte Mildrede (16c.).

Notum sit universis quod ego Ricardus decanus de Codeham concessi, dedi, et hac presenti carta mea confirmavi priori et canonicis Sancti Petri de Gipwico duos solidos annui redditus de mesuagio meo quod teneo de eis in Gipwico pro tribus solidis annuis apud Cotessloh ubi venditur marimium,[1] ita quod ego et assignati mei solvemus in perpetuum quolibet anno dictis priori et canonicis quinque solidos pro dicto mesuagio, videlicet duos solidos et sex denarios ad Pascha, et duos solidos et sex denarios ad festum Sancti Mikaelis. Pro hac vero concessione, donatione, et carta mea confirmatione, concesserunt et dederunt et quietumclamaverunt dicti prior et canonici mesuagium cum pertinentiis quod Osbertus et Hawis uxor eius tenuerunt de eis michi et aliis burgensibus de Gipwico in augmentum et dilata-tionem mansionis fratrum minorum.[2] Et in huius rei testimonium, presenti scripto sigillum meum apposui. Hiis testibus: Domino Radulfo de Blumvill archidiacono Suffolchie, Magistro Gervasio decano de Gipwico, Domino Ricardo capellano de Sancto Laurentio, Petro Eborard et Hugone de Langeston' tunc bailivis, Iohanne Norman, Eliseo et Willelmo et Iohanne filiis eius, Iohanne Costin, Waltero de Leyston', Iohanne de Beumes, Rogero Lyu, Amisio Bolle, Rogero de Langeston', et multis aliis.

1 That the timber (*marimium*) market was in St Mildred's parish is shown by a deed of 25 March 1399 in the Ipswich borough archive: C6/6/1/4 (*IBAC*, pp. 562–63).

2 The Minorite (Franciscan) Order was founded informally in 1209–10, and confirmed by a papal bull of 1223 (Brooke, *Medieval Monastery*, 189). The statement in *VCH Suffolk* (II, 126, citing Weever's *Funeral Monuments*) that the Ipswich house was founded early in the reign of Edward I is clearly incorrect.

Date: Ralf de Blumvill does not appear in the *Fasti* as archdeacon of Suffolk, but *does* appear there as archdeacon of Norfolk, which office he resigned for pluralism in 1237 (*Fasti*, ii, 66). He must have served the Suffolk office for part or all of the *lacuna* in the *Fasti*, i.e., *c.* 1219–1236. This is borne out by the presence of some of the other witnesses, e.g. John Costin and Roger Lyu attest the agreement between Woodbridge Priory and the burgesses of Ipswich concerning the tolls of Woodbridge market on 18 November 1233 (SROI, Iveagh MSS, HD 1538/435/4), while John de Beumes served as bailiff for at least one term between 1227 and 1232, and again in 1233–34. Richard, dean of Coddenham, attests a Dodnash Priory charter dated 28 October 1223 x 27 October 1224 (*Dodnash Charters*, no. 16). The year in which Peter Eborard and Hugh de Langeston served together as bailiffs is unknown.

380. Notification that Gratian son of John the chaplain and Agatha his sister have sold and quitclaimed in perpetuity to Richard, dean of Coddenham, and the brothers Robert, Richard, Henry and Michael, the houses with the ground and appurtenances which they had in Ipswich beside the timber market, which were Edgar the cobbler's and are between the house of Simon Cote and Robert the palmer, for 40s of sterlings; to have and to hold to them and their heirs and assigns, of the prior and convent by the service of 3s *per annum*, namely 18d at Easter and the feast of St Michael, for all services save the king's service of 1d house-rent. Warranty is granted. Sealed in testimony.   [1220s – 1230s]

TNA, E40/3294. 222 × 78mm, 13mm turnup. Seal 1 is a vesica, 28 × 37mm, reddish-brown wax, design of ear of grain on a stalk, legend +SIGILL … RATIAN; tag 70mm. Tag 2 90mm, trace of wax but no seal, reddish-brown also. Endorsed: Gipps', tres solid' ubi venditur meremium (14c.); par' sancte Mildrede (16c.).

Sciant presentes et futuri quod ego Gratianus filius Iohannis capellani et Agatha soror mea vendidimus et quietus [*sic*] clamavimus inperpetuum de nobis et heredibus nostris si quos habuerimus, Ricardo de Codeham decano et Roberto, Ricardo, Henrico et Michaeli, fratribus, domos cum fundo et omnibus aliis perti-nentiis suis quas habuimus in villa Gipwici iuxta forum ubi venditur meremium, que fuerunt Eidgari sutoris et sunt inter domum Simonis Cote et Roberti palmerii, pro quadraginta solidis sterlingorum, habendas et tenendas illis et heredibus eorum vel assignatis, de priore et conventu Sancti Petri de Gipwico, libere, quiete, et hereditarie per servicium trium solidorum per annum solvendorum, scilicet decem et octo denariorum ad Pascha et decem et octo denariorum ad festum Sancti Michaelis, pro omni servicio et demanda salvo servicio domini regis, scilicet uno denario ad hadgabulum. Et nos et heredes nostri si quos habuerimus warantiz-abimus predicto Ricardo et supradictis fratribus et eorum heredibus vel assignatis, domos pretaxatas cum omnibus suis pertinentiis. Et in huius rei testimonium presentem cartam sigillo nostro roboratam eis contulimus. Hiis testibus: Thoma filio Manseri, Amisio vinitario tunc ballivis, Iohanne filio Normanni, Willelmo fratre eius, Iohanne de Beumes, Iohanne Prikehert, Petro filio Eborardi, Philippo de Porta, Iohanne fratre eius, Galfrido Blundel, Willelmo fratre eius, Silvestro filio Walkelini, Laurentio molendinario, Waltero mercatore, Waltero de Leystune,

Rogero Liu, Iohanne filio Costentini, Roberto Paris, Andrea Peper, Petro Peper, Rogero de Langestune, Ricardo Morel, et multis aliis.

Date: Similar to no. 379. Richard, dean of Coddenham is the grantor of one and grantee of the other. Both are witnessed by John de Beumes, Peter (son of) Eborard, Walter of Leiston, Roger Lyu and Roger of Langestune.

381. Notification by Gilbert Haltebe of Ipswich (Gyp') that he and his heirs are bound to the prior and canons and their successors in perpetuity for 32d annual rent for a piece of land with buildings which he held of them containing 43 feet in length and 23 feet in width, lying between his messuage and a certain messuage of Roger Prikehert, one headland abutting upon the messuage which Gilbert sometime held of the canons and resigned to them; to be paid at two terms of the year, namely 16d at Easter and the feast of St Michael; so that if he, his heirs or assigns cease payment of that rent at the said terms, it may be lawful for the cellarer of that house or his attorney to distrain upon him, his heirs and assigns, and even upon the heirs of his assigns and of his heirs [*sic*], both there and in all his principal houses which abut upon the king's market place. He also wills and grants, and firmly confirms by this charter, for him, his heirs, assigns and the heirs of his assigns, that if at any time the prior and canons shall be hindered so that they may not distrain for the rent, it may be lawful for the canons to enter into the piece of land with its buildings and retain them in fee to them and their successors in perpetuity without any impediment of Gilbert, his heirs, assigns and the heirs of his assigns. Sealed in testimony.

Testibus: Matheo de Porta, Semanno Tophole, tunc ballivis de Gyp', Roberto Wlfun, Ricardo Fader, Iohanne Lorekin, Galfrido Horold, Roberto le Taverner, Edmundo le Gros, Nicholao Godeskalc, Thoma le Gros, Iohanne Poperolle and others.

[1250s – 1270s]

TNA, E40/3793. 220 × 119mm, 23mm turnup, 94mm tag. Seal fragment in green wax, 25 × 33mm, unintelligible. Endorsed: xxxiid. de dono Gilberti Haltebe nunc Iohannis Stoke et Iohannis le Man in foro carn' (?15c.). Iohannes le M ... et Iohannes de ?Stokes pro placea quod fuit Gilberti Haltebe (?14c.). par' sancte Mildrede (?15c.). N E (?16c.).

Date: Matthew de Porta is first known to have served as bailiff in 1255, though he may have done so earlier, in a period for which the records are lacking. He last served in 1279. Seman Tophole and Richard Fader served the office together in 1266–67. Gilbert Haltebe the grantor was dead before 1 April 1281 (no. 480).

IPSWICH, ST NICHOLAS

382. Grant by Robert son of Adam of London to the canons, of the messuage which was his father Adam's in St Nicholas, Ipswich, to be held of Robert and his heirs for the annual rent of 1d at the feast of St Michael for all secular exactions pertaining to him saving the king's service of 1d house-rent, 8d *per annum* to the prior of Woodbridge and 2d *per annum* to the dean of Ipswich. For this gift the canons have given a fine of 2 marks of silver. Warranty is granted. Besides, Robert has granted to the canons, for the salvation of his soul and those of his parents, ancestors and successors, in free, pure and perpetual alms, 1d annual rent to be received from John Costin.   [Late twelfth – early thirteenth century]

TNA, E40/3782. 164 × 112mm, 17mm turnup, 72mm tag, no seal. Endorsed: parochia Nich'i priori de Wodebregge viiid' (16c.); par' sancti Nicholai priori sancti Petri (?16c.).

Sciant presentes et futuri quod ego Robertus filius Ade de Londoniis [*sic*] concessi et dedi et hac mea carta confirmavi Deo et ecclesie beatorum apostolorum Petri et Pauli de Gipwico et canonicis ibidem Deo servientibus, totum mesagium [*sic*] quod fuit dicti Ade patris mei in villa de Gipwico, quod scilicet iacet inter mesagium [*sic*] Galfridi Blundel versus aquilonem et regiam viam versus meridiem, in parrochia Sancti Nicholai, cum omnibus pertinenciis suis; habendum et tenendum de me et heredibus meis, libere et quiete; solvendo inde annuatim michi et heredibus meis unum denarium in festo Sancti Michaelis pro omnibus serviciis et consuetudinibus et exaccionibus secularibus que ad me pertinent, salvo servicio domini regis, scilicet haggabulo ad quod unum denarium pertinet, et salvo servicio diversorum, scilicet priori de Wudebrig' octo denarios per annum, et decano de Gipwico duos denarios per annum. Et pro hac concessione et donacione et huius carte confirmacione, dederunt michi prefati canonici duas marcas argenti in gersumiam. Quare ego et heredes mei debemus warantizare predictis canonicis predictum mesagium cum suis pertinenciis per predictum servicium contra omnes homines. Preterea dedi eis redditum unius denarii per annum a Iohanne Costin recipiendum, pro salute anime mee et omnium parentum et antecessorum et successorum meorum, in liberam et puram et perpetuam elemosinam. Hiis testibus: Iohanne, Walkelino, Willelmo filiis Normanni, Thoma Manseri, Willelmo Angoth, Iohanne Costin, Alexandro Baldri, Galfrido, Roberto, Willelmo Blundell', Philippo de Porta, Iohanne fratre eius, Amisio Bolle, Humfrido Starling, Willelmo Herode et multis aliis.

Date: In 1200 John son of Norman was elected one of the two first bailiffs of Ipswich, Philip de Porta one of the first coroners, and Amis Bolle one of the first capital portmen. The absence of the bailiffs from the list of witnesses may perhaps signify a date before 1200. Almost all the witnesses attest other charters in this collection between the 1190s and the early thirteenth century.

383. Quitclaim by Nigel son of Bartholomew the cook to the canons, of the whole of the messuage with its buildings which he held of them in St Nicholas, Ipswich; for which quitclaim they have given him 8s of silver. Sealed in corroboration.
                    [Late twelfth – first third of thirteenth century]

TNA, E40/3664. 172 × 52mm, including folded-out turnup of 11mm, tag 112mm. Seal 35mm, fragment only. Endorsed: par' sancti Nicholai (16c.); Gipewic (16/17c.). There are words on the inner faces of the tag, but only one is clearly legible: Amen.

Sciant presentes et futuri quod ego Nigellus filius Bartholomei coci resignavi et quietum clamavi Deo et ecclesie beatorum apostolorum Petri et Pauli de Gipuico et canonicis ibidem Deo servientibus, totum mesagium [*sic*] meum cum edificiis et pertinentiis quod tenui de eisdem canonicis in villa Gipuici in parochia sancti Nicolai. Pro hac autem resignacione et quieta clamacione dederunt michi predicti canonici viii solidos argenti. Et ut hec resignacio et quieta clamacio firma sit et stabilis, presentem paginam sigillo meo roboravi. Hiis testibus: Iohanne filio Normanni, Petro filio Eborardi, Iohanne de Beumeis, Iohanne filio Costantini, Waltero Scot, Rogero filio Liu, Roberto Paris, Godefrido Godscalc, Hosberto de Belinges, Waltero de Herewic', Normanno Marescallo, Alano Harand, et multis aliis.

Date: On John son of Norman as bailiff, see no. 382. He (nos. 43, 48, 49), Peter son of Eborard (no. 40), John son of Constantine (nos. 40, 43, 48) and Roger [son of] Liu (nos. 43, 44) attest other charters as early as the 1180s or 1190s. Roger Liu was one of the first coroners, and Robert Paris one of the first capital portmen, chosen for Ipswich in 1200. Others do not feature elsewhere before the 1220s, and some appear into the 1240s, notably John de Beumeis, who was bailiff sometime between 1227 and 1232, and again 1233–34, and was a party to legal proceedings before the justices in eyre in 1240 (*CPSE*, no. 1046).

384. Grant in perpetuity by Robert son of Alexander of 'Bruntune' and Nichola his wife, daughter of Edmund son of Charles of Ipswich, to the prior and convent, of the messuage which was Edmund's in St Nicholas, Ipswich, lying beside the highway from the canons' gate to Ipswich market place on the east, for which the prior and convent are to pay 2d *per annum* at the feast of St Michael for all demands save the king's service of house-rent. For this gift the prior and convent have given a fine of 3 marks of silver. Warranty is granted.

[Late twelfth – early thirteenth century]

TNA, E40/3858. 179 × 99mm, 18mm turnup, tag at left 85mm, slit at right for the other tag, now lost. Seal on tag at left, in natural wax, 36mm round, showing an eight-pointed design. Legend lost. Endorsed: Rob' fil' Alexand' Bru'ton (14c.); par' sancti Nicolai (?17c.).

Sciant presentes et futuri quod ego Robertus filius Alexandri de Bruntune et Nicholaa uxor mea, filia Eadmundi filii Karoli de Gipwico, concessimus et dedimus et hac carta nostra confirmavimus priori et conventui Sancti Petri de Gipwico totum mesagium [*sic*] quod fuit predicti Eadmundi in villa de Gipwico, scilicet in parochia Sancti Nicholai, quod iacet iuxta viam regiam que tendit a porta canonicorum Sancti Petri ad forum de Gipwico versus orientem, illis et successoribus eorum tenendum de nobis et heredibus nostris in perpetuum, bene et in pace, libere et quiete; solvendo inde nobis singulis annis duos denarios ad festum Sancti Michaelis pro omnibus serviciis et consuetudinibus et exaccionibus, salvo servicio domini regis, scilicet hagabolo. Pro hac autem concessione et donacione, et huius carte nostre confirmacione, dederunt nobis predicti prior et conventus tres marcas argenti in gersumiam. Quare ego Robertus et Nicholaa uxor mea et heredes nostri debemus warantizare prefatum mesagium prefatis priori et conventui per prefatum servicium contra omnes homines. Hiis testibus: Rogero de Horshage, Galfrido pincerna, Roberto filio eius, Iohanne Sturmin, Eadmundo de Bruntune, Iohanne [*et*] Willelmo filiis Normanni, Thoma Manseri, Iohanne filio Costantini, Waltero mercatore, Willelmo Angoth, Roberto Paris, Eadmundo Goldhevech, Galfrido Blundel et multis aliis.

Date: John son of Norman and Robert Paris: see no. 383. Ten of the witnesses attest other charters of SS Peter and Paul from the 1180s or 1190s to the early thirteenth century, e.g., Roger of Horshage (nos. 31, 43, 44), William son of Norman (nos. 31, 43, 48, 49), John son of Constantine (nos. 40, 43, 48).

385. Confirmation by Nichola daughter of Edmund son of Charles of Ipswich, in her widowhood, of the gift which her late husband Robert son of Alexander of 'Bruntone' made to the prior and convent, of the messuage which was her father Edmund's in St Nicholas, Ipswich; to hold of her and her heirs in perpetuity, on payment of 2d annually at the feast of St Michael for all demands save the king's service of house-rent. For this confirmation the canons have given her 20s of silver and one seam of corn. Warranty is granted.   [First third of thirteenth century]

TNA, E40/3502. 202 × 56mm, 9mm turnup, 90mm tag, seal missing. Endorsed: par' sancti Nicolai (16/17c.).

Sciant presentes et futuri quod ego Nicholaa [*sic*] filia Edmundi filii Karoli de Gypewico, in viduitate mea concessi et confirmavi donum quod Robertus filius Alexandri de Brumtone [*sic*] quondam maritus meus fecit priori et conventui ecclesie apostolorum Petri et Pauli de Gypewico, scilicet totum mesuagium quod fuit predicti Edmundi patris mei in villa de Gypewico, et iacet in parochia Sancti Nicholai, unde unum capud abutat versus mesuagium quod fuit Alexandri Baudri versus orientem, et aliud capud super viam regiam versus occidentem; illis et eorum successoribus tenendum de me et heredibus meis imperpetuum, bene et in pace, libere et quiete, solvendo inde michi et heredibus meis singulis annis duos denarios ad festum Sancti Michaelis pro omnibus serviciis et demandis, salvo servicio domini regis, scilicet hagabelo. Pro hac autem concessione et confirmacione dederunt michi predicti canonici viginti solidos argenti et unam summam frumenti. Quare ego Nicholaa et heredes mei warantizabimus prefatum mesuagium predictis canonicis per prefatum servicium contra omnes. Hiis testibus: Willelmo Godeskalc, Osberto de Foro tunc temporis ballivis, Iohanne de Beumys, Elya filio Iohannis Norman, Hugone de Langestone, Waltero de Leystone, Silvestro filio Wakelini, Amisio vinetario, Iohanne filio eius, Rogero Leu, Hugone filio eius, Osberto de Beling', et aliis.

Date: Later than no. 384 because Nichola's husband Robert has since died; and after 1200 because of the presence of the current bailiffs of Ipswich among the witnesses. William Godeskalc served again as bailiff sometime between the 1230s and the middle of the century. Since he was chosen as one of the first group of capital burgesses under the charter of 1200, and was sufficiently senior to be elected alderman the same year ('Black Domesday, fols 78r., 80v.), a date no later than the 1230s seems likely, especially since some witnesses (e.g., Amis the Vintner and Roger Leu who was also one of the coroners chosen in 1200) attest elsewhere as early as the 1190s (nos. 31 and 43).

386. Grant in free, pure and perpetual alms by John de Beumes to the canons, for the salvation of his soul and those of his parents, ancestors and successors, of 3 shillingsworth of annual rent to be taken from the messuage which was Amphrey the chaplain's in St Nicholas, Ipswich, that is, 18d *per annum* from Hamon Spiking and 18d *per annum* from Alexander of Sudbury, and all the service and fealty due to John from the said messuage without reservation. Sealed for perpetual stability.

[Late twelfth – first third of thirteenth century]

TNA, E40/3665. 203 × 100mm, 27mm turnup, 146mm tag. Seal 37mm round, part missing, perhaps showing a fleur-de-lys. Legend: + SIGILL … NIS. Endorsed: iiis' par' sancti Nicolai (16c.); Gippewic (?17c.).

Omnibus Christi fidelibus ad quos presens scriptum pervenerit, Iohannes de Beumes salutem. Noverit universitas vestra me concessisse et dedisse et hac mea carta confirmasse Deo et ecclesie beatorum Petri et Pauli de Gipeswico et canonicis ibidem Deo servientibus, tres solidatas annui redditus de mesagio [*sic*] quod fuit Amfridi capellani in parochia Sancti Nicholai de Gipeswico percipiendas, scilicet de Hamone Spiking decem et octo denarios per annum, et de Alexandro de Suberia decem et octo denarios per annum, et totum servicium et totam fidelitatem que michi de predicto mesagio debuerunt, sine aliquo retenemento, illis et successoribus eorum inperpetuum, in liberam et puram et perpetuam elemosinam, pro salute anime mee et omnium parentum et antecessorum et successorum meorum. Et ut hec mea concessio et donacio perpetuam habeat firmitatem, presens scriptum eis contuli sigilli mei impressione signatum. His testibus: Radulfo de Pesehalle, Iohanne filio Alexandri, Iohanne filio Normanni, Willelmo de Beumes, Iohanne Costin, Amisio vinitore, Waltero mercatore, Rogero Lyw, Waltero de Leestune, Alexandro filio Galfridi Aci, Iohanne filio Nicholai, Philippo de Porta, Petro filio Eborardi, Iohanne Prekehert, et multis aliis.

Date: Various witnesses including John son of Norman (nos. 43, 49), John Costin (nos. 44, 49), Amis the vintner (no. 31), Roger Lyw (nos. 43, 44), and Philip de Porta (nos. 44, 48, 49) attest other charters in the 1180s or 1190s. John Prekehert served as beadle of Ipswich in 1200. John de Beumes the donor was bailiff sometime between 1227 and 1232, and again 1233–34, and was involved in litigation before the justices at the 1240 eyre (*CPSE*, no. 1046). The charter is perhaps likely to date after 1217 when Ralph II of Peasenhall had succeeded his father Norman II (active 1178–1210: *Sibton Cartularies*, I, introduction, pp. 80–81).

387. Grant by Alan of Tuddenham, chaplain, to Denis del Cley of Ipswich, for his homage and service and a fine of 15s of silver, of all the land which Christian the widow of Waukelin Mauclerch held of the prior and convent in the parish of St Nicholas, Ipswich; to hold to Denis and his heirs of Alan and his heirs in fee and by inheritance. Proviso against gift, sale or assignment to men of religion or Jews. An annual rent of 20d is to be paid to Alan and his heirs in four instalments, for all services and exactions except the king's service of house-rent. Warranty is granted.

[1230s – mid-thirteenth century]

TNA, E40/3393. 165 × 96mm, 14mm turnup, 78mm tag, seal missing. Endorsed: parochia Nich'i xxd' (17c.).

Sciant presentes et futuri quod ego Alanus de Thudeam capellanus concessi, dedi, et hac presenti carta mea confirmavi Dionisio del Cley de Gypewico, pro homagio et servicio suo et pro quindecim solidis argenti quos michi dedit in gersumam, totam terram cum omnibus pertinenciis quam Cristiana quondam uxor Waukelini Mauclerch tenuit de domino priore et conventu Sancti Petri de Gypewico iacentem in parochia Sancti Nicholai de Gypewico inter terram Agnetis quondam uxoris Willelmi clerici et terram Iohannis de Leyham, et unum caput abutat super viam regalem versus aquilonem. Habendam et tenendam illi et heredibus suis de me et heredibus meis vel cuicumque et quibuscumque dare, vendere, vel assignare voluerit, exceptis viris religiosis et Iudeis, libere et pacifice in feodo et hereditate; reddendo inde per annum michi et heredibus meis viginti denarios ad quatuor terminos, videlicet ad Pascha quinque denarios, et ad festum Sancti Iohannis Baptiste quinque denarios, et ad festum Sancti Michaelis quinque denarios, et ad Natale Domini quinque denarios, pro omnibus serviciis, consue-tudinibus et exactionibus, salvo servicio domini regis, scilicet Haggabulo. Et ego Alanus capellanus et heredes mei warantizabimus predictam terram cum omnibus pertinenciis prefato Dionisio et heredibus suis vel assignatis suis et assignatorum heredibus per predictum servicium contra omnes homines et feminas. In huius rei testimonium presenti scripto sigillum meum apposui. Hiis testibus: Silvestro filio Waukelini de Bramfort, Matheo de Porta tunc ballivis de Gypewico, Willelmo Godeschalc, Waltero de Leyst[*un*], Amisio vinitario, Oseberto de Foro, Gileberto Hautebe, Huberto de Saba', Thurstano del Clei, Galfrido Ballard, Alano mercatore, Iohanne Davi, et multis aliis.

Date: Matthew de Porta is known to have served as bailiff at intervals between 1255 and 1279, and probably did so earlier. Silvester son of Wakelin served for at least one term between 1227 and 1232, and is known to have done so in 1254-55. By 1270 Vivian son of Silvester is serving as bailiff, suggesting that his father is now aged or dead. Matthew and Silvester must have served together at some period for which the borough court rolls are lacking: between the 1230s and 1266 or 1267-69. Since the witness Amis the Vintner attests as far back as the 1190s, and William Godeschalc was chosen a capital burgess in 1200, a date in the 1230s or 1240s seems most likely.

388. Grant in free, pure and perpetual alms by Ellis/Elias son of John Norman of Ipswich to the canons, of an annual rent of 18d and four hens which Andrew Cuntasse and John his brother used to pay to him for a messuage in the parish of St Nicholas, with the whole tenement whence the rent issues; the rent to be paid in two instalments at the feasts of St Michael and Easter, and the four hens at the Nativity; provided that the canons remit to Ellis and his heirs in perpetuity 12d *per annum* in which he was bound to them for part of his courtyard beside the cemetery of St Nicholas. Warranty is granted.   [1230s – mid-thirteenth century]

TNA, E40/3688. 144 × 70mm, 13mm turnup, 95mm tag, seal missing. Endorsed: Carta de tenemento Walteri Stampard in parochia Sancti Nicholai nunc Th ... dil Ston modo Schriblond ... (?15c.); modo ten' Pynhe ad ... per ... iiii gallinass xviiid (?16c.).

Sciant presentes et futuri quod ego Elyas filius Iohannis Norman de Gypewico concessi, dedi, et presenti carta mea confirmavi Deo et ecclesie beatorum apostolorum Petri et Pauli de Gypewico et canonicis ibidem Deo servientibus, octodecim denaratas annui redditus, et quatuor gallinas annuas ad unam refectionem, uno die eas deferentis, quos Andreas Cuntasse et Iohannes frater eius michi solverunt per annum, pro quodam mesuagio in parochia Sancti Nicholai cum toto tenemento et eiusdem pertinenciis unde dictus redditus provenit; solvendos ad duos teminos anni, videlicet ad festum Sancti Michaelis novem denarios, et ad Pascha novem denarios, et dictas quatuor gallinas ad Natale Domini; in liberam, puram et perpetuam elemosinam. Ita cum quod dicti canonici remiserunt michi et heredibus meis inperpetuum duodecim denarios annuos in quibus eis tenebar pro quadam parte curie mee ex parte cimeterii Sancti Nicholai. Et ego et heredes mei dictum redditum et tenementum et pertinenciis dictis canonicis warantizabimus inperpetuum. In cuius rei testimonium presenti scripto sigillum meum apposui. Hiis testibus: Willelmo Godeschalk', Matheo de Porta, tunc tempore ballivis de Gypewico, Galfrido de Beumes, Silvestro filio Waukelini, Roberto Wlfun, Hugone de Langestun', Oseberto de Belinges, Waltero de Leystun', Hugone Lyu et aliis.

Date: Matthew de Porta as bailiff: see no. 387. There is no record in the borough court rolls of William Godescalk having served the office. They must have served together at some time for which the court rolls have not survived. Since Godescalk was chosen a capital burgess in 1200, a date beyond the 1240s seems unlikely.

389. Grant by Geoffrey Blundel of Ipswich to his bastard son William, for his homage and service and a fine of one mark of silver, of a messuage with its buildings in St Nicholas, Ipswich, to hold of Geoffrey and his heirs in fee and by inheritance. He is to pay annually to the prior and convent of St Peter's 12d in two instalments, and to Geoffrey and his heirs ½d for all exactions saving the king's service of house-rent. Warranty is granted. Sealed for perpetual stability.

[1230s – mid-thirteenth century]

TNA, E40/3909. 174 × 90mm, 17mm turnup, 75mm tag, seal missing. Endorsed: paroch' Nich' xiid'; paroch' Nich' xiid' (two different hands of 16c. or 17c.).

Sciant presentes et futuri quod ego Galfridus Blundel de Gyppuyco concessi, dedi, et hac presenti carta mea confirmavi Willelmo filio meo bastardo, pro homagio et servicio suo, et pro una marcha argenti quam michi dedit in gersumam, unum mesuagium cum edificiis et omnibus pertinenciis quod iacet in parochia Sancti Nicholai de Gyppuyco inter terram Alani Horold et terram quondam Emme de Stanham; habendum et tenendum de me et heredibus meis, illi et heredibus suis vel cuicumque dare, vendere, legare, vel assignare voluerit, libere, quiete, in feodo et hereditate. Reddendo inde per annum priori et conventui Sancti Petri de Gyppuico duodecim denarios ad duos terminos anni, scilicet ad Pascha sex denarios et ad festum Sancti Michaelis sex denarios, et michi et heredibus meis unum obolum ad eundem terminum pro omni servicio, consuetudine et exactione salvo servicio domini regis, scilicet hagabulo. Et ego prefatus Galfridus et heredes mei warantizabimus predictum mesuagium cum pertinenciis predicto Willelmo et heredibus suis vel suis assignatis et heredibus eorum per predictum servitium contra omnes homines et feminas. Et ut hec mea concessio et donatio et huius carte mee confirmatio rata et stabilis permaneat in perpetuum, presens scriptum impressione sigilli mei robboravi. Hiis testibus: Willelmo Godesk' et Matheo de Porta tunc ballivis, Silvestro filio Walkelini, Osberto de Belings, Osberto de Foro, Petro Peper, Huberto de Saham, Helia Norman, Alano mercatore, Galfrido Ballard, Iohanne Davi, Amisio Pistore, et aliis.

Date: See nos. 387 and 388.

390. Notification by William of Ash, son of Richard formerly rector of Ash church, chaplain, that he has quitclaimed and bequeathed in his last testament, and by this charter confirmed to the canons, for the salvation of his soul, the messuage with buildings in St Nicholas, Ipswich which he formerly held of them; he has also granted to them the remainder of the tenement with its buildings and curtilages which adjoins the messuage on the west, and which he purchased of Alan Horold and Alan the merchant. The prior and convent out of charity have granted that the names of William and his father shall be noted in their book of obits, and that food and drink shall be distributed on William's anniversary day for his soul, as for a professed canon. [*c.* 1250–1267]

TNA, E40/3635. 223 × 76mm, including folded-out turnup of 12mm, 106mm tag. Seal fragment 16 × 24mm, apparently with a device of a branch of a tree. Endorsed: par' sancti Nicolai (16/17c.). Tag made from another deed, apparently a draft of the present text; words legible at ends of lines: Sciant presentes et futuri quod ego Will's … testamento meo legavi et hac presenti *and* carta mea confirmavi Deo et ecclesie beatorum … imperpetuum pro salute anime mee et.

Sciant presentes et futuri quod ego Willelmus de Aechs filius Ricardi quondam rectoris ecclesie de Aechs, capellanus, concessi, reddidi, quietumclamavi, in ultimo testamento meo legavi, et hac presenti carta mea confirmavi, Deo et ecclesie beatorum apostolorum Petri et Pauli de Gypewico et canonicis ibidem Deo servientibus et servituris imperpetuum, pro salute anime mee, quoddam meswagium cum edificiis in parochia Sancti Nicholai de Gypewico, quod de eisdem priore et canonicis aliquando tenui; quod quidem meswagium iacet inter meswagium quod fuit quondam Iohannis le Michele ex una parte et meswagium Ade Cobiten ex altera, et unum capud abutat super regiam stratam versus orientem. Eodem et testamento meo concessi, dedi, et ista eadem carta confirmavi Deo et eisdem priori et canonicis totum residuum fundum cum edificiis et curtilagiis quod eidem meswagio adiacet et parte occidentis [*sic*] quod de Alano Horold et Alano mercatore per particulas adquisivi. Tenendum et habendum predictis canonicis et eorum successoribus et assignatis eorum, libere, quiete, bene, et in pace imperpetuum. Predicti vero prior et canonici communi assensu concesserunt michi caritatis intuitu ut nomen meum cum nomine patris mei in martirologio eorum annotetur, et ut cibus et potus die anniversarii mei detur pro anima mea sicut pro canonico professo. In cuius rei testimonium huic presenti scripto sigillum meum apposui. Hiis testibus: Ricardo Fader, Roberto de Orford tunc ballivis, Hugone de Langestun', Hugone Liu, Nicholao Godescalk', Iacobo Norman, Bond' le Tanur, Rogero de Ponte, Andrea et Iohanne Cusstasse fratribus, et aliis.

Date: This charter, in both versions (nos. 390 and 391), is earlier than the associated demise (no. 505), which dates 8 January 1253 x September 1267. Richard Fader's first known term as bailiff of Ipswich is 1266–67, and Robert of Orford's 1271–72, though they must have served together earlier at any time from *c.* 1250 to 1254 or between 1256 and 1266; the record is incomplete.

391. Notification by William of Ash, son of Richard formerly rector of Ash church, in the same terms as no. 390, but with the omission of the references to William's status of chaplain, to his last testament, and to provision for his soul. The witness list is the same as that of no. 390 except for the omission of Nicholas Godescalk'.

[*c.* 1250 – 1267]

TNA, E40/3636. 189 × 70mm, 11mm turnup, 95mm tag. Fragment of seal 17 × 22mm, design lost. Endorsed: par' sancti Nicholai i s' (16c.), paroch Nich'i (16c.).

Sciant presentes et futuri quod ego Willelmus de Aechs, filius Ricardi quondam rectoris ecclesie de Aess', concessi, reddidi, et quietumclamavi Deo et ecclesie beatorum apostolorum Petri et Pauli de Gypwico et canonicis ibidem Deo servientibus et servituris imperpetuum, quoddam mesuagium cum edificiis in parochia Sancti Nicholai de Gypwico quod de eisdem priore et canonicis aliquando tenui; quod quidem mesuagium iacet inter mesuagium quod fuit quondam Iohannis le Michele ex una parte et mesuagium Ade Cobiten ex altera, et unum capud abutat super regiam stratam versus orientem. Preterea concessi, dedi, et ista eadem carta confirmavi Deo et eisdem priori et canonicis totum residuum fundum cum edificiis et curtilagiis quod eidem mesuagio adiacet ex parte occidentis [*sic*], quod de Alano Horold et Alano mercatore per particulas adquisivi. Tenendum et habendum predictis canonicis et eorum successoribus et assignatis eorum, libere, quiete, bene, et in pace imperpetuum. Predicti vero prior et canonici communi assensu concesserunt michi caritatis intuitu ut nomen meum cum nomine patris mei in martirologio eorum annotetur, et ut cibus et potus die anniversarii mei detur pro anima mea sicut pro canonico professo. In cuius rei testimonium huic scripto sigillum meum apposui. Testibus: Ricardo Fader, Roberto de Orford tunc ballivis, Hugone de Langestun', Hugone Lyu, Iacobo Norman, Bond' le Tanur, Rogero de Ponte, Andrea et Iohanne Cuntasse fratribus, et aliis.

Date: See no. 390.

392. Grant in free, pure and perpetual alms by Robert de [*sic*] Buteler of Hemingstone to the canons, for the salvation of his soul and those of his ancestors and successors, of 6d-worth of annual rent from the yard and buildings formerly of Avis the dyer in St Nicholas, Ipswich, next to the highway, between a messuage of Alan Dunkepot and the street extending to 'Botflod'; to be taken in two instalments. Robert also grants, for him and his heirs, to the canons, free power of entry and distraint for recovery of arrears. Consequently and out of charity the canons have granted to Robert that they will insert his obit in their martyrology, on account of which Robert and his heirs will warrant the rent against all in perpetuity. Sealed in testimony.   [Mid-thirteenth century, probably not after 1260]

Bodl., ms charters Suffolk 207. 178 × 116mm, 21mm turnup. There is one slit but tag and seal are lost. Endorsed: N.P. ii (13/14c.); par' sancti Nichol' vid. (16c.).

Sciant presentes et futuri quod ego Robertus de [*sic*] Buteler de Hemingestun' concessi, dedi, et hac presenti carta mea confirmavi domui beatorum apostolorum Petri et Pauli de Gypewico et canonicis ibidem Deo servientibus, pro salute anime mee et animarum antecessorum et successorum meorum, in liberam, puram, et perpetuam elemosinam, sex denariatos annui redditus de area et edificiis quondam Avicie Tingtricis [*sic, for tinctricis*] in parochia Sancti Nicholai de Gypewico situatis iuxta viam regiam inter quoddam mesuagium Alani Dunkepot ex una parte et vicum extendentem versus Botflod ex altera; tenend' et habend' eisdem canonicis libere et quiete sine omni clamio, cavillatione et demanda. Et per semetipsos vel attornatum eorum absque mediatore vel intrabato de dictis area et edificiis percipiendos ad duos terminos, scilicet ad Pascha tres denarios et ad festum Sancti Michaelis tres denarios, relinquens etiam et concedens eisdem canonicis vel suo attornato pro me et heredibus meis, liberam potestatem intrandi et destringendi dictam aream et dicta edificia per omnimoda catalla ibidem existencia, pro solutione dicti annui redditus quotienscumque contingat eundem redditum prenominatis terminis non persolvi. Exhinc ergo et caritatis intuitu concesserunt mihi predicti canonici obitum meum in suo inseri martilogio [*sic*] propter quod ego et heredes mei warantizabimus dictis canonicis et successoribus suis dictum redditum contra omnes imperpetuum. In cuius rei testimonium presens scriptum sigilli mei impressione roboravi. Hiis testibus: Silvestro Walkelin, Osberto de Foro tunc ballivis de Gypewico, Roberto Wuffum [*sic, for Wulfun*], Hugone Liu, Iohanne Bolle, Nicholao de Foro, Thurstano del Cley, Iohanne de Sancto Georgio, Matheo de Porta, Roberto Godescalc, Iohanne Fader, Semanno Blundel, et aliis.

Date: John of St George was chosen a capital portman of Ipswich in 1200 ('Black Domesday', fol. 78r.), and attests no. 460, 1230s – 1240s, and nos. 372 and 377, mid-thirteenth century; he is unlikely to have been active beyond the 1250s. Silvester (son of) Wakelin served as bailiff (with John de Beaumes) for at least one term between 1227 and 1232 (no. 437), and again with Thurstan del Cley in 1254–55. Silvester's year of office with Osbert of the Market is unknown. Hugh Liu served as bailiff with Matthew de Porta in 1255–56 (no. 354).

393A. Grant in free, pure and perpetual alms by Agatha, widow of John Costent' of Ipswich (*Gypewico*), to the canons, of one messuage with buildings in St Nicholas, lying at 'Solhel' between the messuage of Alexander le Chaluner' and the messuage of Richard Fader; 5s 8d from the messuage of Roger le Cuppere in St Mildred, to be taken at three terms of the year, 30d at the feast of St Michael, 8d at the Nativity, and 30d at Easter; 4s 4d from the messuage of Richard and Michael le Berener' in St Mary of the Tower at two terms, St Michael and Easter; 3s from a messuage of Denis del Cley, sometime of 'Sultedemolot' in the same parish, at St Michael and Easter; half a mark from the quay which Agatha purchased of the heirs of John Costent' her former husband, namely that which Edmund son of Seman Alp held of her in St Mary at the Quay, with the fee, escheat, and all things which by reason of that tenement, fee, or the rents may pertain or accrue to her, at St Michael and

Easter; half a mark and 3d annual rent which the same Edmund granted to the canons in exchange for another half mark which he used to pay her out of the quay, to be paid from the places below-written, namely 18d from the messuage of William Saye lying between the land formerly of John Leg and Edmund's land, at St Michael and Easter; 18d from the messuage of Geoffrey Aldham lying between the messuage of William le Daubur' and a certain cemetery, at St Michael and Easter; 12d from the messuage of Roger the miller lying between the messuage formerly William Angot's and a piece of land formerly Richard Crane's, at St Michael and Easter; 2d from the messuage of William Blacsune lying between the messuage of John of Needham (*Nedham*) and the messuage of Robert Fulwater, at St Michael and Easter; 9d from a house with a kiln of John and Lawrence the sons of the late William Kidenoth, situated between the messuage of John son of Cecilia of Bocking[1] and the messuage formerly Robert le Cuteller's; 12d from a messuage of Agatha's beyond the bridge, between a house of Thomas le Cros and the salt water bank below the bridge, at St Michael and Easter; 8d from the messuage of Robert Cobat lying between a certain messuage of Matilda the wife of Stephen Stric and a certain messuage of Alice the former wife of William Hasting', at St Michael and Easter; 4d from a messuage of Joyce the widow of Thomas Dru, lying between the messuage of William Verdun and a messuage formerly of William Godescalc', at St Michael and Easter. To hold and to have every year at the due terms from the said tenements, freely, quietly, well and in peace in perpetuity on account of Agatha and her heirs and any others who could make any claim in her name. This grant and charter were made by the consent of all the tenants and rent payers. Out of charity the prior and convent, for the souls of Agatha, her ancestors, parents and friends, have granted to her that any one of the canons of the convent shall celebrate Mass in their church four times a week in perpetuity. Warranty is granted against all people in perpetuity. Sealed in testimony.

Hiis testibus: Domino Galfrido de Beumes, Matheo de Porta et Nicholao de Foro tunc ballivis Gypewici, Roberto Wolhund', Nicholao Godescalk', Thurstanno del Glei, Ricardo de Bosco de Ressemere, Hugolino, Herveo de Pleyford', Iohanne filio Lawrencii, Willelmo Testepin, Ricardo Fader et aliis. [1256 x 1269 or 1274 x 1276]

TNA, E40/3776. 264 × 182mm, 16mm turnup, 113mm tag. Seal: 36mm round, showing a fleur-de-lys. Endorsed: N p[i]; Agatha Costyn de Gyppewyc [similar to hand of charter]; tlof[r] de Kayo (?14c.).

  1 Probably the manor of Bocking in Crowfield, near Ipswich, rather than the parish of Bocking in Essex.

Date: Matthew de Porta served as bailiff of Ipswich at intervals between 1255 and 1279; he probably also did so earlier. There is no record in the borough court rolls of Nicholas de Foro having done so. They must therefore have served together for one or more years for which the rolls have not survived, probably between 1256–69 or 1274–76.

393B. Plea heard in the court of Petty Pleas at Ipswich on Wednesday before Palm Sunday, 17 Edward [II],[1] in which Geoffrey Godesup, tailor and Aldith his wife were attached to answer Prior Henry of St Peter's concerning a plea of abatement,[2] whereupon the prior by his attorney claims that unjustly and without judgement they have disseised him of his free tenement in Ipswich, as of the right of his church, namely of 12d annual rent to be taken in perpetuity from a certain messuage which Geoffrey and Aldith hold beyond Stoke Bridge, situated between the house formerly of Thomas le Groos and the salt river bank, of which annual rent William the former prior and his predecessors were seised as of the right of their church. And Philip Harneys now holds the messuage [*illegible*] in arrears of 40s for 40 years past. The same prior has now distrained upon the messuage for his arrears. And Geoffrey and Aldith came and recognised the rent to be the right of the said church, and that it was in arrears for the whole of the said time, by which it is agreed that the prior recover his seisin of the rent and also his damages and arrears, and that Geoffrey and Aldith are in mercy for their disseisin. And be it known that in full court they have attorned to the prior for the rent. 4 April 1324

TNA, E40/3776 [*continued*]. Stitched to no. 393A. 250 × 97mm. No endorsement.

> 1 The regnal year must be that of Edward II, not Edward I, since Prior Henry of Burstall was not elected until 1304, and his successor Henry of Kersey until 1311.
> 2 The plea of abatement was Ipswich borough's version of the assize of Novel Disseisin (*IBAC*, pp. 73, 81).

393C. Plea heard in the Court of Petty Pleas at Ipswich on Wednesday after the feast of the Conception of the BVM, 1 Edward III, John Irp and Richard of Layham (*Leyham*) then bailiffs. An assize comes to declare according to the custom of the town, if Geoffrey Bullok and Cristina his wife unjustly and without judgement disseised the prior of St Peter's of his free tenement in Ipswich, as the prior complains, through a certain abatement, according to the custom of the town, namely of 5s 8d annual rent to be taken from the capital messuage of Geoffrey and Cristina which was [*illegible*] in the parish of St Mildred next to 'le timber-market', placed in view [*illegible*] for that he was distrained on the said messuage [*illegible*] said rent in arrears for several years. And Geoffrey in person and Cristina by Geoffrey [*illegible*] hold the said messuage placed in the view and say that they have made no [*illegible*] and no disseisin thereof. And they place themselves upon the assize. And the assize is taken before John of Akenham, Peter le Fay, John Aluce, Roger Etham, [*illegible*], Richard Fynch, Thomas of Stoke, Thomas Halpeni, Richard Mynyard and Ralph Steward, jurors having viewed etc. They say [*illegible*] that Geoffrey and Cristina hold the messuage of the prior and convent by the service of 5s 8d annual rent, to be paid to them in perpetuity. They say also that the said distraint [*illegible*] to the prior's damage of 20s taxed by the jurors [*illegible*] furthermore if Cristina was [*illegible*] or not, they say that she was not. Therefore it is agreed that the prior recover seisin of the free tenement, namely the annual rent [*illegible*] in seisin by the view of the jurors. And that Geoffrey be in mercy through his disseisin. And that [*illegible*] the prior for a false claim [*illegible*] against Cristina be in mercy. And after [*illegible*]. 10 December 1327

TNA, E40/3776 (continued). Stitched to no. 393A and B. 245 × 109mm. Endorsed: De parochia sancte Mildrede. Document badly stained and discoloured.

394. Grant in free, pure and perpetual alms by Simon Blundel of Ipswich (*Gypewico*), for him and his heirs and successors, to the prior and convent, of 6d annual rent from his messuage lying lengthways between the land of Roger of the bridge (*de Ponte*) on the south and the common street on the north, and widthways between the messuage of William Falleden on the east and the messuage of Nicholas le Kuher on the west, in the parish of St Nicholas, to be taken in two instalments at the feast of St Michael and Easter, without any disturbance or objection. Simon grants that if he, his heirs or successors, cease to pay the rent, the prior and convent or their attorney may have full power to enter and distrain upon the messuage and all the houses within it until full payment and satisfaction for the rent has been made. So that this gift and charter of confirmation may have perpetual warranty, the prior and convent have remitted to Simon and his heirs 6d annual rent which they used to take for a messuage formerly of Nicholas the cooper (*cuparii*) in the parish of St Nicholas which the Carmelite friars now hold. Sealed in testimony.

Hiis testibus: Matheo de Porta, Viviano filio Silvestri tunc ballivis, Galfrido de Beaumes, Ricardo Fader, Hugone Liu, Roberto de Oreford, Iohanne Clement, Hugone Golding, Clemente del Kay, Alano Parminod, Rogero Foht et multis aliis.

[Probably 1278 x 1279]

TNA, E40/3960. 213 × 112mm, 14mm turnup, 110mm tag. No seal or trace thereof. Endorsed: Ioh' Chabot; par' sancti Nicholai (both 15c.); paroch' Nich' vid' (16c.).

Date: The charter refers to a house then held by the Carmelites. This order seems to have been established in Ipswich in 1278, for their settlement here was contemporary with that at Winchester, which took place at that date (*VCH Suffolk*, II, 130). From 1277/78 to 1286 there is only one administrative year, 1278–79, for which the Ipswich bailiffs' names are unknown; this is thus the presumed date of the joint tenure by Matthew de Porta and Vivian son of Silvester. Matthew had served as bailiff probably since the 1240s. He may have been dead by 1286, almost certainly so by August 1290, since a man of his seniority and long experience would surely have been included (with his fellow-bailiff Vivian, who *was*, in the panel of burgesses delegated to re-state the customs of the borough after the theft of the old 'Domesday' roll in 1272, a task long delayed by Edward I's taking the borough for a time into the hands of the Crown.

395. Notification[1] by Henry of 'Bradegrene', son of Nichola the daughter of Edmund Charles of Ipswich (*Gippewyco*), that he has granted, resigned and utterly quitclaimed, for himself and his heirs, to the canons, all right and claim which he had or might have had in a messuage within the canons' courtyard,[2] whether in rent [*illegible*] pertaining to that messuage; to be held by the canons and their successors in free, pure and perpetual alms, without any objection or claim by him or his heirs in perpetuity. Sealed in testimony.

Hiis testibus: Domino Roberto de Bosco milite, Iohanne de la Dale, Martino Iustus, Iohanne Aunsys, Iohanne Clement, Philippo Harneys, Laurentio Horold, Hugone fratre eius, et aliis. At Ipswich on the day of St Bricius, 14 Edward I.

13 or 14 November 1286

TNA, E40/3512. 223 × 66mm, 18mm turnup, 120mm tag. Seal round in 31 × 38mm blob of wax, device of sunburst of leaves. Legend: … NRICI DE BRADEG … Brown Wax. Endorsed: par' sancti Nich'i (17c.). Badly stained; a few words illegible.

1 For related documents, see nos. 384 and 385.

2 The courtyard referred to must be premises owned by the canons, but not part of the priory precinct, which was of course in the parish of St Peter.

IPSWICH, ST PETER

396. Grant in free, pure and perpetual alms by Walkelin son of Norman, for the salvation of his soul and the souls of his wife Matilda and all his ancestors, to the canons, of a piece of land in Ipswich which lies between the land which was Iveta of Alnesbourn's and the land which the grantor gave to his brother William of Belines.

[Late twelfth – early thirteenth century]

TNA, E40/3848. 195 × 59mm, 15mm turnup, 127mm tag. Seal in green wax, 33mm round, showing a sunburst and crescent moon. … AL … only legible of legend. Endorsed: in parochia sancti Petri (?16c.).

Sciant presentes et futuri quod ego Walkelinus filius Normanni concessi et dedi et hac carta mea confirmavi Deo et ecclesie beatorum apostolorum Petri et Pauli de Gipewico et canonicis ibidem Deo servientibus, unam peciam terre in villa de Gipwico, silicet que iacet inter terram que fuit Ivete de Alvesbrunne et terram quam dedi Willelmo de Belines fratri meo, in liberam et puram et perpetuam elemosinam pro salute anime mee et Matildis uxoris mee, et omnium antecessorum meorum. Hiis testibus: Huberto de Bromford, Ada de Ulmo, Tome filio Manseri, Iohanne filio Normanni, Willelmo de Belines, Willelmo Angot, Nicholao et Silvestro fratribus, Roberto Paris, Waltero mercatore, et multis aliis.

Date: John son of Norman was bailiff in 1200, and Robert Paris a capital portman. The donor attests elsewhere (nos. 48, 49) from the 1180s. The absence of the current bailiffs from the witness list may perhaps indicate a date before 1200. At Easter 1201 a plea of land and of *iniuria* brought by Geoffrey de Ambli *v.* Hubert of Bramford and the bailiff of the bishop of Évreux was essoined (*PBKJ*, I, no. 3397, p. 340).

397. Grant in free, pure and perpetual alms by William son of William of Kembroke to the altar of the Blessed Mary in the church of St Peter and the canons, for the provision of an oil lamp before the altar, of 16 pence worth of annual rent in the parish of St Peter, Ipswich, which Geoffrey Cumbrevile used to pay him out of his messuage between the messuages of Robert of Orford and Robert Paris, and the whole fee from which the rent issues, for the salvation of his soul and the souls of his ancestors and successors, quit of all secular service. Warranty is granted.

[1220s – 1230s; perhaps 1233–34]

TNA, E40/3495. 152 × 80mm, 11mm turnup, 32mm tag (fragment only). Seal missing. Endorsed: Will' filius Andree de Sprouton xvid. (14c.); Will' de Kenebrok in supp' xvid. de mesuag' Galfr' Cu'brevil' in parochia sancti Petri (?14c.).

Sciant presentes et futuri quod ego Willelmus filius Willelmi de Kenebroch sancte caritatis intuitu concessi, dedi, et presenti carta mea confirmavi Deo et altari beate Marie quod est in ecclesia Sancti Petri de Gypewico, et canonicis in eadem ecclesia Deo servientibus et in perpetuum servituris, ad exhibendum lumen olei coram dicto altari, sexdecim denariatos annui redditus in burgo de Gypewico, in parochia Sancti Petri, quem scilicet redditum Galfridus Cumbrevile michi solebat annuatim reddere de mesuagio suo quod est inter mesuagium Roberti de Oreford' et mesuagium Roberti Paris, et totum feodum de quo idem redditus provenit, cum omnibus pertinenciis; habendos et tenendos eisdem canonicis et eorum successoribus in liberam, puram, et perpetuam elemosinam, pro salute anime mee et pro animabus antecessorum et successorum meorum, solutam et quietam ab omni seculari servicio et exactione. Et ego Willelmus et heredes mei warantizabimus prefatis canonicis et eorum successoribus prenominatum redditum et feodum cum suis pertinenciis et adquietabimus contra omnes homines. Et in huius rei testimonium huic scripto sigillum meum apposui. Hiis testibus: Galfrido de Beaumes, Iohanne de Beaumes, Rogero Lyu, Silvestro filio Walkelini, Amisio vinitario, Elya Norman, Waltero de Leystone, Constantino Fader, Galfrido Blundel, Oseberto de Beling', Roberto Paris, Thoma Pullegos, et aliis.

Date: Most witnesses do not attest other charters in this collection before the 1220s, though Robert Paris and Roger Lyu occur as early as the 1190s, with Lyu serving as coroner and Paris as a capital portman in 1200. Lyu attests the agreement between Woodbridge Priory and the burgesses of Ipswich on 18 November 1233 (SROI, Iveagh MSS, HD 1538/435/4). Geoffrey and John de Beaumes served together as bailiffs in 1233–34. Their position at the head of the witness list may indicate that the charter was issued during their year of office, though their official status would normally have been specified.

398. Confirmation in free, pure and perpetual alms by John son of Andrew of Sproughton to the canons, in consideration of charity and for the salvation of his soul, of the gift which William son of William of Kembroke made to them of the annual rent of 16d in the parish of St Peter, namely from the messuage which Geoffrey Cumbrevill' sometime held of John's fee, with the whole fee from which the rent issues, quit of exactions by John or his heirs.

[1220s – 1230s; perhaps 1233–34]

TNA, E40/3531. 146 × 53mm, 9mm turnup, 146mm tag. String is wrapped around the tag. Seal missing. No endorsements.

Sciant presentes et futuri quod ego Iohannes filius Andree de Sproutone intuitu caritatis et pro salute anime mee concessi et presenti carta mea confirmavi pro me et heredibus meis canonicis ecclesie Sancti Petri de Gypewico, totum donum quod Willelmus filius Willelmi de Kenebroch eis fecit de annuo redditu sexdecim denariorum cum pertinenciis in burgo de Gypewico, in parochia Sancti Petri, videlicet de mesuagio quod Galfridus Cumbrevill' aliquando tenuit de feodo meo, quod scilicet mesuagium est inter mesuagium Roberti de Oreford et mesuagium Roberti Paris. Habendum et tenendum eisdem canonicis et eorum successoribus cum toto feodo de quo redditus ille provenit, in liberam puram et perpetuam elemosinam, sicut carta dicti Willelmi quam inde habent testatur, quiete et solute ab omni clamio et exactione mei vel heredum meorum. Et ut hec mea concessio et presentis carte mee confirmacio perpetuam obtineat stabilitatem, eam sigilli mei apposicione roboravi. Hiis testibus: Iohanne de Beaumes, Galfrido de Beaumes, Rogero Lyu, Silvestro filio Wakelini, Amisio vinitario, Elya Norman, Waltero de Leyston', Oseberto de Beling', Roberto Paris, Thoma Pullegos, et aliis.

Date: See no. 397, which this charter confirms. The lists of witnesses are almost identical, and the charters may well have been issued at the same time.

399. Notification of resignation and quitclaim by Walkelin son of Norman to the church and canons of SS Peter and Paul, of the messuage which Albert held of him in the parish of the same church, and another messuage in St Nicholas, which Richard de la Grene, cobbler, held of him; both of which messuages Walkelin held of the canons. For this quitclaim the canons have given him 20s. Warranty is granted.   [Post-1200 – 1230s]

TNA, E40/3857. 159 × 81mm, 17mm turnup, 113mm tag. Seal in green wax, 33mm round, showing a sunburst and crescent moon. Legend: SIGILL' WALKELINI FIL' NORM'. Endorsed: [*two illegible words*] in par' sancti Petri; aliud in par' sancti Nicolai (?17c.).

Sciant presentes et futuri quod ego Walkelinus filius Normanni resignavi et quietumclamavi Deo et ecclesie Beatorum Apostolorum Petri et Pauli de Gypewico et canonicis ibidem Deo servientibus, totum mesuagium cum pertinenciis quod Albertus tenuit de me in parochia eiusdem ecclesie, et quoddam aliud mesuagium cum pertinenciis in parochia Sancti Nicholai de Gypewico quod Ricardus de la Grene, sutor, tenuit de me, que scilicet mesuagia ego tenui de eisdem canonicis, et totum ius et clamium quod habui vel habere potui in eisdem mesuagiis, sine aliquo retenemento, pro viginti solidis quos prefati canonici michi dederunt. Quare ego et heredes mei warantizabimus predictis canonicis dicta mesuagia cum pertinenciis contra omnes homines. Et in huius rei testimonium presens scriptum sigillo meo confirmavi. Hiis testibus: Rogero Lyu, Amisio vinitario, tunc ballivis de Gypewico, Iohanne fratre meo, Petro filio Eborardi, Waltero mercatore, Iohanne filio Constantini, Galfrido de Beaumes, Iohanne de Belmes, Rogero de Langestone, Laurencio molendinario, Willelmo Herode, Iohanne Fot et multis aliis.

Date: After 1200 because of the presence of the bailiffs of Ipswich among the witnesses. Walkelin son of Norman and all but four of the witnesses attest as early as the 1190s elsewhere in this collection, making a date after 1240 unlikely. John brother of Walkelin (usually known as John son of Norman) was bailiff in 1200, and Roger Lyu a coroner the same year, and in 1233 attested an agreement concerning the tolls of Woodbridge market (see no. 397, note on dating). Geoffrey and John de Beaumes/Belmes were bailiffs in 1233–34.

400. Grant by Richard, dean of Coddenham to the canons, in consideration of charity and for the salvation of his soul, of a messuage in the parish of St Peter, abutting east on the highway leading from the market towards the bridge, and west on the house of Thomas Pullegos, for 12d annual rent in two instalments to Rose Godeskalc and her heirs, for all demands save the king's service of house-rent.

[Early – mid-thirteenth century]

TNA, E40/3674. 164 × 84mm, 14mm turnup, 65mm tag. Seal 44 × 37mm, showing the Agnus Dei. Legend: + S' RICARDI DECANI CODEHA'. Endorsed: De mesuagio in parochia sancti Petri quondam Ric'i decani de Codeha' per servicium xiid' (14c.); de uno mesuagio in par' sancti Petri (14c., different hand); par' sancti Petri (16c.).

Sciant presentes et futuri quod ego Ricardus decanus de Codeham dedi et concessi et presenti carta mea confirmavi Deo et ecclesie apostolorum Petri et Pauli de Gypewico et canonicis ibidem Deo servientibus, caritatis intuitu et pro salute anime mee, unum mesuagium in parochia Sancti Petri cum pertinenciis, cuius unum capud abutat super regiam viam que tendit a foro versus pontem ex parte orientis, et aliud abutat super domum Thome Pullegos versus occidentem. Reddendo inde annuatim Roysie Godeskalc et heredibus suis duodecim denarios ad duos terminos, scilicet ad Pasca sex denarios, ad festum Sancti Michaelis sex denarios, pro omni servicio et demanda salvo servicio domini regis, scilicet hagable. Et in huius rei testimonium presens scriptum sigilli mei apposicione corroboravi. Hiis testibus: Iohanne de Beaumes, Silvestro, Costantino Fader, Rogero Leu, Amisio Boll', Willelmo Godeskalc, Elya filio Normanni, Galfrido Blundel, Iohanne Prikeherte, et multis aliis.

Date: Richard, dean of Coddenham, attests a Dodnash Priory charter (*Dodnash Charters*, no. 16) dating 28 October 1223 x 27 October 1224; at the 1240 eyre in Suffolk he is accused, along with Prior Gilbert of St Peter's and William Godeskalc (capital burgess and alderman of Ipswich in 1200), of unjustly disseising Master Robert of Coddenham of his free tenement in Ipswich (*CPSE*, no. 640).

401. Quitclaim by Matilda, relict of John de Bewmes, in the time of her widowhood, to the canons, of all right of dower she might have in the lands and rents which her late husband gave to them. For this the canons have given her two marks of silver. Matilda has promised and sworn, touching holy relics, that henceforth she will lay no legal claim to any right in either lands or rents.

[Mid-thirteenth century, after May 1240]

TNA, E40/3732. 192 × 72mm, 16mm turnup, 66mm tag. Seal 32 × 18mm, design of a head in profile, legend mostly gone. Endorsed: par' sancti Petri (16c.).

Sciant presentes et futuri quod ego Matildis relicta Iohannis de Bewmes in tempore viduitatis mee concessi et quietumclamavi Deo et ecclesie apostolorum Petri et Pauli de Gipewico et canonicis ibidem Deo servientibus, totum ius meum et clamium quod habui vel habere potui nomine dotis in terris [*et omitted*] in redditibus quod Iohannes de Bewmes quondam maritus meus eisdem canonicis dedit et concessit. Pro hac autem concessione et quietaclamatione dederunt michi predicti canonici duas marcas argenti. Et ego predicta Matildis fideliter promisi et sacrosanctis[1] tactis iuravi, quod de cetero nec in terris nec in redditibus aliquid ius vendicabo. Et ut hec predicta mea concessio et quieta clamacio rata et stabilis permaneat, ad maiorem securitatem huic presenti scripto sigillum meum apposui.

Hiis testibus: Willelmo Godeskach, Matheo de Porta, tunc temporis ballivis de Gipewico, Galfrido de Bewmes, Silvestro filio Wakelini, Willelmo de Holebroc, Baldewino de Pesehal', Roberto Wlfhun, Hugone Lyu, Oseberto de Foro, Oseberto de Belinges, Stephano Strich, et multis aliis.

> 1 Perhaps including the fragment of the 'true cross' mentioned as being in the possession of the priory in no. 365.

Date: John de Bewmes, Matilda's deceased husband, was alive in May 1240, when he was a party to a dispute concerning lands claimed as free alms by Gilbert the parson of St Nicholas, Ipswich (*CPSE*, nos. 275, 282).

402. Grant in perpetuity by James of Knapton and Clemence his wife to the prior and convent, of their messuage in St Peter, Ipswich, paying to the capital lords of the fee the due and accustomed services in respect thereof. Warranty is granted.
[Mid- or later thirteenth century]

No witnesses named; ?unexecuted. TNA, E40/3712. 217 × 63mm, 18mm turnup. Left and right tags both 55mm. No seals. Endorsed: mesuagium paroch' Petri (?15c.). Gippewic (16c.).

Sciant presentes et futuri quod nos Iacobus de Knapetone et Clemencia uxor mea concessimus, dedimus, et hac presenti [carta *omitted*] nostra confirmavimus priori et conventui Sancti Petri de Gyppewyco et eorum successoribus totum mesuagium nostrum cum pertinenciis quod habuimus in willa de Gyppewyco in parochia Sancti Petri. Habendum et tenendum predicto priori et eiusdem loci conventui et eorum successoribus imperpetuum, faciendo capitalibus dominis feodi servicia inde debita et consueta. Et nos predicti Iacobus et Clemencia et heredes nostri warantizabimus predictum mesuagium cum pertinenciis predicto priori et conventui et eorum successoribus imperpetuum. In cuius rei testimonium huic scripto sigilla nostra apposuimus.

Date: Thomas of Knapton, probably the son of Augustine of Rushmere, held various lands in Hintlesham during the first half of the thirteenth century. Thomas married Alice, sister of Baldwin *medicus*, and they had a son James (presumably the grantor of this charter) living in 1283, though Thomas was by then dead (Plunkett, 'Machells', p. 91, citing TNA, Ancient Deeds, E40/3361).

403. Notification by Walter Pullegos that for the salvation of his soul he has granted and confirmed, and bequeathed by his testament, to the canons, towards their pittance, 2s annual rent to be taken from the messuage and houses of Hugh son of Robert Davy which he held of Walter in St Peter, Ipswich, to be paid in four instalments; to be held to them and their successors in perpetuity, in free, pure and perpetual alms. Sealed for perpetual validity, by the consent and will of Hugh.
[*c.* 1250 – *c.* 1280]

TNA, E40/3540. 146 × 82mm, 17mm turnup, 100mm tag. Seal 32mm round, no counterseal, device of heads of corn. Legend at right gone, POLLEGOS legible at left. Endorsed: Gypewic (14c.), iid' par' sancti Pet' (16c.). Oddly, another tag is attached to the tag on this charter by a blade of grass tied around it. The meaning is unclear, but probably another charter linked to the same property was tied to this one by the tags, but has now become detached from its own tag.

Sciant presentes et futuri quod ego Walterus Pullegos pro salute anime mee concessi, dedi, et hac presenti carta mea confirmavi et in testamento meo legavi, Deo et ecclesie beatorum apostolorum Petri et Pauli de Gypewico et canonicis ibidem Deo servientibus et inperpetuum servituris, ad eorum pictanciam, duos solidos annui redditus percipiendos de meswagio et domibus Hugonis filii Roberti Davy quod de me tenuit in parochia Sancti Petri de Gypewico, scilicet inter meswagium meum et meswagium quondam Ade Bothman, ad quatuor terminos anni, videlicet ad festum Sancti Michaelis sex denarios, ad festum Sancti Andree sex denarios, ad Pascha sex denarios, et ad Nativitatem Sancti Iohannis Baptiste sex denarios. Tenendos et habendos illis et successoribus suis imperpetuum in liberam, puram, et perpetuam elemosinam. Et ut testamentum meum in hoc, et ista concessio, donacio, et huius carte confirmacio perpetuam habeant stabilitatem, de consensu et voluntate dicti Hugoni huic scripto sigillum meum apposui. Hiis testibus: Domino Ricardo decano de Gypewico, Ricardo Fader, Matheo de Porta, Roberto Davy et Hugone filio suo, Osberto de Foro, Semanno Tophol, Galfrido Horold, Ricardo de Foro, Hugone Golding, et aliis.

Date: There are five witnesses in common with no. 529.

404. Notification by Seman Becmane of Ipswich (*Gypewico*) that he has granted, assigned and by this present charter confirmed to the prior and convent of the apostles Peter and Paul of the order of St Augustine, 4d annual rent which they used formerly to take from part of his messuage in Ipswich, to have and take henceforth from his capital messuage which was sometime the capital messuage of Adam Becman and Langliva his wife, Seman's mother, in the parish of St Peter, which lies lengthways between a messuage of Hugh Davy on the east and the messuage of Robert Baudekyn on the west, the north end abutting on the highway leading from the new mill towards the bridge of Ipswich; which messuage of Seman's he charges henceforth with the said 4d annual rent to the religious and their successors towards their pittance at four annual terms in perpetuity, namely 1d at the feasts of St Michael, the Lord's Nativity, Easter and the Nativity of St John the Baptist. He gives to them and to their collector of rents full power, without licence of any bailiff, to enter the messuage and to distrain in it, as often as necessary for arrears of rent unpaid at any term. Sealed in testimony.

Hiis testibus: Iohanne Lyu et Thoma Clement tunc ballivis de Gypewico, Iohanne Clement, Philippo Harneys, Iohanne filio suo, Thoma Aylred, Nicholao le Clerk', Alexandro Lovegod, Roberto Davy, Henrico Rotun, Herveo de Baudreseye, Petro fabro, et multis aliis. At Ipswich, Friday next before the feast of St Felix, 22 Edward I.

5 March 1294

TNA, E40/3414. 155 × 164mm, including folded-out turnup of 13mm, 95mm tag, seal missing. Endorsed: paroch' sancti Petri; ad pitanciam iiiid' (15/16c.).

405. Grant by Selona who was the wife of Hugh Golding of Ipswich (*Gippewyco*), by the assent and will of John [*illegible*], to Adam Bolle of Ipswich, for his service and for a fine of 16s of silver, of her messuage with its buildings in St Peter, Ipswich, next to Adam Bolle's messuage on the north and the curtilage of Philip Harneys on the south, abutting east on the highway and west on the curtilage formerly of Sir Laurence of Creeting (*Cretingge*), chaplain; to have and to hold of Selona and her heirs, to him and his heirs and assigns, freely, quietly, rightly, in peace, in fee and by inheritance, and to give, sell, bequeath or assign to whomsoever he may wish; rendering annually to Selona and her heirs or assigns 2d, that is, 1d at the feast of St Michael and Easter, and to the prior and convent of St Peter of Ipswich [*missing*] pence at the said terms, for all services and secular demands, save the king's service of house-rent. Warranty by the grantor and his heirs against all people in perpetuity. Sealed in testimony.

Hiis testibus: [Thoma Stace[1]] et Iohanne le Mayster tunc ballivis Gippewyci, Philippo Harneys, Iohanne filio suo, Ricardo Lyeu, Iohanne Lyeu, Elya Coco, Rogero Pachet, Willelmo filio [*illegible*] de la Grene, et aliis. At Ipswich, ?12[2] April, 29 Edward I.   ?12 April 1301

TNA, E40/3391. 242 × 107mm, including folded-out turnup of 14mm. Seal and tag missing. One illegible early modern endorsement. Poor condition, badly discoloured in places, some text missing.

    1 Illegible, but known from the borough Portmanmote roll to have been bailiff at this time.
    2 Of the day of the month, only 'duo' remains.

406. Notification by Hugh Horold of Ipswich (*Gypwyco*) that he has granted and utterly quitclaimed, for himself and his heirs, to the prior and convent and their successors, all right and claim that he had or might have had in a piece of land in Ipswich, on the north side of the priory of St Peter, which was sometime Thurstan del Cley's, for a certain sum of money which they have given to Hugh in cash as a fine; to be held to the prior and convent and their successors, freely, quietly, well and in peace, in fee and by inheritance in perpetuity. On condition that neither Hugh nor his heirs, nor anyone on his behalf, may henceforth have any right or lay claim to the said piece of land. Sealed in testimony.

Hiis testibus: Laurentio Cobbe, Iohanne Leu tunc ballivis Gypwici, Laurentio Horold, Iohanne le Maister, Nicholao clerico, Thoma le Rente, Alexandro Margarete, Henrico le Rotoun, Ada de Holebrok et aliis. On the morrow of the Exaltation of the Holy Cross, 31 Edward I.   15 September 1303

TNA, E40/3697. 207 × 87mm, 13mm turnup, 75mm tag. Seal 25 × 20mm, detail mostly gone. Endorsed: par' sancti Petri mesuag'; tenementum ex parte boriali prioratus (14c.).

407. Grant in perpetuity by Sayeva Lew of Ipswich (*Gypp'*)[1] to God and the Holy Cross of the church of the apostles Peter and Paul and the prior and convent, of 40d-worth of annual rent to be taken from the messuage sometime of William of

London in the parish of St Peter, Ipswich, towards the maintenance of a lamp to burn daily before the cross in the church; to be held to the prior and convent and their successors in perpetuity. Warranty by the grantor and her heirs against all men in perpetuity. The prior and convent, for them and all their successors, have granted that they are bound to maintain the lamp to burn daily in the church on account of the rent in perpetuity. For the faithful performance of which, the prior and convent grant that they may be appealed and compelled through any ecclesiastical judge if they do not perform it in the form abovesaid. In testimony whereof the parties have sealed each other's copy of this chirograph.

Hiis testibus: Thoma Stace, Thoma le Rente ballivis Gypp', Thoma de Petra, Alexandro Margrete, Elya Koco, Roberto Clement, Hugone Scoht, Thoma clerico et aliis. At Ipswich, on the eve of St Andrew the Apostle, 1310. 29 November 1310

TNA, E40/3587. 214 × 110mm maximum, top edge indented. Parts of CYROGRAPHUM can be seen. 13mm turnup, 55mm tag. Seal missing. Endorsed: par' sancti Pet' xld' (16c.).

1 Sayeva Lew (there are various spellings) was doubtless a member of the family of that name which produced several bailiffs of Ipswich in the second half of the thirteenth and the early years of the fourteenth century. In addition to her gift to SS Peter and Paul, in 1315 she bequeathed the rents from several of her tenements in the town to maintain tapers and lamps to burn in the chapel of All Saints (later Our Lady's Chapel, popularly known as Gracechurch, in St Matthew's parish), and lamps before the Rood and the altar of St Mary in St Matthew's parish church itself (Blatchly and MacCulloch, *Miracles in Lady Lane*, pp. 2–5, citing Martin, *Recognizance Rolls*, p. 60).

408. Grant in perpetuity[1] by Sayeva Lew of Ipswich to God and the Holy Cross of the church of the apostles Peter and Paul and the prior and convent, of 40d-worth of annual rent to be taken yearly from the messuage sometime of Roger of London in the parish of St Peter, Ipswich, towards the maintenance of a lamp to burn daily before the cross in the church; to be held to the prior and convent and their successors in perpetuity. Warranty by the grantor and her heirs against all men in perpetuity. The prior and convent, for them and all their successors, have granted that they are bound to maintain the lamp to burn daily in the church on account of the rent in perpetuity. For the faithful performance of which, the prior and convent grant that they may be appealed and compelled through any ecclesiastical judge if they do not perform it in the form abovesaid. In testimony whereof the parties have sealed each other's copy of this chirograph.

His testibus: Thoma Stace, Thoma le Rente ballivis Gypp', Thoma de Petra, Alexandro Margrete, Elya Koco, Roberto Clement, Hugone Scoht, Thoma clerico et aliis. At Ipswich, on the eve of St Andrew the Apostle, 1310. 29 November 1310

TNA, E40/3586. 262 × 98mm maximum, indented at top, with part of CYROGRAPHUM visible, turnup 18mm, 103mm tag, seal missing. Endorsed: paroch' Petri xld' (16c.).

1 The text of this charter differs from that of no. 407 in that the rent is payable from the messuage sometime of *Roger* of London, not from that sometime of *William* of London.

409. Counterpart of 408.   29 November 1310

TNA, E40/3589. 257 × 113mm maximum, indented at top with part of CYROGRAPHUM visible. Turnup 15mm, tag 110mm, seal missing. Endorsed: par' sancti Petri (16c.).

410. Assignment (*assignavi*) by Sayeva Leu, for her and her heirs, of her tenant Adam Bolle, concerning 40d-worth of annual rent issuing from a messuage[1] formerly Roger of London's (*de Loundres*), to be paid annually to the prior and convent and their successors in perpetuity. Sealed in testimony.

Hiis testibus: Thoma Stace, Thoma le Rente, ballivis Gyppewici, Thoma de Petra, Alexandro Margret', Elya Koco, Hugone Scoht et aliis. At Ipswich, on the eve of St Andrew the Apostle, 1310.   29 November 1310

TNA, E40/3588. 250 × 57mm, including folded-out turnup, 14mm. Two slits for tags, left empty, but right possessing a tag 73mm long. No seal. No endorsements.

1 In St Peter's parish: see no. 408 of the same date.

411. Duplicate (not a counterpart, since neither document is indented) of no. 410.
                                                                   29 November 1310

TNA, E40/3638. 200 × 54mm, 13mm turnup, 75mm tag. Endorsed: iiis' iii[*sic*]d' (14c.); villa Gipwici (?14c.).

412. Notification by John de la Dale that he has granted, remitted and utterly quitclaimed, for himself and his heirs, to the prior and convent and their successors, all right and claim which he had or could have in future in the messuage with its buildings and all its other appurtenances which he lately purchased from Emma the wife of the late Hugh Esboyt in the parish of St Peter, Ipswich (*Gyppewyco*), between the messuage of John Drayl on the south and the highway on the north, abutting east on John Drayl's messuage and west on the highway; to be held of the capital lord of the fee, by the due and accustomed services, to the prior and convent and their successors, freely, quietly, rightly and in peace, in perpetuity, so that neither John de la Dale nor his heirs, nor anyone through or for him, may henceforth claim any right therein. Sealed in testimony.

Hiis testibus: Thoma Stace, Thoma le Rente, Iohanne de Watlefeude, Waltero de Westhale, Hugone Horold, Alexandro Margarete, Henrico Rotoun, Ada de Holebrok', Roberto de le Lane, Rogero Fabro, et aliis. At Ipswich, on the feast of the Exaltation of the Holy Cross, 5 Edward II.   14 September 1311

TNA, E40/3618. 224 × 112mm, 16mm turnup, 133mm tag. Fragment of seal, 13 × 16mm. Endorsed: Gippewic (17c.).

413. Notification by Joan Wolston, daughter of Walter Wolston of Brundish (*Borndysh*), that she has remitted and quitclaimed, for herself and her heirs, to the prior and canons and their successors in perpetuity, all right and claim which she had or in any way might have had, in all the lands and tenements which the prior and canons hold of her in Ipswich (*Gypewyco*), or which pertain or might pertain to her in any way whatsoever. Furthermore she has remitted and quitclaimed, for herself and her heirs in perpetuity, to the prior and canons and their successors, all right and claim which she had, or in any way might have in future, in all the rent which she was accustomed to take annually from the prior and canons out of all those tenements which they hold of her in the parish of St Peter, Ipswich; so that neither she nor her heirs, nor anyone in their name, may henceforth be able to make any claim in the aforesaid tenements and rent in perpetuity. Sealed in testimony.

Hiis testibus: Iohanne de Whatefeld, Thoma de la Rente, Gilberto Roberd, Thoma Stace, Henrico le Rotoun, Rogero le Smhyt, Milone le Smhyt, Semanno de Merihel, Iohanne Hyrp, Alexandro Margarete, Thoma clerico et aliis. At Ipswich, Tuesday next after the feast of SS Nereus and Achilleus, Martyrs, 15 Edward II.

18 May 1322

TNA, E40/3871. 232 × 113mm, 28mm turnup, 50mm tag with three seals attached to it by parchment ties. Seal at left in dark red wax, 25mm round, showing a bird sitting on a branch, legend lost. Seal in centre in dark green wax, 30mm round, showing a fleur-de-lys, legend lost. Seal at right in dark red, 20mm round, with design and legend both lost. Endorsed: Relaxatio reddit' per Ioh'm Wolston'.

414. Grant and confirmation by Walter of Bures, chaplain, to the prior and canons, of the whole of his messuage which he lately purchased of Robert Drayl, in the parish of St Peter, Ipswich (*Gippewyco*); to be held of the capital lords of that fee, to the prior and canons and their successors in fee and by inheritance, for the services which pertain to it in perpetuity. Warranty by the grantor and his heirs against all people in perpetuity. Sealed in testimony.

Hiis testibus: Ricardo Loen, Thoma le Rente, Waltero de Westhale, Thoma Stace, Laurentio Cobbe, Henrico le Rotoun, Gilberto Roberd, et aliis.   [1304 x 1323]

TNA, E40/3268. 217 × 74mm, 12mm turnup, 93mm tag. Seal fragment 16 × 18mm, brown wax, legend and device unclear. Endorsed: H prior iixx (13c.); in Gypp' (?16c.).

Date: After the election of Prior Henry of Burstall in 1304, or perhaps after that of Henry of Kersey in 1311 (see endorsement), and before the death of Thomas le Rente in 1323. Le Rente first appears in the records in 1281; he was a member of the committee appointed on 10 August 1290 to re-state the borough customs (see Alsford, 'Thomas le Rente', *PSIAH*, XXXV Part 2 (1982), 105–15).

415. Grant by Adam Bolle of Ipswich (*Gippewyco*) to Prior Henry and the canons, of his messuage in Ipswich between the curtilage of Alice Pachat on the south and the curtilages of John of Claydon (*Cleydone*) and William Sperlyng on the north, one end abutting on the highway from the priory of St Peter to the fish market[1] and the other on the curtilage of William Fyn; to be held to the prior and canons and their successors, of the capital lords of that fee by the due and accustomed services. Warranty by the grantor and his heirs against all people in perpetuity. Sealed in testimony.

Hiis testibus: Iohanne Irp, Iohanne de Prestone tunc ballivis ville Gippewyci, Iohanne de Whatefelde, Thoma Stace, Elis' Coco, Milone Fabro, Semanno de Meriehil et aliis. At Ipswich, Sunday next after the Purification of the Blessed Mary, 18 Edward II.   3 February 1325

TNA, E40/3392. 212 × 96mm, 16mm turnup, 80mm tag. Seal missing. Endorsed: Ad' Bolle (15c.); Gypp' d' Boll' (16c.).

> 1 The fish market is shown in the bird's eye plan of Ipswich from Speed's 1611 map of Suffolk. It lay at a point in the present Buttermarket at the junction with Dial Lane. That it occupied the same site in the medieval period is shown from two grants of common soil in the borough archive, dated 1395 and 1499 (SROI, C/3/8/3/1 and C/3/8/3/7). The highway from the priory passed through the parishes of St Peter, St Stephen and St Lawrence. No. 415 could relate to any of the three parishes, though no. 416 suggests that the property lay in St Peter's.

416. Notification by Adam Bolle [*illegible*] that he has granted [*illegible*] and utterly quitclaimed, for himself and his heirs, to Prior Henry and the canons, all right and claim which he had, might have had, or could in future have, in a messuage in the parish of St Peter, Ipswich (*Gippewico*), between the curtilage of John Hattele and the messuage of William le Toke, [?one end abutting *illegible*] on the messuage of John Thedam, and the other upon the highway extending from the priory of St Peter [*illegible*] to the fish market of Ipswich, so that neither he nor his heirs [?nor anyone *illegible*] in their name may [?henceforth *illegible*] claim any right therein. Sealed in testimony.

Hiis testibus: Iohanne Irp, Ricardo de Lei' tunc ballivis ville Gippewici, Thoma de Whitefelde, Henrico le Rotun iuniore, Milone le Sur [*illegible*]. At Ipswich, Sunday after the feast of St Hillary, [*regnal year illegible*] Edward III.

[17 January 1328]

TNA, E40/3390. Poor condition, badly galled and rubbed. 206 × 100mm, 19mm turnup, 85mm tag. Seal in blob of wax 23 × 21mm, seal impression 15mm round. Unintelligible design, dark wax. Endorsed: par' sancti Petri (16/17c.); H prior ii Ad' Belle (15c.).

Date: John Irp served several terms as bailiff of Ipswich, but only one in conjunction with a Richard: with Richard of Leyham/Layham from September 1327 to September 1328 (SROI, Ipswich Portmanmote roll C/2/1/1/36; *IBAC*, p. 49).

417. Grant in perpetuity by Thomas of Rougham to God, the church of St Peter and the prior and canons, for a certain sum of money cash down, of a piece of land with a windmill constructed on it, with its site, mount and ditches, and free entry and exit to and from the mill, and all its appurtenances, in the parish of St Peter, Ipswich (*Gippewyco*), between the land of the prior and canons on the north and the land formerly of Robert West on the south, one headland abutting east on the pasture called 'le Cokyspyhtil', the other abutting west upon the highway from Ipswich towards 'Coldone'.[1] He has also granted and confirmed to them a piece of meadow fit to mow in Sproughton (*Sprouton'*) between [*sic*] the river bank which extends from Sproughton towards Handford (*Haneford*) bridge on the north, abutting east upon the meadow of Robert of Boss Hall (*Bordeshowe*). He has also granted and confirmed to them 4s annual rent in perpetuity, to be taken from the capital messuage of John Gyloun in the parish of St Peter, that is, between the place of the prior and canons on one side and the messuage of Richard Ficat on the other; and also 5s rent to be taken annually from the capital messuage of Richard Fycat next to the said messuage of John Gyloun. To have and to hold to the prior and canons and their successors, freely, quietly, rightly and in peace, in fee and by inheritance, of the capital lords of the fees, by the services by right due and accustomed. Warranty by the grantor and his heirs against all people in perpetuity.

Hiis testibus: Iohanne de Whatefelde, Ricardo de Leyham, Galfrido Costyn, Thoma de Whatefelde, Willelmo Malyn, Iohanne de Akenham, Alano Davy, Willelmo de Kenebrok', Willelmo Deyse et aliis. At Ipswich, Sunday the feast of St Peter *in cathedra*, 6 Edward III.   22 February 1332

TNA, E40/3290. 306 × 159mm, 21mm turnup, 138mm tag. Seal 27mm round, green wax, showing Agnus Dei, legend ECCE ... at right. Endorsed T de Rouham (14c.); Gippewic' (16c.); par' sancti Petri (16c.); Belstede (17c.).

 1 ?In Belstead; see endorsement.

418. Grant by Thomas of Rougham to the prior and canons, in the same terms as no. 417, though of later date.

Hiis testibus: Iohanne de Whatefelde, Ricardo de Leyham, Galfrido Costyn, Thoma de Whatefelde, Willelmo Malyn, Iohanne de Akenham, Alano Davy, Willelmo de Kenebrok', Willelmo Deyse et aliis. At Ipswich, Sunday next before the feast of St Ambrose, 6 Edward III.   29 March 1332

TNA, E40/3863. 299 × 236mm, including a turnup of 17mm which has been folded out. One set of slits for tag. Endorsed: Inde habemus aliam cartam[1] (14c.); Tho'e de Rouham (15c.); paroch' Petri (16c.); par' sancti Petri de monte molendina [*sic*] et aliis redditibus (17c.).

 1 The 'other charter' referred to is no. 417, dated 22 February 1332. The hands are not the
  same.

419. Notification by William of Brandeston (*Brandiston'*) of Ipswich (*Gyppwyco*) that he has granted, remitted and utterly quitclaimed, for himself and his heirs, to Prior Henry of Kersey, the canons, and their successors, all right and claim which he had, has, or in any way might have had or may have, in a piece of land in the suburb of Ipswich, in St Peter's parish, next to the prior's land, 5 perches in length and 3 perches in width on the west, which was held of the prior by the service of one halfpenny *per annum*; so that neither William nor his heirs, nor anyone in his name, may henceforth in future claim any right therein. Warranty is granted against all people in perpetuity. Sealed in testimony.

Hiis testibus: Iohanne Haltebe, Willelmo de Kenebrock', Thoma le Mayster, Roberto de Bordeshowe et Roberto Cok' et aliis. At Ipswich, Thursday the feast of St John the Baptist, 13 Edward III.   24 June 1339

TNA, E40/3868. 234 × 100mm, 16mm turnup, 97mm tag. Seal in dark green wax, 25 × 35mm, of mysterious design. Endorsed: Brandiston xld' (15c.); de una pecia terre in subberbio [*sic*] Gipp' (16c.).

420. Notification by John Goldhauk', wine drawer of London (*wyndrawer London'*), and Joan his wife, who was the wife of Walter Langeleye of Ipswich (*Gippewico*), that they have remitted, released and utterly quitclaimed, for themselves and their heirs in perpetuity, to Prior William and the convent, all their right and claim which they ever had, have, or in whatever manner might be able to have, in a tenement with a curtilage and all its appurtenances, situated in the parish of St Peter of Ipswich, between the tenement of the prior and convent which Sarra Irp formerly held on the south side and the garden of the prior and convent on the north side, abutting east upon 'le Gesthalle' and west on the highway; which tenement and curtilage Joan, together with Walter her former husband, now deceased, took and held of John the late prior and the convent at fee-farm for the term of one hundred years, for an annual rent of 3s of silver, to be paid yearly, and into which tenement and curtilage Prior William and the convent re-entered in their original state during the term of three years last past before the date of these presents, because the rent was in arrears, as they were rightly allowed to do according to the grants made in respect thereof; so that neither John Goldhauk' and Joan his wife, nor their heirs, nor any other for them or in their name, may make any claim to the tenement and curtilage in the future, but be excluded from all right, title, claim or action whatsoever in perpetuity by the presents. Sealed in testimony.

Hiis testibus: Iohanne Rous, Roberto Lucas, tunc ballivis ville Gippewici, Iohanne Bernard, Hugone Hoo, Willelmo Debenham, Willelmo Russell, Ricardo Joye, Henrico Heyward, et aliis. At Ipswich, 18 May, 11 Henry IV.   18 May 1410

E40/3479. 257 × 150mm, 17mm turnup, 110mm tag at right, seal 20mm round, red wax; 35mm tag at left, seal missing. Endorsed: per' (16c.).

IPSWICH, UNNAMED PARISH AND SUBURBS

421. Confirmation by Geoffrey de Beumes, son of William de Beumes, to the canons, of the gift which William his father made to them, namely 12d annual rent towards their pittance on the anniversary day of his death, to be taken in perpetuity from Geoffrey and his heirs from the messuage which is between that which was William Belwether's and that of Thomas Gynchun. If Geoffrey or his heirs default in payment, the canons may distrain.   [1220s – 1240s]

TNA, E40/3730. 165 × 76mm, 17mm turnup, 150mm tag. Endorsed: Galfrid' Beumes de Gypewic' (14c.).

Sciant presentes et futuri quod ego Galfridus de Beumes filius Willelmi de Beumes concessi et hac mea carta confirmavi canonicis Sancti Petri de Gypewico, donum quod predictus Willelmus pater meus eis fecit, scilicet duodecim denarios annui redditus ad eorum pictanciam in anniversario die obitus sui in perpetuum recipiendos de me et heredibus meis de mesuagio quod est inter mesuagium quod fuit Willelmi Belwether, et mesuagium Thome Gynchun. Ita quidem quod si ego vel heredes mei cessaverimus in solucione dicti redditus, quod absit, liceat dictis canonicis dictum mesuagium usque ad plenam solucionem restringere. Hoc autem eis feci pro salute anime mee et anime dicti Willelmi patris mei et antecessorum et successorum meorum omnium. Et ut hec mea concessio et huius carte mee confirmacio firma sit et stabilis inperpetuum, presenti scripto sigillum meum apposui. Hiis testibus: Iohanne de Beaumes et Silvestro filio Walkelini tunc ballivis de Gypewico, Iohanne filio Normanni, Petro filio Eborardi, Iohanne filio Constantini, Rogero Lyu, Amisio Vinitario, Waltero de Leeston, Constantino Fader, Roberto Paris, Oseberto de Belinges, Edmundo Goldhavech, et multis aliis.

Date: John de Beaumes and Silvester son of Walkelin served at least one term together as bailiffs of Ipswich between 1227 and 1232. In 1200, John son of Norman was a bailiff, Roger Lyu a coroner, and Robert Paris a capital burgess ('Black Domesday', fols 77r.–78r.). Together with Peter son of Eborard, John son of Constantine and Amis the vintner, they all attest from the 1190s, making it unlikely that they would still be active after the 1240s; John de Beaumes, however, was a party to a land dispute at the eyre of 1240 (*CPSE*, nos. 275, 282).

422. Grant in free and perpetual alms by William son of William of Kembroke to the canons, towards the improvement of their pittance, of a piece of land in the suburb of Ipswich, lying lengthways next to the way extending towards Horsewade, one headland abutting on the messuage of Robert Shuruard and the other on the land of Geoffrey Cayward, and which William sometime held of Robert Blundel by the annual service of 18d; for the salvation of his soul and those of his ancestors, rendering 18d annually to Robert Blundel and his heirs, in two instalments, for all secular demands save the king's service, namely house-rent. Warranty is granted.
[Early – mid-thirteenth century]

TNA, E40/3731. 163 × 70mm, 13mm turnup, 80mm tag. Seal design is difficult to interpret, perhaps a spray of flowers. Legend: … GILL' WILLELM … Counterseal also difficult to interpret. Endorsed: De terris iuxta Horswaud (14c.).

Sciant presentes et futuri quod ego Willelmus filius Willelmi de Kenebroch concessi et dedi et hac mea carta confirmavi Deo et ecclesie beatorum apostolorum Petri et Pauli de Gypewico et canonicis ibidem Deo servientibus, ad eorum pitanciam emendandam, unam peciam terre in suburbio de Gypewico que iacet in longum iuxta viam que tendit versus Horsewade, cuius unum capud abutat super mesuagium Roberti Shuruard et aliud super terram Galfridi Cayward, quam scilicet peciam tenui aliquando de Roberto Blundel per servicium annuum octodecim denariorum, cum edificiis et pertinenciis suis, illis et eorum successoribus tenendam et habendam in liberam et perpetuam elemosinam, pro salute anime mee et pro animabus antecessorum meorum. Reddendo inde annuatim predicto Roberto Blundel et heredibus suis octodecim denarios, scilicet ad Pascha novem denarios, et ad festum Sancti Michaelis novem denarios, pro omnibus serviciis, consuetudinibus et demandis secularibus, salvo servicio domini regis, scilicet hadgabulo. Et ego Willelmus et heredes mei warantizabimus predictis canonicis et eorum successoribus predictam peciam terre cum pertinenciis, per prenominatum servicium, contra omnes homines. Hiis testibus: Petro filio Eborardi et Hugone de Langestun' tunc ballivis de Gipewico, Iohanne filio Normanni, Iohanne de Beaumes, Iohanne filio Constantini, Waltero de Leestun', Roger Lyu, Amisio Vinitario, Galfrido Blundel, Iohanne Prekehert, Reginaldo filio eius, Roberto Shuruard et multis aliis.

Date: Robert Blundel (and others: see dating note to no. 421) attest other charters from the 1190s. John Prekehert was beadle in 1200 ('Black Domesday', fol. 79v.). None of them is likely to have been active beyond the mid-thirteenth century. For John de Beaumes, bailiff between 1227 and 1232, and 1233–34, and participating in the 1240 eyre, see no. 421, n.

IPSWICH AND ELSEWHERE

423. Grant in perpetuity by Nicholas Bonde of Freston[1] (*Frestone*) to Prior Henry and the canons, of two tofts, 48 acres of land and two acres of pasture in Ipswich (*Gippewyco*), Wherstead (*Wherstede*), Belstead (*Belstede*), Thurleston (*Thurlestone*) and Hintlesham (*Hyntlesham*), to have and to hold of the capital lords of that fee, freely, quietly, in fee and by inheritance, by the services pertaining to the same tenement in perpetuity. For this grant and present charter of confirmation the prior and canons have given £20 of sterlings. Sealed in testimony.

Hiis testibus: Fulcone Baroun, Ricardo de Coppedok', Iohanne de Coppedok', Petro Annoys, Stephano de Bramford, Rogero Tyvel, Mansero clerico et aliis. At Ipswich, 10 December, 14 Edward II.   10 December 1320

TNA, E40/3424. 224 × 90mm, 15mm turnup, 110mm tag, no seal. Endorsed: H prior ii (14c.); ii hund? (15c.); Wested Belsted Thwrlistwin [*sic*] Hyntelisham (16c.).

  1 Of the family which held the manor of Bonds in Freston.

424. Notification by Thomas of Rougham that he has granted, remitted and utterly in perpetuity quitclaimed, for himself and his heirs, to Sir Henry the prior, the canons and their successors, all right and claim which he had or in any way might have had, or might have in the future, in all the lands and tenements which they have by the gift of Nicholas Bonde in the townships of Ipswich (*Gippewici*), Wherstead (*Wherstede*), Belstead (*Belstede*), Thurleston and Hintlesham (*Hyntlesham*), which tenements Nicholas and Thomas purchased jointly in those towns; so that neither he nor his heirs, nor anyone in his or their name, may be able to claim any right therein in perpetuity. Sealed in testimony.

Hiis testibus: Fulcone Baroun, Ricardo de Coppedok', Iohanne de Coppedok', Stephano de Bramford, Rogero Tyvel, Mansero clerico, Willelmo le Fuller' et aliis. At Ipswich, 20 January, 14 Edward II.   20 January 1321

TNA, E40/3558. 229 × 100mm, 15mm turnup, 97mm tag. Seal 21mm round but fragment only. Endorsed: Gipwic Wetsted Bested Hintesham et Thurliston (17c.).

425. Notification by Nicholas Bonde of Freston that he has conceded, remitted and utterly in perpetuity quitclaimed, for himself and his heirs, to Sir Henry the prior, the canons and their successors, all right and claim which he had or in any way might have had, or might have in future, in all the lands and tenements which they have and hold in the townships of Wherstead (*Wherstede*), Belstead (*Belstede*), Thurleston, Hintlesham (*Hyntelsham*) and Ipswich (*Gippewyco*), so that neither he nor his heirs, nor anyone in his or their name, may in any way be able to claim any right therein in perpetuity. Sealed in testimony.

Hiis testibus: Fulcone Baroun, Ricardo de Coppedok', Iohanne de Coppedok', Stephano de Bramford, Rogero Tyvel, Mansero clerico, Willelmo le Fullere et aliis. At Ipswich, 20 January, 14 Edward II. 20 January 1321

TNA, E40/3940. 229 × 84mm, 13mm turnup, on the underside of which is the following line of text: 'Sciant presentes et futuri quod ego Nicholaus Bond de Frestone concessi et dedi et hac presenti …', apparently the top line of a draft or rejected copy of the text of no. 423. Tag 90mm. Seal once 25mm round, no legend, heraldry in an architectural frame. Endorsed: H' prior iis' (?14c.).

RAYDON

426. Grant in free and perpetual alms by Hugh son of Hugh of Polstead to the canons, for the salvation of his soul and the souls of his ancestors and successors, of all the land, rent, meadow and pasture which Alwin Lykepani of Raydon held of Hugh's father in Raydon; to hold and to have of Hugh and his heirs, free from all secular service and demand, saving the king's due and accustomed service. Warranty is granted. [Second quarter of thirteenth century]

TNA, E40/3332. 171 × 96mm, 125mm tag, much mangled. Seal unusual: a triangle with rounded corners, much abraded; shield in centre cross-hatched with an unidentifiable device superimposed. Endorsed: Campeis de Pyde (?15/16c.).

Sciant presentes et futuri quod ego Hugo filius Hugonis de Polestede concessi, dedi, et hac presenti carta mea confirmavi Deo et ecclesie apostolorum Petri et Pauli de Gypwico et canonicis ibidem Deo servientibus, in liberam et perpetuam elemosinam pro salute anime mee et animabus antecessorum et successorum meorum, totam terram redditum pratum et pasturam cum pertinenciis quam Alwinus Lykepani de Reydune tenuit de patre meo in villa de Reidune. Tenendas et habendas de me et heredibus meis illis et eorum successoribus libere quiete bene et in pace, absolute ab omni servicio seculari et demanda, salvo servicio domini regis debito et consueto. Et ego Hugo et heredes mei warantibimus [*sic*] et defendemus dictam terram redditum pratum et pasturam cum pertinenciis contra omnes inperpetuum. Hiis testibus: Domino Galfrido de Badele, Domino Willelmo filio Roberti de Reydune, Willelmo de Holebroc, Ricardo de Bordeshoe, Gerardo de Sproutune, Willelmo Testepyn, Baldewino de Pesehal', Ricardo de Berhot, Edmundo de Polsted, Alano le Herun de Polstede et aliis.

Date: Sir Geoffrey III of Badley was admitted a forinsec burgess of Ipswich in 1233–34 ('Black Domesday', fol. 84r.). William of Holbrook attests no. 539, 16 September 1235 x 23 May 1248. William Testepin attests no. 83, 1227–32, and is party to a final concord of 1219–20 (Rye, *Fines*, no. 92); he is a pledge to prosecute in no. 321, 31 May 1238.

427. Notification by William of Ramsey (*Ramesey*) that, whereas there was a dispute between him and the prior and canons concerning an annual rent of 4s to be taken from a tenement of his which was formerly Robert Ascelyn's in Raydon (*Reydone*), for which rent they often distrained upon the said tenements [*sic*], he wills and grants, for himself and his heirs, that the prior and canons henceforth may have the 4s annually in equal instalments at the four usual terms, for the payment of which to the prior and canons and their successors in perpetuity he binds himself and his heirs and all his tenements for distraint by them in perpetuity. Sealed in testimony.

Hiis testibus: Iohanne de Reymes, Roberto de Reymes, Waltero Baldewyn', Willelmo dil Holt de Reydone, Nicholao de Lafham et aliis. At Ipswich, 4 May, 26 Edward I.

4 May 1298

TNA, E40/3333. 228 × 116mm, 18mm turnup, 95mm tag. There is a small seal, 22mm round, showing the device of a bird, but with the legend wholly lost. Endorsed: W. de Ramesei (in same hand as text); Reidone (16c.).

SPROUGHTON

428. Notification by Robert de Blancheville to John, bishop of Norwich, his archdeacons and clergy, that he has given to the church and canons of SS Peter and Paul in perpetual alms, all the land of Sproughton with all the appurtenances to which he has proved his title as his inheritance in Suffolk by the king's precept, which [*missing*] his grandmother held in the same township; free from all exactions except the service of the king and the lords of the foundation. This he has done for the salvation of his soul and those of his heirs and ancestors, and out of brotherly love because the canons have granted that they will receive his body on his death.

[1175 – c. 1198]

No details of dimensions or seals are available. Endorsed: Rob't de Blanchevilla de terris in Sprutton. The text is printed in *Collectanea Topographica et Genealogica*, IV, 242–43, to which it was contributed by 'L.B.L.' (probably the antiquary the Revd Lambert Blackwell Larking, 1797 – c. 1868: Dr S.J. Plunkett, *pers. comm.*). The charter is said to be from the muniments of the Cotton family; its present location is unknown.

Venerabili patri suo Iohanni Dei gratia Norwicensi episcopo et archidiaconis suis universisque clericis sibi subiectis et omnibus sancte matris ecclesie filiis, Rodbertus [*de Blanchevi*]lla salutem. Sciatis me concessisse et dedisse ecclesie apostolorum Petri et Pauli de Gypewico et canonicis eiusdem loci, totam terram de Sproutunia cum omnibus pertinentiis quam ego diracionavi ut hereditatem meam

in comitatu Sudfolchie precepto domini regis et quam [*missing*]ivena mea ava
tenuit in eodem villa Sproutuniae, in perpetuam elemosinam, liberam et quietam
ab omnibus consuetudinibus et exactionibus que ad me pertinent, salvo servitio
domini regis et dominorum fundi. Hanc concessionem et donationem feci ecclesie
prenominate pro salute anime mee et heredum meorum et parentum meorum, et
pro fraternitate quia michi concesserunt in obitu meo ad corpus meum suscipi-
endum. His testibus: Wimar' capellano, Hamone Reginold, Willelmo Raddulfus,
Hamone capellano, A[*missing*], Roberto de Willavesham,[1] Willelmo filio Hervei,
Radulfo de Bedding',[2] Willelmo Vis de lu, W[*missing*] Fulch'r, Cedric' de Tudeham
et Roberto de Tudeham, Roberto de Burnedis,[3] Roberto Nep', Clemente Reginold'
carpentario, Roberto de Blunvill.

1 Willisham.
2 Bedingfield.
3 Brundish.

Date: Wimar the chaplain occurs from 1165 (*Dodnash Charters*, p. 4) to 1198
(no. 484 in the present edition). John, bishop of Norwich is thus almost certainly
John of Oxford (cons. 14 December 1175, d. 2 June 1200), rather than his successor
John de Gray.

429. Grant in free, pure and perpetual alms by Manser of Gusford to the canons,
for the salvation of his soul and those of his ancestors, of two acres of land in
Sproughton, lying between the land which William H'lewin gave to the church in
alms and the land of Richard son of Hubert.   [1180s – early thirteenth century]

TNA, E40/3404. 200 × 57mm, 24mm turnup, 104mm tag, seal missing. Endorsed:
Manseri de Gu[th]elesford (13/14c.).

Sciant presentes et futuri quod ego Manserus de Guthelesford' dedi et concessi et
hac presenti carta mea confirmavi Deo et ecclesie beatorum apostolorum Petri et
Pauli de Gypewico et canonicis ibidem Deo servientibus, pro salute anime mee et
parentum meorum, duas acras terre in Sproutune que iacent inter terram quam
Willelmus H'lewin dedit predicte ecclesie in elemosinam et terram Ricardi filii
Huberti, in liberam, puram et perpetuam elemosinam. His testibus: Ricardo filio
Huberti, Hugone Talemache, Ada de Ulmo, Mansero de Bordeshoe, Gerardo de
Ripa, Willelmo fratre suo, Martino de Guthelesford, Rogero fratre suo, Willelmo
Angot, et multis aliis.

Date: Manser of Gusford attests no. 433 (late twelfth century – *c.* 1202), along with
Eustace of Brantham (occ. 1165–1202). Hugh Talemache I attests three charters
of Dodnash Priory (*Dodnash Charters*, nos. 13, late twelfth – early thirteenth
century; 14, early thirteenth century before 1221; and 35, late 1226; and occurs
1210–12 (*Bk Fees*, 134). Adam of the Elm attests no. 43, after Easter 1180 and before
October 1198 but probably close to 1180, and other charters of SS Peter and Paul
1180s – early thirteenth century. The absence of a warranty clause suggests a
twelfth-century date.

430. Grant in free and pure and perpetual alms by Warin son of Osbert the clerk
of Sproughton to the canons, for the salvation of his soul and those of all his

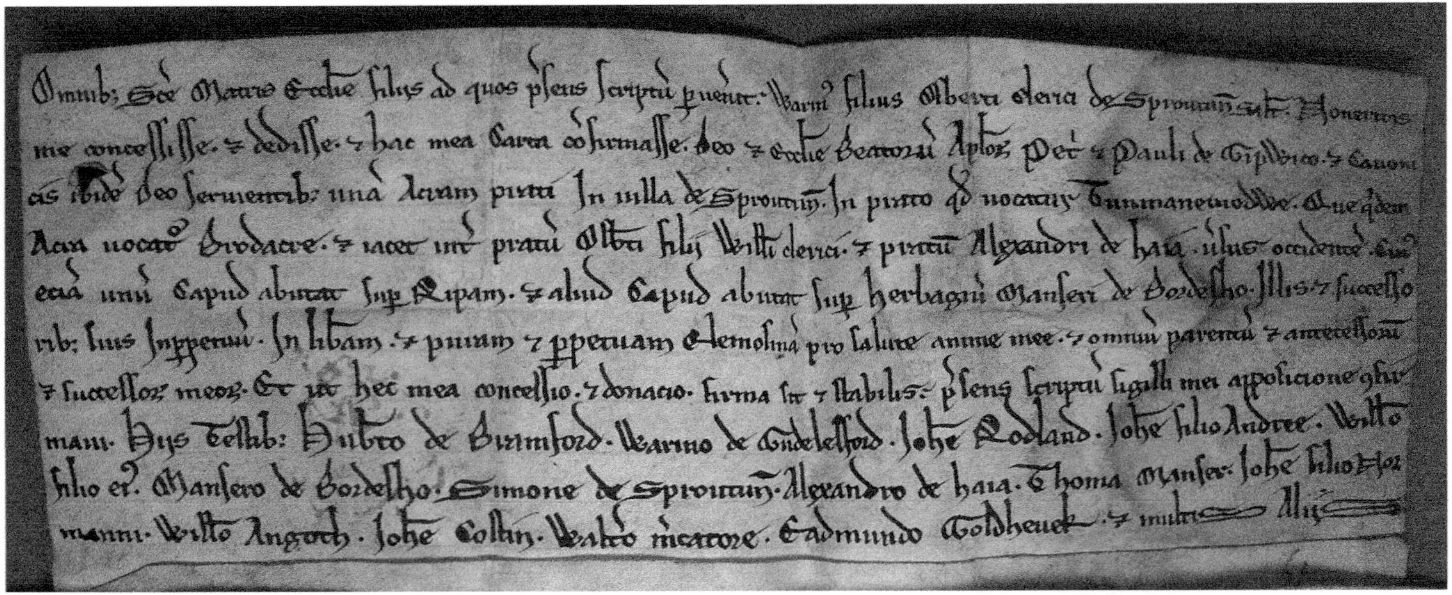

Fig. 3 Grant in free, pure and perpetual alms by Warin son of Osbert the clerk to the canons, of 'Brodacre' in 'Tunmanemedwe' in Sproughton, 1180s – early thirteenth century (no. 430). London, The National Archives, E40/3853.

grandparents, ancestors and successors, of one acre of meadow called 'Brodacre' in the meadow called 'Tunmanemedwe' in Sproughton, between the meadow of Osbert son of William the clerk and that of Alexander Hay, one headland abutting on the river bank, the other on the pasture of Manser of Boss Hall.

[1180s – early thirteenth century]

TNA, E40/3853. 184 × 82mm, 14mm turnup, 118mm tag. Tag has on it a fragment of musical notation, so has obviously been reused from an unwanted liturgical manuscript, which in turn suggests that the charter was written by a priory scribe on behalf of the donor. Seal missing. Endorsed: Warinus fil' Osberti (15c.); de Sprowton (16/17c).

Omnibus sancte matris ecclesie filiis ad quos presens scriptum pervenerit, Warinus filius Osberti clerici de Sproutun' salutem. Noveritis me concessisse et dedisse et hac mea carta confirmasse Deo et ecclesie beatorum apostolorum Petri et Pauli de Gipwico et canonicis ibidem Deo servientibus, unam acram prati in villa de Sproutun', in prato quod vocatur Tunmanemedwe, que quidem acra vocatur Brodacre, et iacet inter pratum Osberti filii Willelmi clerici et pratum Alexandri de Haia versus occidentem, cuius etiam unum capud abutat super ripam, et aliud capud abutat super herbagium Manseri de Bordesho; illis et successoribus suis inperpetuum, in liberam et puram et perpetuam elemosinam pro salute anime mee et omnium parentum et antecessorum et successorum meorum. Et ut hec mea concessio et donacio firma sit et stabilis, presens scriptum sigilli mei apposicione confirmavi. Hiis testibus: Huberto de Bramford, Warino de Gudelesford, Iohanne Rodland, Iohanne filio Andree, Willelmo filio eius, Mansero de Bordesho, Simone de Sproutun', Alexandro de Haia, Thoma Manser, Iohanne filio Normanni, Willelmo Angoth, Iohanne Costin, Waltero mercatore, Eadmundo Goldhevek, et multis aliis.

Date: Various witnesses attest other charters in the collection for these years, e.g. Hubert of Bramford (no. 43, between Easter 1180 and October 1198) and Warin of Gusford (no. 49, 1180s). A plea of land brought by Geoffrey de Ambli against Hubert of Bramford and the bailiffs of the bishop of Évreux was essoined until Sunday *post clausum Pasche*, 1201 (*PBKJ*, I, no. 3397). John son of Norman was a bailiff of Ipswich in 1200 ('Black Domesday', fol. 77r.).

431. Grant in perpetuity by Warin son of Osbert the clerk of Sproughton to the canons, of one acre of meadow called 'Brodacre' in Sproughton, in the meadow called 'Tunmanemedwe', to hold of Warin and his heirs, rendering 12d annually in two instalments for all secular exactions. For this grant the canons have given him 20s of sterlings. Warranty is granted. [1180s – early thirteenth century]

TNA, E40/3525. 152 × 112mm, including folded-out turnup of 10mm, 103mm tag, seal missing. Endorsed: Warinus filius Osb' clerici de Sprouton (14c.); Sprowton (17c.). The hand is different from that of no. 430.

Omnibus sancte matris ecclesie filiis ad quos presens scriptum pervenerit, Warinus filius Osberti clerici de Sproutune salutem. Noverit universitas vestra me concessisse et dedisse et hac presenti carta mea confirmasse Deo et ecclesie beatorum apostolorum Petri et Pauli de Gipwico et canonicis ibidem Deo servientibus, unam acram prati in villa de Sproutune, in prato quod vocatur Tunmanemedwe, que quidem acra vocatur Brodacre, et iacet inter pratum Osberti filii Willelmi clerici versus orientem, et inter pratum Alexandri de Haia versus occidentem, cuius etiam unum capud abutat super ripam, et aliud capud abutat super herbagium Manseri de Bordesho; illis et successoribus suis habendum et tenendum de me et heredibus meis inperpetuum, in bono [*sic*] et pace, libere et quiete et honorifice, reddendo inde michi annuatim duodecim denarios, ad duos terminos, scilicet ad Pascha sex denarios, et ad festum Sancti Mikaelis sex denarios, pro omnibus serviciis, consuetudinibus, et secularibus exaccionibus. Pro hac igitur concessione et donacione et huius carte mee confirmacione, prefati canonici dederunt michi viginti solidos sterlingorum in gersumiam. Quare ego Warinus et heredes mei warantizabimus prefatam acram prati predictis canonicis per prenominatum servicium contra omnes homines. Hiis testibus: Huberto de Bramford, Warino de Gudeleford, Iohanne Rolland, Iohanne filio Andree, Willelmo filio eius, Mansero de Bordesho, Roberto filio eius, Simone de Sproutun', Alexandro de Haia, Thoma Manser, Iohanne filio Normanni, Willelmo Angot, Iohanne Costin, Waltero mercatore, et multis aliis.

Date: The witness list is almost identical with that of no. 430.

432. Grant in perpetual alms by Joce son of Reginald of Cotton to the canons, of 30 acres of Ware[1] called Chebbeleslond in Sproughton, with his cousin John son of Manser of Gusford who has taken the habit of a religious at the priory, and for the salvation of Joce's soul and the souls of his ancestors, free of all secular demands pertaining to him, saving the service of the lord of the fee. [Late twelfth century]

No details of dimensions, seal or endorsements are available. The text is printed in *Collectanea Topographica et Genealogica*, IV, 243, and is said to be from the muniments of the Cotton family; its present location is unknown: see no. 428.

Omnibus sancte matris ecclesie filiis presentibus et futuris, Ioce filius Reginaldi de Cottune salutem. Sciatis me dedisse et concessisse et presenti carta mea confirmasse Deo et ecclesie apostolorum Petri et Pauli de Gipeswico et canonicis ibidem Deo servientibus, xxx acras de Ware cum omnibus pertinentiis in Sproutune que appellantur Chebbeleslond, cum Iohanne cognato meo filio Manseri de Guthelesford qui ibi habitum religionis accepit et pro salute anime mee et antecessorum meorum, libere et quiete in perpetua elemosina ab omnibus secularibus serviciis que ad me pertinent, salvo servicio domini de feudo. Huius autem donationis et confirmationis testes sunt: Ricardus presbiter de Cottune, Warinus de Navelt',[2] Radulfus de Huntefeld, Manser de Guthelesford, Martinus filius eius, Ricardus filius Ioce, Warinus filius Manseri, Rogerus frater eius, Iohannes filius Edmundi, Manser de ponte, Willelmus filius Angod, Edmundus Goldhavec, Ricardus de Panit'[3] et multi alii.

1 'War-land': land liable to payment of geld.
2 Naughton.
3 Pannington in Wherstead.

Date: Manser of Gusford attests various charters of SS Peter and Paul from the 1180s
and 1190s (e.g. nos. 340, 349, 429), Martin his son is presumably the 'Martinus de
Guthelesford' who wrote his name on the flyleaf of a late twelfth-century volume
of *XII Prophetae* formerly at Bury Abbey, now in Pembroke College Library: see
M.R. James's Pembroke Catalogue (1905 edn), item 65, pp. 57–58 (Dr S.J. Plunkett,
pers. comm.). William son of Angod (as William Angod) attests no. 482 in October
1198; Edmund Goldhavec attests no. 43, *c.* 1180.

433. Grant in perpetuity by Manser of Boss Hall to the canons, on the petition of
a friend of his kinsman, of 30 acres of Ware[1] called 'Kebelleslond' in Sproughton,
which Baldwin of Sproughton held of Manser's father Robert; to hold of Manser
and his heirs, paying 8s of sterlings annually for all services and secular exactions
pertaining to him, saving the service of the king and capital lord. For this grant
the canons have given him half a mark of silver.   [Late twelfth century – *c.* 1202]

TNA, E40/3524. 163 × 67mm, 13mm turnup, 150mm tag, seal missing. String on tag.
Endorsed: Ma'seri de Bordesho (?), Sprowton, Sproutune (both 16/17c.).

Universis sancte matris ecclesie filiis presentibus et futuris, Manserus de Bordesho
salutem. Sciatis me concessisse et hac carta mea confirmasse peticione socii cognati
mei Deo et ecclesie apostolorum Petri et Pauli de Gypeswico et canonicis ibidem
Deo servientibus, xxx^ta acras de Ware cum pertinentiis in Sproutune que vocantur
Kebelleslond, quas Baldewinus de Sproutune tenuit de Rodberto patre meo;
tenendas de me et heredibus meis in perpetuum, solvendo inde michi et heredibus
meis singulis annis viii^to solidos sterlingorum pro omnibus serviciis et exaccionibus
secularibus quas ad me pertinent, salvo servicio domini regis et capitalis domini.
Pro hac autem concessione et confirmatione dederunt michi predicti canonici
dimidiam marcam argenti. His testibus: Eustachio de Braham, Ricardo de
Bromford, Ranulfo le Bra', Philippo de Winestun, Mansero de Gutlesford, Ioce de
Cottune, Martino filio Manseri, Warino fratre suo, Ricardo de Panitune, Ricardo
de Tivile, Willelmo filio Angod, Edmundo filio Goldhavec et multis aliis.

1 'War-land': land liable to payment of geld.

Date: Eustace of Brantham occurs 1165–1202 (*Dodnash Charters*, no. 31, n.).
Richard de Tivile is party to a final concord quitclaiming the land of Pannington in
Wherstead to the priory in May 1196 (no. 309), and with Edmund son of Goldhavec
attests no. 482 in October 1198.

434. Grant in free, pure and perpetual alms by Roger son of William of Bramford
to the canons, for the salvation of his soul and those of Cecily his wife and all his
parents, ancestors and successors, of half an acre of meadow in Sproughton, in the
meadow called 'Brademedwe', which lies lengthways next to the lords' meadow.
Warranty is granted.   [Late twelfth century – 1220s]

TNA, E40/3419. 172 × 76mm, 26mm turnup, 105mm tag, seal missing. Endorsed:
Rogeri de Bromford (13c.); Sprowton (17c.).

Sciant presentes et futuri quod ego Rogerus filius Willelmi de Bromford concessi
et dedi et hac mea carta confirmavi, Deo et ecclesie beatorum apostolorum Petri

et Pauli de Gypewico et canonicis ibidem Deo servientibus, dimidiam acram prati in villa de Sproutune, in prato quod vocatur Brademedwe, quod scilicet iacet in longitudine propinquius prato dominorum; in liberam et puram et perpetuam elemosinam, pro salute anime mee et Cecilie uxoris mee et omnium parentum et antecessorum et successorum meorum. Et ego et heredes mei warantizabimus predictam dimidiam acram prati predictis canonicis contra omnes homines. Et ut hec mea concessio et donatio et huius carte mee confirmatio firma sit et stabilis, eam sigilli mei apposicione roboravi. Hiis testibus: Galfrido de Baddele, Huberto de Bromford, Rogero de Baddele, Willelmo filio Gregorii, Roberto de Nortwde, Symone de Sproutone, Mansero de Bordleshowe, Alexandro de Heia, Iohanne filio Andree, Willelmo filio eius, Warino de Guthelesford, Osberto filio Ade, Warino filio Osberti, Rogero Kalmodin, et multis aliis.

Date: The charters (nos. 40, 44) of Geoffrey II of Badley date *c.* 1180. Roger of Badley's grant (no. 31) to the canons of his part of Handford Mill dates 1190s – 1203, and he was dead before Easter 1230 (Introduction, p. 59). In Easter Term 1201 a plea of land by Geoffrey de Ambli against Hubert of Bramford and the bailiffs of the bishop of Évreux was essoined (*PBKJ*, I, no. 3397).

435. Grant in free, pure and perpetual alms by Roger son of William of Bramford to the canons, for the salvation of his soul and those of all his parents, ancestors and successors, of half an acre of meadow in Sproughton, in 'Tunmanemedwe', between the meadow formerly of Edmund son of Ailwi and that formerly of Roger's uncle Osbert. Warranty is granted. [Late twelfth century – 1220s]

TNA, E40/3551. 183 × 83mm, 13mm turnup, 60mm tag, seal missing. Endorsed: Roger de Bramford (13c.); di' acr' in p'ato voc' Tunmanesmedwe (15c.); Sproutun (15c.).

Sciant presentes et futuri quod ego Rogerus filius Willelmi de Bramford concessi et dedi et hac mea carta confirmavi Deo et ecclesie beatorum apostolorum Petri et Pauli de Gipwico et canonicis ibidem Deo servientibus, dimidiam acram prati in villa de Sproutun', in prato quod vocatur Tunmanemedwe, que scilicet dimidia acra iacet inter pratum quod fuit Eadmundi filii Ailwi et inter pratum quod fuit Ade filii Osberti avunculi mei, in liberam et puram et perpetuam elemosinam, pro salute anime mee et omnium parentum et antecessorum et successorum meorum. Et ego et heredes mei warantizabimus predictam dimidiam acram prati predictis canonicis contra omnes homines. Et ut hec mea concessio et donacio et huius carte mee confirmacio firma sit et stabilis, eam sigilli mei apposicione roboravi. Hiis testibus: Roberto de Baddele, Huberto de Bramford, Rogero de Baddele, Willelmo filio Gregorii, Mansero de Bordesho, Warino de Gudelesford, Iohanne filio Andree, Simone de Sproutune, Alexandro de Haia, Warino filio Osberti, Rogero Kalmodin, Roberto de Norwde, Osberto filio Ade, Iohanne Mori, et multis aliis.

Date: Similar to Roger's charter no. 434, with which it has eleven witnesses in common.

436. Grant in free and perpetual alms by Roger Bramford of Sproughton to the canons, for the salvation of his soul and those of his ancestors and successors, of

2½ acres of land in Sproughton, between the canons' land on the west and the lane from his house towards the highway called 'Wrabessclohg' on the east, one headland abutting on his land, the other on the lane from the canons' house to 'Wrabessclohg'; to hold of Roger and his heirs, rendering to them annually 5d in three instalments, for all services. Warranty is granted. [1220s – 1250s]

TNA, E40/3841. 178 × 95mm, 15mm turnup, 70mm tag. Seal shows a fleur-de-lys, 40 × 37mm. Legend: + SIGILL' ROGERI DE BROMEFORD. No endorsements.

Sciant presentes et futuri quod ego Rogerus Bromford de Sproutun' concessi, dedi, et hac presenti carta mea confirmavi Deo et ecclesie apostolorum Petri et Pauli de Gypewico et canonicis ibidem Deo servientibus, in liberam et perpetuam elemosinam pro salute anime mee et antecessorum et successorum meorum, duas acras terre et dimidiam cum pertinentiis in parochia de Sproutun', que iacent inter terram dictorum canonicorum ex occidentali parte et venellam que tendit a domo mea versus viam regiam que vocatur Wrabessclohg' ex parte orientali, et unum capud habutat super terram meam et aliud super venellam que tendit a domo dictorum canonicorum versus viam regiam que vocatur Wrabessclohg'; tenendas et habendas illis et eorum successoribus de me et heredibus meis, libere, quiete, bene et in pace; reddendo inde annuatim michi et heredibus meis quinque denarios ad tres terminos, scilicet ad Pascha duos denarios, ad festum Sancti Iohannis Baptiste unum denarium, et ad festum Sancti Michaelis duos denarios, pro omnibus serviciis, consuetudinibus et demandis. Et ego dictus Rogerus et heredes mei warantizabimus dictam terram cum pertinenciis dictis canonicis et eorum successoribus per predictum servicium contra omnes inperpetuum. In huius rei testimonium presens scriptum sigilli mei apposicione roboravi. Hiis testibus: Domino Roberto de Aungerwile, Domino Nicholao filio eius, Ricardo decano de Codeham, Roberto le Buteler, Radulfo fratre eius, Ricardo de Bordesho, Mansero fratre eius, Ricardo del Hel, Roberto fratre eius, Alexandro Grigorie, Roberto de Nortwde, Willelmo Angot et aliis.

Date: Another of Roger Bramford's charters (no. 139) dates from between the 1220s and the 1250s. He was dead perhaps before 1260, certainly before August 1264 (no. 138, by the time of which his daughter Agnes has inherited her late father's land in Sproughton). Richard, dean of Coddenham attests a Dodnash Priory charter (*Dodnash Charters*, no. 16), 28 October 1223 x 27 October 1224, and in the 1240 eyre is accused, along with others, of unjustly disseising Master Robert of Coddenham of his free tenement in Ipswich (*CPSE*, no. 640).

437. Grant in free, pure and perpetual alms by Warin of Gusford to the canons, for the salvation of his soul and those of Alice his wife and all his ancestors and benefactors, of 9s annual rent to be taken from the hand of his brother Roger and his heirs in three instalments, for 27 acres of land which Roger held of their brother Martin in Sproughton, which 9s their brother Decimus the chaplain used to receive for life from Roger by Martin's gift. Proviso for distraint by the canons in case of arrears in payment. Warranty is granted. [29 April 1227 x 11 June 1232]

TNA, E40/3846. 165 × 113mm, 18mm turnup, 94mm tag, seal missing. Endorsed: Sprowton (16c.).

Sciant presentes et futuri quod ego Garinus de Guthesford concessi et dedi et hac mea carta confirmavi, pro me et heredibus meis, Deo et ecclesie beatorum apostolorum Petri et Pauli de Gypewico et canonicis ibidem Deo servientibus, pro salute anime mee et Alicie uxoris mee, et omnium parentum et benefactorum meorum, novem solidos annui redditus recipiendos per manum Rogeri fratris mei et heredum suorum ad tres anni terminos, scilicet ad Pascha tres solidos, et ad festum Sancti Iohannis Babtiste [*sic*] tres solidos, et ad festum Sancti Michaelis tres solidos, de viginti septem acris terre cum pertinenciis quas predictus Rogerus tenuit de Martino fratre meo in villa de Sprouton', quos scilicet novem solidos Decimus capellanus, frater meus, recipere debuit quoad viveret de eodem Rogero ex dono predicti Martini fratris mei, illis et successoribus suis; habendum de me et heredibus meis et tenendum in liberam et puram et perpetuam elemosinam, libere et quiete, et solute ab omni seculari servicio et demanda. Et si forte predictus Rogerus vel heredes sui predictum redditum ad prefatos terminos non reddiderint, licebit predictis canonicis distringere ipsum Rogerum et heredes suos per predictam terram donec predictum redditum eis persolverint. Et ego Garinus et heredes mei warantizabimus prenominatis canonicis et eorum successoribus predictum redditum contra omnes homines. Et ut hac mea concessio et donacio firma sit et stabilis in perpetuum, presens scriptum sigillo meo confirmavi. Hiis testibus: Domino Herberto de Alicun tunc vicecomite Suffolchie et Norfolchie, Domino Galfrido de Badel', Domino Sewalo de Neuton', Roberto de Angervill', Iohanne filio Normanni, Silvestro filio Walkelini et Iohanne de Beumes tunc ballivis de Gypewico, Rogero de Horshag', Hugone filio Mabilie, Ricardo de Bordeshowe, Oseberto de Sprouton', Alexandro de Haya, Iohanne Rodland, Waltero Wicher, et multis aliis.

Date: Sir Herbert de Alencun sheriff.

438. Notification by Warin of Gusford to the canons that, for the salvation of his soul and those of Alice his wife and all his ancestors and benefactors, he has quitclaimed all right which he had in 27 acres of land which Roger his brother formerly held of him in Sproughton, with Roger's homage and all the services which he owed to Warin for the land, without reservation. Warranty is granted.

[29 April 1227 – 1230s]

TNA, E40/3844. 171 × 69mm, 16mm turnup, 114mm tag. Fragments of green wax attached to tag, but seal missing. The tag is written on re-used parchment; 'dedisse et hac carta' is legible on the inner face.

Sciant presentes et futuri quod ego Garinus de Guthlesford concessi et dedi et quietum clamavi Deo et ecclesie beatorum apostolorum Petri et Pauli de Gypeswico et canonicis ibidem Deo servientibus, pro salute anime mee et Alicie uxoris mee, et omnium parentum et benefactorum meorum, totum ius quod habui in viginti et septem acris terre cum pertinenciis quos Rogerus frater meus aliquando tenuit de me in villa de Sproutun', cum homagio predicti Rogeri et omnibus serviciis que michi debuit de terra predicta, sine aliquo retenemento, predictis canonicis et successoribus suis habendum et tenendum de me et heredibus meis, libere, et integre, et solute ab omni seculari servicio, in puram et liberam et perpetuam elemosinam. Et ego Garinus et heredes mei warantizabimus predictam terram cum serviciis et omnibus pertinenciis predictis canonicis et successoribus suis contra omnes homines, et eam defendemus de regalibus serviciis, et de omnibus aliis serviciis. Et ut hec mea concessio et quietaclamatio firma sit et stabilis, huic scripto sigillum meum apposui. Hiis testibus: Domino Roberto de Angervill, Roberto de Northwude, Osberto filio Ade de Sproutun, Rogero de Brumford, Roberto de Stanbrege, Willelmo Gregori, Toma de Remes, Alexandro de la Ha, Hamundo le Bretun, et multis aliis.

Date: Made either at the same time as, or somewhat later than Warin's grant in free alms of the rent on the property (no. 437). Warin occurs as a witness to other charters from *c.* 1180 (no. 49) and would have been an old man by the 1230s.

439. Notification by Alice, widow of Warin of Gusford, that she has purchased from the prior and convent a piece of meadow in Sproughton, one headland of which abuts on the bank of Gusford, the other on the high street extending to Gusford bridge towards Ipswich, to hold of the canons while she lives, and to revert to them without objection after her death. [Late 1220s – 1230s]

TNA, E40/3845. 210 × 46mm, 9mm turnup, 87mm tag. Seal of brown wax, 23mm round, mostly destroyed. Endorsed: N pⁱ (late medieval).

Sciant presentes et futuri quod ego Alicia relicta quondam Warini de Guthelesford adquisivi quamdam peciam prati a priore et conventu Sancti Petri de Gypwico, iacentem in parochia de Sproutun, cuius unum capud abutat super ripam de Guthelesford et aliud capud super regiam stratam extendentem se usque ad pontem de Guthelesford versus Gypwicum. Tenendum et habendum predictum pratum michi quoad vixero, de predictis canonicis in tota vita mea, libere, quiete, bene, et in pace. Post decessum autem meum predicta pecia prati cum suis pertinenciis predictis canonicis et eorum successoribus sine impedimento vel contradictione alicuius solute et quiete revertetur. In cuius rei testimonium huic scripto sigillum meum apposui. Hiis testibus: Oseberto de Sproutun, Willelmo filio eius, Willelmo de Northwde, Willelmo le Fre, Rogero Warin, Laurentio Rodland, Rogero de Ripa et aliis.

Date: After no. 437 and no. 438. Warin of Gusford was still alive when Sir Herbert de Alencun commenced his shrievalty on 29 April 1227, and perhaps when his term of office ended on 11 June 1232 (no. 437).

440. Grant in free, pure and perpetual alms by Richard of Boss Hall to the canons, for the salvation of his soul and those of all his ancestors and successors, of 3s 1½d annual rent from the annual rent of 8s which they were accustomed to pay him from the land which William son of Gregory holds of them in Sproughton, free from all secular service and demand. [1220s – 1230s]

TNA, E40/3277. 177 × 53mm, 10mm turnup, 83mm tag. Seal 39mm round, including where restored with modern wax at left. Device a sunburst of leaves. Legend: … GILL' RICA … . Endorsed: Bordyshowe (16c.).

Sciant presentes et futuri quod ego Ricardus de Bordeshowe concessi et dedi et hac mea carta confirmavi Deo et ecclesie beatorum apostolorum Petri et Pauli de Gypewico et canonicis ibidem Deo servientibus, tres solidos et tres obolos annui redditus de redditu annuo octo solidorum quem michi solebant reddere de terra quam Willelmus filius Gregorii tenet de ipsis in parochia de Sproutune, pro salute anime mee et antecessorum et successorum meorum omnium, illis et successoribus eorum in perpetuum. Tenendos et habendos de me et heredibus meis in liberam et puram et perpetuam elemosinam, libere et quiete et solute ab omni seculari servicio et demanda. Et ut hec mea concessio et donacio et huius carte mee confirmacio firma sit et stabilis in perpetuum, huic scripto sigillum meum apposui. Hiis testibus: Domino Galfrido de Badele, Domino Roberto de Angervill', Domino Sewallo de Neutone, Iohanne filio Normanni, Iohanne de Beaumes, Petro filio Eborardi, Alexandro de Haya, Oseberto filio Adam', Iohanne filio Andree, Iohanne Rodland, Roberto de Norewude, Rogero de Ripa et multis aliis.

Date: Richard of Boss Hall attests various charters in this collection, including no. 437 (1227–32) and no. 45 (1230s or 1240s). Sir Sewell of Newton attests no. 371 between 1227 and 1232. John son of Norman, a bailiff of Ipswich in 1200, attests from the late twelfth century (nos. 48, 49) to the 1230s (no. 458).

441. Grant in perpetuity by Thomas Testepin to the canons, of the piece of meadow in Sproughton which Roger Calmodin gave to him in exchange for the meadow which he ought to have warranted to Thomas before the king's justices, lying below the wood of 'Helewrthe' between Roger's meadow and the river bank; to hold to them and their successors of Thomas and his heirs, rendering 4d annually in three instalments for all services, customs and demands. For this gift and confirmation the canons have given him 14s of sterlings and 8d for a fine. Warranty is granted.

[1220s – 1240s]

TNA, E40/3412. 165 × 78mm, 8mm turnup, 90mm tag, seal missing. No endorsements.

Sciant presentes et futuri quod ego Thomas Testepin concessi, dedi, et hac presenti carta mea confirmavi Deo et ecclesie beatorum apostolorum Petri et Pauli de Gibvico [*sic*] et canonicis ibidem Deo servientibus, totam peciam prati cum pertinenciis in parochia de Sproutone quam Rogerus Calmodin michi dedit in excambiam pro prato quod warantizare michi debuit coram iusticiariis domini regis, iacentem sub bosco de Helewrthe inter pratum dicti Rogeri Calmodin et ripam. Tenendam et habendam illis et eorum successoribus in perpetuum de me et heredibus meis, libere et quiete, bene et in pace, reddendo inde annuatim michi et heredibus meis quatuor denarios ad tres terminos, scilicet ad Pascha unum denarium, et ad festum Sancti Iohannis Baptiste duos denarios, et ad festum [Sancti *omitted*] Michaelis unum denarium, pro omnibus serviciis, consuetudinibus et demandis. Pro hac autem concessione, donatione, et huius carte mee confirmatione, dederunt michi predicti canonici quatuordecim solidos sterlingorum et octo denarios in gersumam. Et ego predictus Thomas et heredes mei warantizabimus predictam peciam prati predictis canonicis et eorum successoribus cum pertinentiis per prenominatum servicium contra omnes. In huius rei testimonium huic presenti scripto sigillum meum apposui. Hiis testibus: Osberto filio Ada', Iohanne filio Andree, Gerardo Richold, Roberto de Northewde, Alexandro de la Haie, Rogero de Bromford, Alexandro Gregor', Ricardo de Bordeshoue, Nicholao fratre suo, Iohanne de Beumes, Silvestro filio Wakelini, Helia Stalim, Rogero le Porter et multis aliis.

Date: Thomas Testepin the donor, with his brothers John and William, attests no. 93, ?1230s – 1240s. John de Beumes and Silvester son of Wakelin served together as bailiffs of Ipswich sometime between 1227 and 1232; Silvester served again in 1254–55. Roger of Bramford was probably dead by 1260 and certainly before 1264 (no. 138). Since several other witnesses attest as early as the 1190s, a date after the 1240s seems unlikely.

442. Grant by Roger of Sproughton to the canons, of three pieces of land in Sproughton, in the field called 'Blakesunel lond'; to hold of Roger and his heirs, rendering 15d annually in three instalments for all services, customs and demands, saving the king's service of 2d in 20s scutage. For this gift and confirmation the canons have given a fine of 55s of silver. Warranty is granted.   [1220s – ?1240s]

TNA, E40/3418. 198 × 106mm, 17mm turnup, 120mm tag, seal missing. Endorsed: Sprouton (17c.)

Sciant presentes et futuri quod ego Rogerus de Sproutone concessi et dedi et hac carta mea confirmavi Deo et ecclesie beatorum apostolorum Petri et Pauli de Gypewico et canonicis ibidem Deo servientibus, tres pecias terre mee cum pertinenciis in parochia de Sproutone, in campo qui vocatur Blakesunel lond, quarum una pecia iacet inter terram dictorum canonicorum ex una parte et terram meam ex altera parte, et unum capud abutat super terram dictorum canonicorum versus aquilonem et aliud capud super terram meam versus austrum; et alia pecia iacet inter terras Oseberti de Sproutune ex utraque parte, et unum capud abutat super viam que vocatur Wrabesloth, et aliud super viam que tendit a domo dictorum canonicorum usque ad viam que vocatur Wrabesloth; et tercia pecia que vocatur Koboldeswude que iacet inter terram dictorum canonicorum ex una parte, et terram meam, et terram Oseberti de Sproutone, et terram Willelmi de Bosco ex altera parte, et unum capud abutat super terram Warini Koket versus occidentem, et aliud capud se extendit versus orientem inter terras dictorum canonicorum, et abutat super terram eorum que vocatur Langelond; tenendas et habendas illis et eorum successoribus de me et heredibus meis, libere, quiete, bene et in pace; reddendo inde annuatim michi et heredibus meis quindecim denarios, ad tres terminos, scilicet ad Pascha quinque denarios, et ad festum Sancti Iohannis Baptiste quinque denarios, et ad festum Sancti Michaelis quinque denarios, pro omnibus serviciis, consuetudinibus et demandis, salvo servicio domini regis, scilicet ad scutagium viginti solidorum duos denarios, et ad plus, plus et ad minus, minus. Pro hac autem donacione et huius carte mee confirmacione, dederunt michi dicti canonici quinquaginta quinque solidos argenti in gersumiam. Et ego Rogerus et heredes mei warantizabimus dictis canonicis et eorum successoribus prefatam terram cum pertinenciis per prenominatum servicium contra omnes homines inperpetuum. Et in huius rei testimonium sigilli mei apposicione roboravi. Hiis testibus: Domino Roberto de Aungevil milite, Oseberto filio Ade de Sproutone, Alexandro de la Haye, Ricardo de Bordesh', Roberto de Northwde, Willelmo filio eius, Iohanne filio Andree, Alexandro Gregor', Roberto de Stanbreg', Willelmo de Badele, Gerardo Richold, Warino Koket, et multis aliis.

Date: Osbert of Sproughton occurs 1227–32 and 1255–56 (nos. 437, 446), and Sir Robert de Angerville from the 1220s (nos. 75, 120). William of Badley is a pledge to prosecute in 1238 (no. 321), and is a party to two pleas of *novel disseisin* at the 1240 eyre (*CPSE*, nos. 287, 427). He does not occur after the 1240s.

443. Grant in free, pure and perpetual alms by Richard of Boss Hall to the canons, of one acre of meadow in Sproughton, in the pasture of 'Grauford', lying across the acre of meadow of Rose the daughter of Beatrice of Wagemere; for the salvation of his soul and the souls of all his ancestors and successors, quit of all secular service and demand. Warranty is granted.   [*c.* 1220s – 1240s]

TNA, E40/3435. 157 × 68mm, 10mm turnup, 84mm tag. Seal 40mm round, green wax; legend: + SIGILL' RICARDI DE … . Design of leaves in sunburst pattern. Endorsed: Sprouton (16/17c.).

Sciant presentes et futuri quod ego Ricardus de Bordeshowe concessi, dedi, et hac presenti carta mea confirmavi Deo et ecclesie apostolorum Petri et Pauli de Gipewico et canonicis ibidem Deo servientibus, unam acram prati in villa de Sproutone in pastura de Grauford, iacentem in transverso acre prati Roysie filie Beatricis de Wagemere, cuius unum capud abutat super pratum quod vocatur le Holm ex parte australi, et aliud capud abutat super pasturam dicti Ricardi ex parte aquiloni. Habendam et tenendam eisdem canonicis et eorum successoribus de me et heredibus meis in liberam, puram et perpetuam elemosinam, pro salute anime mee et pro animabus antecessorum et successorum meorum, quietam et solutam ab omni servicio seculari et demanda. Et ego Ricardus et heredes mei warantizabimus dictis canonicis et eorum successoribus predictam acram prati contra omnes homines. Hiis testibus: Domino Roberto de Angerwill', Domino Galfrido de Badel', militibus, Iohanne Rodlond, Roberto de Northwude, Alexandro de la Haye, Roberto Wlffun, Iohanne de Sancto Georgio, Iohanne de Beaumes, Galfrido de Beaumes, Elya Norman, Iohanne Prikehert, Willelmo Godescalc, et multis aliis.

Date: Geoffrey II de Badele may have died in 1233 or 1234, when his son Geoffrey III was admitted a forinsec burgess of Ipswich (Introduction, p. 61). John of St George, John Prikehert and William Godescalc all held office in the town in 1200. Prikehert attested an agreement between the Ipswich burgesses and the prior of Woodbridge in 1233 (SROI, HD 1538/435/4), while Godescalc was accused, with others, at the 1240 eyre, of disseising Master Robert of Coddenham of his free tenement in Ipswich (*CPSE*, no. 640). John and Geoffrey de Beaumes served together as bailiffs for 1233–34.

444. Grant in free, pure and perpetual alms by Richard of Boss Hall, son of Manser of Boss Hall, to the canons, of two acres of meadow in Sproughton, in the pasture called 'Crauford', between Richard's meadow on both sides, with right of free entry and exit; free from all secular service and demand. Warranty is granted.

[Early – mid-thirteenth century]

TNA, E40/3272. 152 × 67mm, 14mm turnup, 13mm tag. Seal 42mm round. Device, a sunburst of leaves; restored at edges. Legend: + SIG'... DE BORDES. Endorsed: 'Sprouton' (16c.).

Notum sit omnibus hoc scriptum inspecturis et audituris quod ego Ricardus de Bordeshowe filius Manseri de Bordeshowe concessi et dedi et hac carta mea confirmavi Deo et ecclesie apostolorum Petri et Pauli de Gypewico et canonicis ibidem Deo servientibus, in liberam, puram et perpetuam elemosinam, duas acras prati cum pertinenciis in villa de Sproutune in pastura que vocatur Crauford, iacentes inter prata mea ex utraque parte, et unum caput abutat versus austrum super pratum quod vocatur Holm et super acram Roysie filie Beatricis, et aliud caput abutat versus aquilonem super terram et mesuagium Rogeri de Bordeshowe, cum libero introitu et exitu. Tenendas et habendas illis et eorum successoribus in perpetuum, libere, quiete, pure et absolute ab omni servicio seculari et demanda. Et ego Ricardus et heredes mei warantizabimus predictum tenementum cum pertinenciis dictis canonicis et eorum successoribus contra omnes in perpetuum. Hiis testibus: Domino Galfrido de Badele, Domino Nicholao de Aungervill', Hoseberto de Sprutun, Rogero de Bramford', Petro de Bramford, Ricardo del Hel, Willelmo Testepin, Silvestro filio Wakelini, Iohanne de Beaumes, Baldewino de Pesehal, Vincencio de Rubroc et aliis.

Date: Richard's charter no. 440 dates from the 1220s or 1230s. Sir Nicholas de Angerville and Roger of Bramford were both dead by 1265 and perhaps by 1260; charter no. 138 which Roger's daughter Agnes granted to the canons, 1260 x 1265, concerned her inheritance from her late father, and by this time Sir Nicholas's heirs had succeeded him as lords of the fee.

445. Notification by William of Northwood, son of Robert of Northwood, that he has quitclaimed to the canons, for himself and his heirs, all right and claim which he had or could have had in 10 acres of land in Sproughton which he claimed to be his right and inheritance by the king's Writ of Right; to have and to hold to them and their successors without any demand and claim by William or his heirs in perpetuity. Sealed in testimony.   [Mid-thirteenth century]

TNA, E40/3847. 177 × 69mm, 20mm turnup, 100mm tag. The tag has been re-used; 'Sciant presens' is legible on one inner face, 'in perpetuum' (line 1) and 'deo et ecclesie beatorum apostolorum' (line 2) on the other. Seal missing. Endorsed: Sprouton (16c.).

Sciant presentes et futuri quod ego Willelmus de Northwde filius Roberti de Norwde concessi, quietumclamavi, et hac presenti carta mea confirmavi, pro me et heredibus meis, Deo et ecclesie beatorum apostolorum Petri et Pauli de Gypwico et canonicis ibidem Deo servientibus et servituris imperpetuum, totum ius et clamium quod habui vel habere potui in decem acris terre cum pertinenciis in villa de Sproutune, quas clamavi esse ius meum et hereditatem pre breve domini regis de recto: habendas et tenendas dictis canonicis et eorum successoribus, bene, quiete, et in pace, sine omni exactione et clamio mei vel heredum meorum imperpetuum. In cuius rei testimonium huic scripto sigillum meum apposui. Hiis testibus: Ricardo de Holebroc, Galfrido de Dodenes, Arnaldo de Colevil', Rogero Warin, Rogero de Ripa, Roberto Andreu, Roberto de Predes, Laurencio Rodland, Warin' Coket, et aliis.

Date: There are three witnesses in common with no. 449 (late 1250s – 1260s). Geoffrey of Dodnash occurs towards the middle of the century and was probably dead by 1257 when Hugh Tollemache confirmed to the canons of Dodnash all the land which Geoffrey had granted to them of his fee (*Dodnash Charters*, pp. 8–9 and nos. 24, 24A).

446. Grant in free, pure and perpetual alms by Hugh of Langestun to the canons, of 32d annual rent which Robert Costard used to pay him for a messuage and four acres of land with adjoining meadow, pasture and other appurtenances which he held of him of the canons' fee in Sproughton (*Sproutun'*); by Robert's consent, with homages, reliefs, exactions and all other revenues without any reservation to Hugh and his heirs; to be taken at four terms of the year, namely 8d at the feasts of Easter, St John the Baptist, St Michael and St Andrew; to have and to hold to the canons and their successors, freely and quit of all secular service. Warranty by the grantor and his heirs against all men, Christians and Jews, in perpetuity. Sealed in testimony.

Hiis testibus: Domino Galfrido de Badele, Osberto de Sproutun', Ricardo de Bordesho, Willelmo de Norwode, Gerardo Richoud, Matheo de Porta, Hugone Lyu tunc ballivis de Gipewico, Silvestro filio Wakellini, Iohanne Bolle, supradicto Roberto Costard, et aliis.   [Probably 29 September 1255 x 28 September 1256]

TNA, E40/3648. 203 × 90mm, 15mm turnup, 125mm tag, seal missing. On the inside of the tag is the top line of a charter, which reads: Sciant presentes et futuri quod ego Hugo de Langestun' dedi et hac presenti carta mea confirmavi Deo et ecclesie beatorum apostolorum Petri … : perhaps a draft of the present charter. No endorsements.

Date: The administrative year Michaelmas 1255 – Michaelmas 1256 is the only term during which Matthew de Porta and Hugh Lyu are known to have served together as bailiffs of Ipswich, though they could have done so on other occasions. Hugh's last-known year of office is 1269–70 (with Richard Fader), Matthew's is 1278–79 (with Vivian son of Silvester).

447. Notification by Robert Costard that he and his heirs are bound to pay to the prior and convent at four terms of the year in perpetuity, 32d annual rent, namely that which Robert used to pay to Hugh of Langestun' for a messuage and four acres of land with meadow, pasture and other appurtenances in Sproughton (*Sproutun'*), which he sometime held of Hugh, of the canons' fee. Sealed in testimony.

Hiis testibus: Domino Galfrido de Badele, Osberto de Sproutun', Ricardo de Bordesho, Willelmo de Norwode, Gerardo Richoud, Matheo de Porta, Hugone Lyu tunc ballivis de Gipewico, Silvestro filio Wakellini, Iohanne Bolle, Surstano [*sic, for Thurstano*] del Cley, et aliis.

[Probably 29 September 1255 x 28 September 1256]

TNA, E40/3646. 135 × 79mm, 17mm turnup, 84mm tag. Seal missing. Endorsed: Sprouton (15c.); xxxiid' in Sprouton' (16c.).

Date: See no. 446. The same bailiffs are in office, and the witness lists are identical, except that in no. 447 Thurstan del Cley has been substituted for Robert Costard, since it is Robert who binds himself for payment. Both documents were almost certainly issued on the same day, though the hands are not the same.

448. Grant in free and perpetual alms by Roger Bramford of Sproughton to the canons, of five acres of land in the field called 'Hunerhuselond' in Sproughton, four acres lying in one piece between the land of Robert of Hastings and the land of Adam of Sproughton, chaplain, the fifth acre between the above piece and the land of Robert of Hastings on one side and Roger's land on the other; rendering annually to Roger and his heirs 10d in three instalments, for all service saving the king's service of 2d scutage, more or less. Warranty is granted.

[Mid-thirteenth century – c. 1260]

TNA, E40/3434. 170 × 101mm, 21mm turnup, 105mm tag. Seal 40mm round in green wax, design perhaps a fleur-de-lys, but broken. Endorsed: Sprouton Sprowton (16/17c.).

Sciant presentes et futuri quod ego Rogerus Bromford de Sproutune concessi, dedi, et hac presenti carta mea confirmavi Deo et ecclesie apostolorum Petri et Pauli de Gypewico et canonicis ibidem Deo servientibus, in liberam et perpetuam elemosinam, quinque acras terre cum pertinentiis in parochia de Sproutune, in campo qui vocatur Hunerhuselond, quarum quatuor acre iacent in una pecia inter terram Roberti de Hasting' et terram Ade de Sproutune capellani, et quinta acra iacet inter prenominatam peciam et terram dicti Roberti de Hasting' ex una parte et terram meam ex altera, et unum capud abutat versus aquilonem super viam regiam, et aliud versus meridiem super terram dicti Ade de Sproutune capellani. Tenendas et habendas illis et eorum successoribus de me et heredibus meis, libere, quiete, bene, et in pace, reddendo inde annuatim michi et heredibus meis decem denarios ad tres terminos anni, videlicet ad Pascha quatuor denarios, ad festum Sancti Iohannis Bapptiste [*sic*] duos denarios, et ad festum Sancti Michaelis quatuor denarios, pro omnibus serviciis, consuetudinibus et demandis, salvo servicio domini regis, scilicet ad scutagium quando super illud feudum evenerit duos denarios, ad plus et ad minus. Et ego dictus Rogerus et heredes mei warantizabimus dictam terram cum pertinentiis dictis canonicis et eorum successoribus per predictum servicium contra omnes in perpetuum. Hiis testibus: Domino Nicholaus de Aungevil', Oseberto filio Ade de Sproutune, Roberto de Northwde, Willelmo filio eius, Ricardo de Bordeshowe, Mansero, Nicholao, Rogero fratribus, Willelmo Andr', Rogero de la Haye, Gerardo Richold, et multis aliis.

Date: Roger Bramford was dead before 1264 and probably by 1260 (see the grant (no. 138) of Agnes his daughter from her inheritance). The same charter shows that Sir Nicholas de Angerville was also dead by then, since it describes his heirs as capital lords of the fee.

449. Notification by Agnes, widow of the late Roger Bramford of Sproughton (*Sproutun'*), that she has granted and quitclaimed to the canons and their successors in perpetuity, all the land with rent and all other appurtenances which she at any time had or might have had in the name of dower in Sproughton, to hold and to have to the canons and their successors freely, quietly and free from all claim by her in perpetuity. For this gift and quitclaim the canons have given her 40s of silver. Sealed in testimony.

Hiis testibus: Willelmo de Northwode, Rogero Warin, Rogero de Ripa, Roberto Andreu, Symone le Vineter, Nicholao del Hil, Roberto Testepin, Thoma de Cnapetun', Warin Coket, et aliis.   [Late 1250s – 1260s]

TNA, E40/3843. 297 × 50mm, but turnup now folded out; once 38mm high with a 12mm turnup. Tag 100mm. Seal in green wax, 34mm round. Legend: ... ETIS FIL'GERA ... . Endorsed: N pⁱ (late medieval, as for no. 439); Sprouton (16c.).

Date: Near-contemporary with no. 138; Roger was probably dead by 1260, certainly before August 1265.

450. Confirmation by Laurence, son of John Rodlond of Stoke-by-Ipswich (*Stokes*), to the canons and their successors, of all the land which Agnes, daughter of the late Roger Bramford of Sproughton (*Sproutun'*), held of the fee of Laurence's father and of himself in Sproughton and sold to the canons and confirmed by her charter; to hold and to have to them and their successors, as Agnes's charter, which they have, attests. Sealed in testimony.

Hiis testibus: Domino Herveo de Stanhoe tunc vicecomite Suffolchie et Norfolchie, Domino Galfrido de Badele, Domino Willelmo Thalebot, Domino Iacobo Lemveyse, Ricardo de Holebroc, Willelmo de Northwode, Rogero Warin, Symone le Vineter, Roberto Wlfun, Willelmo Testepin, Rogero de Rypa, Roberto Andreu, Rogero de Cnapetun', Nicholao del Hyl, Thoma de Cnapetun', Roberto de Sparkeford, Warino Koket, et aliis.   [9 January 1260 x 28 August 1265]

TNA, E40/3400. 204 × 90mm, 23mm turnup, 125mm tag. Seal 40mm round, flower design; legend SIGILL' LAURENCII RODLAUN ... . Endorsed: Rodland in Sprouton; H Prior; xx sol. (various hands, 14–15c.).

Date: Sir Hervey de Stanhoe commenced his account as sheriff on 9 January 1260, and was succeeded on 9 July 1261 by Philip Marmyun. He served again 27 June 1264 – 28 August 1265.

451. Confirmation by Berta Bramford of Sproughton (*Sprutun'*) in her maidenhood to the canons, for the salvation of her soul and that of her sister Agnes, of the gift which Agnes made to them, namely a piece of land in Sproughton, lying between the land of William of the Wood (*de Bosco*) on one side and the land of William and Berta on the other, one headland abutting on the canons' land, the other on William's marsh; to hold and to have to them and their successors in perpetuity, rightly, in peace and in fee. Sealed so that this concession and charter of confirmation may be valid.

Hiis testibus: Domino Galfrido de Badele, Petro de Bramford, Baldewino de Pesehal, Osberto filio Ade, Roberto de Northwde, Willelmo filio eius, Ricardo de Bordeshowe, Mansero, Nicholao, Rogero fratribus suis, Willelmo Andreu, Rogero de la Haye, Gerardo Riclod,[1] Alexandro Gregorie, et multis aliis.   [1260s]

TNA, E40/3592. 220 × 47mm, 9mm turnup, 113mm tag. Seal of ears of corn, legend gone. Tag made from draft of text, parts legible at either end of lines:

Sciant presentes et fu ...	... deo et ecclesie beatorum
apostolorum Petri et P ...	... Agnes soror mea
eis fecit, videlicet ...	... eiusdem Will'i de Berte [*sic*]

Endorsed: Sprouton (16c).

   1 *Sic*: 'Richoud' in other Sproughton charters.

Date: Not before 9 January 1260, the earliest date by which Berta's sister Agnes could have made the grant (no. 138) to the canons of her inheritance in Sproughton after the death of her father Roger.

452. Grant and quitclaim by Simon le Vineter of Sproughton (*Sprouton'*) to the canons, present and future in perpetuity, for 20s of silver which they have given him at his promotion, of all right and claim which he had or could have had in two acres of land in Sproughton, whereof one acre lies between the lands of the canons on either side and the other lies towards 'Wrabbeslow' between the canons' land and that formerly of Osbert son of Adam of Sproughton; which two acres Wakelin le Vineter purchased of Roger Bramford; to have and to hold to the canons and their successors in free, pure and perpetual alms, freely, quietly, rightly and in peace, without any claim by Simon or his heirs, in perpetuity. Sealed in testimony by Simon and his brother John, who has given his assent and consent to this deed.

Hiis testibus: Roberto de Bordeshowe, Willelmo del Haye, Willelmo Waryn, Ricardo de Clink, Ricardo Hervey, Ricardo Bunne, Iohanne Manser, et aliis. At Ipswich, Wednesday next after the feast of the Conception of the Blessed Virgin Mary, 16 Edward I.   10 December 1287

TNA, E40/3579. 226 × 85mm, 16mm turnup. Tag at left 86mm, blob of wax approx. 15mm round; tag at right 98mm, seal 36mm round, ... LE VINET ... legible of legend, device of leaves. Endorsed: Sprouton' (16c.).

453. Notification by Agnes, daughter and heir of Roger Bramford of Sproughton (*Sproutone*) and widow of Geoffrey Ingenolf of Little Waldingfield (*Waudingfeud' Parva*), that in the legal power of her widowhood she has granted, confirmed, remitted and utterly in perpetuity quitclaimed, for herself and her heirs, to the prior and convent and their successors in perpetuity, all right and claim which she had or might have had, or in any way might in future have, in the lands, tenements, homages, rents, services, escheats, wards, reliefs, and the capital messuage with all its other appurtenances, which were formerly Roger her father's in Sproughton, and which they have and hold by her gift and those of any others whomsoever of her predecessors, by her charter of feoffment and those of the others, which they granted to them; to have and to hold to the prior and convent and their successors according to the tenor of her charter and whatsoever others they have in their possession, so that neither Agnes nor her heirs, nor anyone in her name or the names of her heirs, may henceforth in perpetuity claim any right therein. For this quitclaim the prior and convent have given her 100s of silver in cash. Sealed in testimony.

Hiis testibus: Viviano filio Silvestri et Laurencio Horold tunc ballivis Gyppwici, Magistro Ricardo Lenebaud, Iohanne de la Dale, Hugone Horold, Willelmo de Northwode, Roberto de Bordeshowe, Willelmo Soyllard, Iacobo de Gothelesford', Willelmo Andreu, Roberto Eustace, Willelmo Nicole, Iohanne Mylland, Willelmo de Blakeshale, et aliis. Given in the chapter house before many trustworthy men, 8 Id. April 1295 and 23 Edward I.   6 April 1295

TNA, E40/3267. 210 × 151mm, 21mm turnup, 110mm tag with shreds of green wax attached. Endorsed: Sprouton' (16c.); Sprouton (16c.); Sprouton (17c.).

454. Notification by Agnes, daughter and heir of Roger Bramford of Sproughton (*Sproutone*) and widow of Geoffrey Ingenulf of Little Waldingfield (*Waudyngfeld' Parva*), that, in the legal power of her widowhood she has granted, remitted and utterly in perpetuity quitclaimed, for herself and her heirs, to the prior and convent and their successors in perpetuity, all right and claim which she had or might have had in any way in the lands, tenements, homages, rents, services, escheats, and wards, with all other appurtenances, and with the capital messuage which was Roger her father's, in Sproughton, which they have and hold by her gift through the charter of feoffment which she made to them; to have and to hold to the prior and convent and their successors according to the tenor of her charter which they have in their possession, sealed with her seal; so that neither Agnes nor her heirs, or anyone [*missing*] may henceforth in perpetuity claim any right therein. [*Missing*] remission and quitclaim the prior and convent have given her 100s of silver in cash. Sealed in testimony.

Hiis testibus: Taleboto de Hynclesham, Thoma del Hel de eadem, Willelmo de Norwode, Roberto de Bordeshowe, Willelmo Warin, Hugone Horold, Willelmo Andreu, Iacobo de Guthelesford, Roberto Eustace, Willelmo Nicole de Gretingham, Iohanne Suyllard, Willelmo de Blakeshale, et aliis. At Ipswich, Wednesday next after the feast of Ambrose the Bishop, 23 Edward I, in the month of April.
                                                                              6 April 1295

TNA, E40/3578. 228 × 95mm, 17mm turnup, 89mm tag; two small holes have destroyed a few words of the text. Seal 30 × 40mm, good condition; legend: S AGNETE FIL' ROGERI BRANFORD; device of sheaf of corn. Endorsed: Spruton (16c.); Sprowton (17c.). Nos. 453 and 454, which are in almost identical terms, have a number of differences in the witness list, and are written in markedly different hands.

455. Notification by John Rodlond, son and heir of the late Reginald Rodlond, that whereas the prior and convent had and held of him certain tenements in Sproughton (*Sproutune*) by the service of 4s annual rent, in respect of which John is mesne tenant between them and the heirs of Sir Roger Loveday, John, for himself and his heirs, has granted and assigned the prior and convent and their successors in perpetuity to the payment of the rent of 4s to the heirs or assigns of the said Roger Loveday at the due and accustomed terms; so that neither John nor his heirs, nor anyone in his name may henceforth have any right or claim in the tenements or rent in perpetuity. Sealed in testimony.

Hiis testibus: Roberto de Bordeshow, Willelmo Warin, Willelmo de le Hay, Laurentio Horold, Hugone Horold, Ricardo de Clinc', Petro Anneys, Iohanne de Godelisford, Iacobo de Godelisford, et aliis. Saturday the feast of the Nativity of the Blessed Mary, 30 Edward I.   8 September 1302

TNA, E40/3318. 217 × 96mm, 7mm turnup, 66mm tag. Small green wax seal with device of an eagle displayed with wings inverted. No endorsements.

456. Notification by John, son and heir of Reginald Rodlond, that he has granted, remitted and utterly quitclaimed in perpetuity, for himself and his heirs, to the prior and convent and their successors, all right and claim which he had or in any way could have had in 4s annual rent in which they were bound to him for all the lands and tenements which they held of him in Sproughton (*Sprouton'*), wheresoever they lie; so that neither he nor his heirs, nor anyone in his name, may henceforth claim any right either in the rent or in the lands and tenements. For this grant and quitclaim the prior and convent have given him 10s in cash. Sealed in testimony.

Hiis testibus: Laurentio Horold, Hugone Horold, Iohanne de Godelisford, Iacobo de Godelisford, Roberto de Bordhowe, Willelmo Warin, Willelmo de le Haye, Petro Anneys, Thoma de le Hyl, Ricardo de Clink, Rogero le Vyneter, et aliis. On the morrow of the Nativity of the Blessed Mary, 30 Edward I.   9 September 1302

TNA, E40/3715. 228 × 114mm, 15mm turnup, 80mm tag, seal missing. Endorsed: Sprouton (16c.).

457. Grant in perpetuity by John son of Richard Haltebe of Ipswich (*Gippewyco*) to Thomas of Rougham and Henry, prior of the church of St Peter, of all the lands and tenements which he held in Sproughton (*Sprouton'*) on the day of the making of this charter, by the gift and feoffment of Michael Bertram and Alice his wife and by the quitclaim of Robert son of Robert of Sparkeford, which were lately Robert of Sparkeford's; to have and to hold to Thomas and the prior and the heirs and assigns of Thomas, of the capital lords of that fee by the services pertaining to those tenements in perpetuity. Moreover he has granted, sold and delivered to Thomas and the prior all his goods and chattels, moveable and immoveable, on the said lands and tenements, to have to them and their assigns whomsoever, without any reservation. Sealed in testimony.

Hiis testibus: Nicholao Bonde, Iohanne Horold, Gilberto Roberd de Gippewyco, Iohanne de Baliol de eadem, Bartholomeo Debeney de eadem, Thoma Horold, Iohanne Andreu de Sprouton', Iohanne le Vyneter de eadem, Roberto de Bordehowe de eadem, Iohanne Waryn, et aliis. At Sproughton, Sunday next after the feast of St Hillary, 20 Edward I.   18 January 1327

TNA, E40/3759. 249 × 114mm, 16mm turnup, 111mm tag. Armorial seal, legend not legible; 22mm round in blob of wax 27mm, attached back to front. Endorsed: Concessi etiam et dedi et hac carta mea confirmavi predictis priori et Thome quatuor denarratas [*sic*] annui redditus singulis annis imperpetuum percipiendas ad quatuor terminos anni usuales et uno cotagio et curtilag' adiacenti in Sprouton' quod predictus Robertus de Sparkeford de me tenet in predicta villa de Sprouton'. Et est dictum mesuagium … iuxta pontem de Sparkeford ex parte borealis [fourteenth century].

THURLESTON

458. Grant in free, pure and perpetual alms by Robert of Claydon to the canons, of all the rent which Baldwin of Pintoun paid him annually, namely 5d, and the whole fee out of which the rent issues; to hold and to have of Robert and his heirs, for the salvation of his soul and those of his parents, free from all secular service and demand. Warranty is granted.   [Midsummer 1232 x Michaelmas 1239]

TNA, E40/3280. 193 × 65mm, 15mm turnup, 84mm tag. Seal 44mm round, green wax with fleur-de-lys design. Legend: +SIGILL' ROB'… . No endorsements.

Sciant presentes et futuri quod ego Robertus de Cleydun' dedi et concessi et hac carta mea confirmavi Deo et ecclesie beatorum apostolorum Petri et Pauli de Gypeswico et canonicis ibidem Deo servientibus, totum redditum quem Baldewinus de Pintoun' michi solebat annuatim reddere, scilicet v denarios ad duos terminos, ad Pasca duos denarios et obolum et ad festum Sancti Michaelis duos denarios et obolum, et totum feudum unde predictus redditus pervenerit;[1] eis et successoribus eorum in perpetuum, tenendum et habendum de me et heredibus meis illiberam [*sic, for* in liberam] et puram et perpetuam elemosinam pro salute animarum mee et parentum meorum, quiete et solute ab omni seculari servitio et demanda. Et ego Robertus et heredes mei warantizabimus predictum redditum predictis canonicis contra omnes gentes. Hiis testibus: Roberto de Brus tunc vicecomite Norfolchie et Suffolchie, Domino Galfrido de Badele, R[oberto *missing*] de Angervill', Baldewino de Peresenhale, Iohanne filio Normanni, Iohanne de Beaumes, Amisio Bolle, Rogero Lyu, Waltero de Leestun, [*missing*] mercatore, et multis aliis.

    1 Probably in Thurleston: 'Pintoun' was in Thurleston – see no. 254, 'in villa de Thurlestune … apud Pintone'.

Date: Robert de Briws/de Briwes/de Brus sheriff Midsummer 1232 – May 1234 and 7 December 1237 – Michaelmas 1239.

459. Grant in free, pure and perpetual alms to the priory, of property in Thurleston, [?lying between] the messuages and lands of William and the land of Adam the merchant, free from all secular services. Warranty is granted. [Before April 1240]

TNA, E40/3281. 143 × 67mm, 12mm turnup, 122mm tag, seal missing. The charter has a modern parchment backing as reinforcement, and no endorsements are visible. The text is much damaged by damp, and much of the document has been lost. The following partial lines are legible, but not much else.

... et ecclesie apostolorum Petri et Pauli de/
... parochia de Thurleston quos scilicet Willelmus .../
... mesuagia et terr' eiusdem Willelmi et terra Ade mercatoris .../
... successoribus et liberam, puram et perpetuam/
... et solutam ab omni seculari servicio/
... warantizabimus predictis canonicis et eorum successoribus prenominatam .../
... testimonium presens scriptum sigilli mei appositione roboravi. Hiis testibus,
Balde[wino]/
... Ada de Blanchevill, Augustino de Westefeld, Adam [*sic*] mercator, Roberto de
Ry, Iusto de Thurlestun, Iohanne/
... et multis aliis.

Date: Adam de Blancheville was alive on 31 May 1238 (no. 321), but dead by April
1240, when at the Suffolk eyre his son and heir William was vouched to warranty;
the suit was deferred because of William's minority (*CPSE*, no. 278).

460. Quitclaim in free, pure and perpetual alms by Robert, son of Baldwin of
Claydon, to the canons, for his soul and those of his ancestors, of all the lands, rents,
meadows, grazing lands, ways, paths and obventions which they or their tenants
hold of his fee in Thurleston or beyond; to hold to them and their successors, free
from all secular service or demand. Warranty is granted.   [?1230s – 1240s]

TNA, E40/3310. 229 × 76mm, small hole at bottom left. Endorsement faint and
illegible, but probably early modern; ends ... ton.

Sciant presentes et futuri quod ego Robertus filius Baldewini de Cleydon concessi,
quietumclamavi, et hac presenti carta mea confirmavi Deo et ecclesie beatorum
apostolorum Petri et Pauli de Gipewico et canonicis ibidem Deo servientibus, et
in perpetuum servituris, in liberam, puram et perpetuam elemosinam, pro anime
mee et animabus antecessorum et successorum meorum, totas terras, redditus,
prata, pascua, cum viis, semitis, boscis, cum eventionibus et omnibus pertinentiis quas ipsi vel eorum tenentes tenent de feodo meo in villa de Thurlestone
vel extra vel ubicumque fuerint sive in planis vel in boscis vel a quibuscumque
illas acceperint. Tenendas et habendas illis et eorum successoribus, libere, quiete,
pure et absolute ab omni servicio seculari et demanda. Et ego dictus Robertus et
heredes mei warantizabimus predictis canonicis et eorum successoribus predictas
terras cum redditibus, pratis, pascuis, viis, semitis, boscis, eventionibus, et cum
omnibus pertinentiis contra omnes in perpetuum. Et in huius rei testimonium
huic presenti scripto sigillum meum apposui. Hiis testibus: Domino Galfrido de
Badele, Baldewino de Pesehale, Willelmo de Cleydone, Augustino de Westerfeld,
Ada' filio decani, Galfrido Carbonel, Radulfo filio eius, Roberto Deri, Hugone Liu,
Roberto de Bosco, Iohanne Sancti Georgii, Alano filio Iusti, et aliis.

Date: Robert of Claydon, son of Baldwin, occurs as grantor of no. 458 (1232–39).
Geoffrey Carbonel, who attests between the 1220s and 1240s (nos. 214, 219), held one
and a half fees of the earl of Oxford in Great Waldingfield in 1242–43 (*Bk Fees*, 920).

461. Grant in free, pure and perpetual alms by William Colle of Thurleston to the
altar of the Blessed Mary in the church of SS Peter and Paul, of 12d annual rent in

perpetuity, to be paid in two instalments from two pieces of land in Thurleston, one lying between the canons' land and that of the parson of Whitton, the other between the canons' land and the land of Geoffrey son of Ordmar in 'Suthwodemere'. Warranty is granted. The canons may hold the land in their demesne in perpetuity, without claim of the grantor or his heirs; and they are to pay the rent to the altar as often as the grantor or his heirs do not.   [1220s – mid-thirteenth century]

TNA, E40/3684. 169 × 95mm, 13mm turnup, 95mm tag, seal missing. Endorsed: Will's Colle de Thurleston' pro duabus peciis terre in eadem villa xiid' (14c.).

Sciant presentes et futuri quod ego Willelmus Colle de Thurleston' concessi, dedi, et hac presenti carta mea confirmavi Deo et altari Beate Marie in ecclesia apostolorum Petri et Pauli de Gypewiz, in liberam, puram et perpetuam elemosinam, duodecim denarios annui redditus imperpetuum, solvendos ad duos terminos anni, scilicet ad Pascham sex denarios, et ad festum Sancti Michaelis sex denarios, de duabus peciis terre iacentibus in parochia de Thurlestun', quarum una pecia iacet inter terram canonicorum Sancti Petri de Gypewiz et terram parsone de Witenton', et altera iacet inter terram ipsorum canonicorum et terram Galfridi filii Ordmari in campo qui vocatur Suthwodemere. Et ego Willelmus et heredes mei warantizabimus predictum redditum predicto altari contra omnes imperpetuum. Concessi et canonicis Sancti Petri de Gypewiz tenere et habere totam predictam terram in dominio suo imperpetuum sine omni reclamacione mei et heredum meorum, et quod ipsi solvant predictum redditum predicto altari quandocumque ego sive heredes mei eundem redditum ad terminos statutos plenarie non solverimus. In huius rei testimonium presens scriptum sigillo meo singnavi. Hiis testibus: Galfrido de Badel' milite, Baldewino de Pesehal, Iohanne Roulod, Augustino de Westerfeud, Roberto de Cleydun', Willelmo de Badel', Roberto de Stanbrigg', Ada mercatore, Iusto de Thurleston', Roberto Gulle, Andrea de Chatesham, Roberto Swith, et multis aliis.

Date: William of Badley, who first occurs in the 1180s or 1190s (no. 43), is a pledge to prosecute in 1238 (no. 321), and a party to two pleas of *novel disseisin* in 1240 (*CPSE*, nos. 287, 427); he is thus unlikely to have lived beyond 1250. Justus of Thurleston is still alive in September 1241 (no. 463), but probably dead by 1250. On these families, see Introduction, pp. 59–60, 64–5.

462. Grant in perpetuity by Gilbert Haltebe to the canons, of four pieces of land in Thurleston, of which one piece lies next to the land of Baldwin de la Dale, abutting on the land of Adam Pithsweyn, and on Baldwin's meadow; another piece lies next to the land of Roger Lyu, abutting east on the said meadow and west on 'Langemedwe'; the third lies next to Baldwin's land, abutting north on 'Suthmedwe' and south on the land of Adam Pithsweyn; and the fourth piece lies next to the land of William Cole, abutting south on 'Suthmedwe' and east on the croft of William Cole. Moreover he has granted to the canons 2s annual rent, to be paid in two instalments from a messuage in St Stephen's parish in Ipswich, between the messuage of Roger Lageman and the street extending to the churchyard on the south; to have and to hold to them and their successors in perpetuity, free from all service. Warranty is granted. For this gift the canons have given 100s of sterlings.

[1230s – *c.* 1250]

TNA, E40/3677. 216 × 102mm, 20mm turnup, 102mm tag. Shreds of green wax remain on the tag. Endorsed: De Thurleston (15c.); par' Sancti Stephani (16c.); Thurleston et de parochia Sancti Stephani (17c.).

Sciant presentes et futuri quod ego Gilbertus Haltebe concessi, dedi, et hac presenti carta mea confirmavi Deo et ecclesie apostolorum Petri et Pauli de Gipewico et canonicis ibidem Deo servientibus, quatuor pecias terre cum pertinenciis in villa de Thurleston', quarum una pecia iacet iuxta terram Baldewini de la Dale, et unum caput habutat super terram Ade Pithsweyn, et aliud caput super pratum predicti Baldewini. Alia vero pecia iacet iuxta terram Rogeri Lyu, et unum caput habutat super predictum pratum versus orientem, et aliud caput versus occidentem super pratum quod vocatur Langemedwe. Tercia vero pecia iacet iuxta terram predicti Baldewini, et habutat super Suthmedwe versus aquilonem, et super terram predicti Ade Pithsweyn versus austrum. Quarta vero pecia iacet iuxta terram Willelmi Cole, et habutat super predictum pratum de Suthmedwe versus occidentem, et super cruftam predicti Willelmi Cole versus orientem. Preterea concessi, dedi, et confirmavi prefatis canonicis duos solidos annui redditus de me et heredibus meis annuatim percipiendos ad duos terminos anni, scilicet ad Pascha duodecim denarios, et ad festum Sancti Michaelis duodecim denarios, de uno mesuagio iacente in parochia Sancti Stephani de Gipewico, inter mesuagium Rogeri Lageman et vicum qui tendit usque in cimiterium predicte parochie ex parte austri, et habutat super viam regiam; quod mesuagium fuit Simonis Caperun aliquo tempore. Tenendas et habendas illis et eorum successoribus inperpetuum, libere et quiete ab omni servicio et demanda. Et ego Gilbertus Haltebe et heredes mei warantizabimus predictam terram et predictum redditum cum omnibus perti-nenciis predictis canonicis contra omnes inperpetuum. Pro hac autem donacione et carte mee confirmatione dederunt michi predicti canonici centum solidos sterlingorum. In huius rei testimonium huic scripto sigillum meum apposui. Hiis testibus: Domino Galfrido de Badele, Domino Nicholao de Aungervill', militibus, Willelmo de Holebroc, Baldewino de Pesehale, Iohanne Rowlond, Iohanne de Beumes, Osberto de Beling', Semanno de Ponte, Thomas [*sic*] Ruch, Galfrido Ballard, Iusto de Thurlestun, et aliis.

Date: John de Beumes was bailiff of Ipswich probably in 1232–33 (no. 437) and in 1233–34; he was a surety at the eyre of 1240 (*CPSE*, no. 1046). Justus of Thurleston, alive on 10 September 1241 (no. 463), does not occur after 1250. Adam Pithsweyn and Roger Lyu occur in the 1190s, and are thus not likely to have lived beyond 1250. Since Haltebe's widow Wymark was still alive as late as 1281 (no. 480), a date in the late 1240s seems likely.

463. Notification by Robert and Baldwin, sons of Godard of Thurleston, and Claricia his widow, that they have demised and leased to the prior and canons a piece of meadow called 'le Northmedue' in Thurleston, free of all secular exaction and demand, for nine years from the feast of St Michael 1242, for 11s 6d in cash and ½d each year of the term. Any grievance of the prior and canons is to be satisfied by arbitration.   10 September 1241

TNA, E40/3415. 158 × 88mm, 19mm turnup, 3 tags all 95mm approx., no seals, no endorsements.

Sciant presentes et futuri quod ego Robertus et ego Baldewinus filii Godardi de Thurlestun', et ego Claricia relicta dicti Godardi, dimisimus et locavimus [*sic*] Domino Priori et canonicis Sancti Petri de Gipewico, unam peciam prati cum suis pertinenciis in parochia de Thurlestun' que vocatur le Northmedue, cuius unum capud abutat super pratum Sefuch'l de Thurlestun et aliud capud super pratum nostrum quod est de feodo de Bramford: habendam et tenendam libere, quiete et absolute ab omni seculari exaccione et demanda, a festo Sancti Michaelis anni vicessimi sexti regni regis Henrici filii Iohannis usque in finem novem annorum continue sequentium; pro undecim solidis et sex denariis quos dederunt nobis premanibus, et pro uno obolo quem nobis dabunt quolibet anno dicti termini. Et si forte quod absit dicti prior et canonici per negligenciam nostram vel defectum super dicto tenementum fuerint aliquo modo gravati, nos eis super dicto gravamine satisfaciemus competenter arbitrio bonorum virorum. Et ad hoc astricti sumus fide media. Et ut omnia supradicta debitum habechit [*sic*] effectum nos presenti scripto sigilla nostra apposuimus. Acta apud Sanctum Petrum de Gipewico, quarto Idus Septembris pontificatus domini Gregorii Pape noni anno quintodecimo. Hiis testibus: Baldewino de Pesenh', Augustino de Westerfeld, Roberto Gulle, Adam [*sic*] mercatore, Vincencio de Rubroc, Roberto de Ry, Iusto, et aliis.

Date: The dating by papal year is very unusual for English private deeds. Though the term of the lease was to begin on 29 September 1242, the document must date to September the previous year. Pope Gregory IX's fifteenth year ran from 19 March 1241 until his death on 22 August 1241 (*HBD*, p. 37). Presumably the news of his death had not reached England by 10 September. See also the quitclaim of the property (no. 241) by Robert and Claricia, conditional upon repayment to the canons of the price of one seam of barley on the day or the morrow of the feast of Holy Cross in autumn (14 or 15 September 1241), which the canons lent them on 4 June the same year.

464. Quitclaim by Christiana, widow of Justus of Thurleston, to the canons, of all right and claim, both in her marriage portion and in the other lands which descended to her in the name of dower through the death of her late husband, for 3s which they have given her in cash, half an acre of land at 'Burbelot' which they have granted to her for life, and one seam of corn annually for life, namely half a seam of wheat and half a seam of barley, that is, 2 bushels of wheat and 2 bushels of barley at Christmas, 2 bushels of wheat at Whitsun and 2 bushels of barley at the Nativity of St John the Baptist.

[Mid-thirteenth century; after 10 September 1241]

TNA, E40/3598. 166 × 91mm, 15mm turnup, 116mm tag. Seal 40mm round, device a fleur-de-lys, legend gone. Endorsed: Burbelot (16/17c.).

Sciant presentes et futuri quod ego Christiana relicta Iustus [*sic*] de Thurlestun' in viduitate mea constituta concessi et quietum clamavi Deo et ecclesie apostolorum Petri et Pauli de Gypwico et canonicis ibidem Deo servientibus et inperpetuum

servituris, totum ius et clamium quod habui vel habere potui tam in maritagio meo
quam in aliis terris michi per mortem Iustus [*sic*] quondam viri mei nomine dotis
descendentibus, pro tribus solidis quos michi dederunt premanibus et dimidia acra
terre apud Burbelot quam dicti canonici ad totam vitam meam michi concesserunt
et pro una summa bladi michi annuatim quamdiu vixero solvenda, scilicet pro
dimidia summa frumenti et dimidia summa ordei, videlicet ad Natale Domini
duos bussellos frumenti et duos bussellos ordei, et ad Pentecosten duos bussellos
frumenti, et ad Nativitatem Sancti Iohannis Baptiste duos bussellos ordei; et post
decessum meum dicta dimidia acra terre ad dictos canonicos soluta et quieta
sine aliqua contradictione heredum meorum vel alicuius alterius revertetur. Et
ut omnia predicta firma et inconcussa remaneant, hoc presens scriptum sigilli
mei impressione roboravi. Hiis testibus: Willelmo de Holebroch, Baldewino de
Pesehale, Gerardo Richoud, Willelmo Testepyn, Willelmo de Cleydun', Augustino
de Westrefeud, Ada filio decani de Westrefeud, Roberto de Ri, Roberto de Bosco,
Iohanne Ade, et aliis.

Date: Justus of Thurleston was still alive on 10 September 1241 (no. 463). Adam
son of the dean, Robert de Ri and Robert de Bosco/Dubois/of the Wood do not
occur after the 1240s; de Bosco acted frequently as surety and juror at the 1240
eyre (*CPSE*, nos. 127, 145, 159 etc.). Justus does not occur after the 1240s, and was
probably dead by 1250.

465. Grant in free, pure and perpetual alms by Geoffrey Gulle, son of Robert
Gulle of Thurleston, to the canons, for the salvation of his soul and the souls of
his ancestors and successors, of 4d annual rent to be taken by the cellarer in two
instalments, from a piece of land in Thurleston lying between the canons' land and
that of Roger Stenekere, abutting south on the canons' land and north on that of
Osbert of the Market; for the maintenance of a light before the altar of the Blessed
Virgin Mary in the priory church. Warranty is granted.

[Mid-thirteenth century]

TNA, E40/3395. 157 × 88mm, 13mm turnup, 79mm tag, seal missing. No
endorsements.

Sciant presentes et futuri quod ego Galfridus Gulle, filius Roberti Gulle de
Thurlestune, concessi, dedi, et hac presenti carta mea confirmavi, pro me et
heredibus meis, Deo et ecclesie beatorum apostolorum Petri et Pauli de Gypewico
et canonicis ibidem Deo servientibus et inperpetuum servituris, in liberam, puram
et perpetuam elemosinam, pro salute anime mee et pro animabus antecessorum et
successorum meorum, quatuor denarios annui redditus percipiendos per manum
selerarii dicte domus ad duos terminos anni, scilicet ad festum Sancti Michaelis
duos denarios, et ad Pascha duos denarios, de una pecia terre in villa de Thurlestune
iacente inter terram dictorum canonicorum et terram Rogeri Stenekere, cuius
unum capud habutat super terram dictorum canonicorum versus austrum, et aliud
capud super terram Osberti de Foro versus aquilonem; habendum et tenendum
dictum redditum dictis canonicis et eorum successoribus ad sustentacionem
luminis coram altare beate Marie virginis in eadem ecclesia, de me et heredibus
et assignatis meis, libere, quiete, bene, et in pace. Et ego et heredes mei vel assignati

mei warantizabimus et defendemus dictum redditum dictis canonicis et eorum successoribus ad dictum lumen sustinendum contra omnes inperpetuum. Et ut hec mea concessio et huius carte mee confirmacio firmam habeat stabilitatem, huic presenti scripto sigillum meum apposui. Hiis testibus: Baldeuino de Pesehal, Willelmo filio eius, Augustino de Westerfeld, Iohanne filio eius, Roberto de Cleyd', Iohanne Bartelmeu de Tudeham, Roberto de Ry, Thurstanno del Cley, Rogero Paris de Blakeham, Ada filio decani de Westerfeld, Iohanne Bus, Humfrido de Wytentune, Alano Iustus, et aliis.

Date: Geoffrey Gulle the grantor is named (as Geoffrey Culle) in a writ of 31 May 1238 (no. 321). He is present when the plea is heard before the justices at the 1240 eyre (*CPSE*, no. 275), and attests no. 287, which dates after September 1242. Adam son of the dean of Westerfield attests between the 1230s and mid-century (nos. 286, 460, 464).

466. Notification by John son of Robert of the Wood (*de Bosco*) of Akenham and his heirs, that they are bound to pay to the prior and convent 14d annual rent, to be taken from the tenements which they hold and ought to hold of them in Thurleston (*Thurlestone*) and Whitton (*Witingtone*), of which tenements two pieces lie in 'Lunfeld', whereof one is called 'the[1] Wroncgehalfacre' and lies between the land of William Blanchevile and the land formerly John May's, its south headland abutting on the land of the rector of Whitton church; and the other called 'the[1] Sortehalfacre' lies at the headland of the land of Baldewyn of Peasenhall (*Pesehale*); and the third piece lies between the land of Alan Justus and the land formerly Robert Letherwine's, its east headland abutting on the meadow of Alan Justus; the fourth piece lies between the lands of Baldewyn of Peasenhall, one headland abutting on the land of Martin Justus and the other on the land formerly John May's; the fifth piece lies between the lands of Robert Lolt, one headland abutting on the land of Martin Justus and the other on the land formerly John May's. They are also bound to pay 23d annual rent, namely towards the pittance of the prior and convent, to be taken from two pieces of land and one piece of meadow, of which one piece of land lies between the lands of Robert Frost, one headland abutting on Baldewin's land, the other on the land of Richard Selune; the other piece of land lies between the land of Robert Blakeman and 'Oldwallestrik', one headland abutting on the meadow called 'Oldwalle', the other on the way extending from Westerfield (*Westerfeld*) as far as 'Crakeford'; and the piece of meadow called 'Oldewalle'. And to the king's precept, as much and as often as it is pleaded by his writ in their court; and they owe suit of court. Sealed in testimony.

Hiis testibus: Domino Willelmo de Henleye, Domino Iohanne de Luvetot, Roberto de Cleydone, Baldewyno de Pesehale, Roberto de Crakeford, Willelmo de Ri, Roberto Lumbekin, Alano Iustus, Adam [*sic*] de Cleydone, Iohanne Ade, Iohanne Siward et multis aliis.   [Mid-thirteenth century – 1260s]

TNA, E40/3728. 182 × 106mm, 13mm turnup, 80mm tag. Seal 37mm round, brown wax, design of five stars emanating from one point, legend S ... BOSCO. Endorsed: 'Thurleston' (16c.).

1 'The' is in English, with the 'thorn' rune.

Date: Sir William of Henley held one knight's fee in Henley in 1242–43 (*Bk Fees*, p. 915), and was a juror at the 1240 eyre (*CPSE*, no. 1096); he attests no. 138, datable to 1260–61 or 1264–65. Sir John de Luvetot sued Geoffrey son of Thomas concerning his holding in Tattingstone in 1268–69 (Rye, *Fines*, p. 69, no. 14). William de Blancheville was vouched to warranty at the 1240 eyre, but the case was postponed because of his minority (*CPSE*, no. 277). Alan Justus attests between the 1240s and 1260s or 1280s (e.g., nos. 286, 535), and Robert of Crakeford attests on 23 April 1270 (no. 520).

467. Notification by Ysouda, widow of William Colle of Thurleston (*Thurlestune*), that in her widowhood she has granted and quitclaimed to the canons in perpetuity, all right and claim which she had or could have had in the name of dower in the lands and rents which descended to her after the death of her late husband, for 2s which the canons have given to her in cash. Sealed in testimony.

Hiis testibus: Baldewino de Pesehal, Roberto de Cleydune, Adam [*sic*] de Aula, Alano Iustus, Martino Iustus, Iohanne Ade, Eadmundo Guthloch, Symone Snel et aliis. [1250s – 1270s]

TNA, E40/3396. 185 × 42mm, 14mm turnup, 107mm tag, seal missing, no endorsements.

Date: Baldwin of Peasenhall attests other priory charters as late as 1277 (no. 469); Robert of Claydon also occurs 1230s – 1270s (nos. 458, 460, 520); but since Martin Justus occurs as late as 1290 (nos. 359, 471, 536), this charter is unlikely to date before 1250. This view is reinforced by the dating of William Colle's charter no. 461.

468. Grant by Margery, daughter of Robert Verd of Foxhall (*Foxhole*), to Martin Justuse of Thurleston (*Thurlestone*), for his homage and service and two marks of silver which he has given her for a fine, of all her land and newly-won land (*incrementum*), together with the meadows, pastures, ways, paths, homages, rents, reliefs, wards, escheats and other appurtenances which came or ought to have come to her by inheritance in Thurleston after the death of her uncle John Oyrman, chaplain; to have and to hold of her and her heirs or assigns, to him and his heirs or assigns, or to whomsoever he may wish to give, sell, bequeath or assign them, freely, quietly, rightly, in peace, in fee and inheritance; rendering annually to the capital lords of the fee the due service and custom, namely to the prior and convent of St Peter 2s, 6d at each of the four terms of St Michael, St Andrew, Easter and the Nativity of St John the Baptist, and to Margery and her heirs one rose at the Nativity of St John the Baptist, for all services, customs, suits of court and secular demands. Warranty by the grantor and her heirs or assigns against all people in perpetuity. Sealed in testimony.

Hiis testibus: Baldewino de Wille, Ade de Aula, Roberto de Crakeford, Willelmo de Ry', Galfrido de Blanchevile, Ricardo Algor, Martino de Akenham, Augustino Brid, Iordano Galle et aliis. [1250s – 1270s]

TNA, E40/3934. 192 × 148mm, the latter dimension including a 12mm turnup which has been folded out; 80mm tag, seal missing. No endorsements.

Date: Although the grantee, Martin Justus, occurs from the 1260s (no. 535), if not before, and attests as late as 8 September 1290 (no. 536), most witnesses to this charter overlap in date between the 1250s and 1270s, e.g., Adam of the Hall, Martin of Akenham and Richard Algor (no. 337).

469. Grant in free, pure and perpetual alms by Richard de Breuse, knight and Alice his wife to the canons serving now and in perpetuity, of a piece of land lying in Thurleston in the field called 'Stowefeld', between the canons' land on either side, with free right of entry and exit, one headland abutting on the donors' meadow on the south, the other on their land on the north; to have and to hold to the canons and their successors, or to whomsoever they may wish to give, sell or assign it, freely, quietly, in fee and peacefully. Moreover they have granted, confirmed and utterly quitclaimed, for themselves and their heirs, to the canons and their successors, similarly in pure, free and perpetual alms, all the lands and tenements which the canons have by the feoffment of Edmund Duelle and Justus his brother, of the donors' fee in Thurleston, so that neither they nor their heirs may henceforth exact or claim anything thereof, either in rents, suits of court or other secular exactions whatsoever. Warranty by the grantors and their heirs against all in perpetuity. Sealed in testimony.

Hiis testibus: Domino Ricardo de Holebroch, Domino Roberto de Bosco, militibus, Baldewyno de Pesehale, Ricardo de Henleye, Adam [*sic*] de Cleydone, Roberto de Crakeford, Galfrido de Blancheville, Martino de Akenham, Martino Iustuse clerico, et multis aliis. 5 Kal. May, A.D. 1277.   27 April 1277

TNA, E40/3948. 173 × 121mm, 21mm turnup, 2 slits for tags, that at left empty, that at right with 60mm tag, with small fragment of natural wax. Seals missing. Endorsed: Thurleston (15/16c.).

470. Duplicate (not a counterpart; neither document is indented) of no. 469, in a similar, but not identical, hand.   27 April 1277

TNA, E40/3771. 177 × 140mm, including turnup now folded out, which adds 17mm to the height. Three slits where the text indicates only two seals; perhaps both were originally attached on the same plaited laces. Endorsed: Ric' Breuse [*illegible*] Thurleston [*illegible*] (both 16/17c.).

471. Grant in free, pure and perpetual alms by John, son of Baldwin of Peasenhall (*Pesehale*), to the canons, for his soul and the souls of Baldwin his father, Agnes his mother and Alexander Wulfun, of half a mark of annual rent towards the canons' pittance, to celebrate the anniversary of John, Baldwin, Agnes and Alexander annually in perpetuity on 17 Kal. November [16 October] without delay, performing John's obit on the same day just as if a canon had died; namely the half mark annually from William de Hernes and his heirs or assigns for four pieces of land which John gave to him and his heirs or assigns in Thurleston (*Thurlestun*); or if the half mark shall not be paid for any reason, the said tenement is to revert in fee and inheritance to the canons, as the indenture which John made to him and he to John attests. Sealed in testimony.

Hiis testibus: Domino Ricardo de Breuse, Domino Iohanne de Lovetot, Domino Roberto de Bosco, Domino Ricardo de Holebrok, militibus, Iohanne Clement, Viviano filio Silvestri tunc ballivis Gypwici, Philippo Harneis, Thoma Ailred, Philippo de Boking', Willelmo de Thornegg', Martino Iustus, Iohanne Aunsis, et multis aliis. At Ipswich (*Gyppwycum*) on the day of the Translation of St Edmund the Archbishop, 18 Edward I. **9 June 1290**

TNA, E40/3888. 276 × 160mm, 21mm turnup, 95mm tag, seal missing. Endorsed: prioris sancti Petri de terra Thurlston' (?15c.).

472. Grant by John, son of Baldwin of Peasenhall (*Pesinhale*), to the canons, of a piece of land containing four acres more or less, with grazing of a certain way extending from Thurleston church towards Ipswich (*Gippewycum*), as the land lies lengthways on the north [*sic*], and lengthways between the way and the prior's land, one headland abutting on the way from Whitton (*Whytington'*) church to Thurleston church on the west; being the piece of land which he formerly purchased of Geoffrey Gulle in Thurleston; to have and to hold of the capital lords of that fee, to the prior and canons and their successors, towards the canons' pittance, by the due and accustomed services in perpetuity, and performing annually in respect thereof on 17 Kal. November [16 October] an anniversary for John's soul and the souls of Baldwin his father, Agnes his mother, Alexander Wolfoun and John's brother Thomas, in all things just as for a canon, in perpetuity. Warranty by the grantor and his heirs to the prior and canons and their successors towards the canons' pittance as aforesaid, against all people in perpetuity. Sealed in testimony.

Hiis testibus: Nicholao de Shrybelound, Thoma de Westerfeld, Baldewyno fratre eius, Rogero Iustous, Willelmo dil Holeweye, Iohanne Iustous, Nicholao Bonde et aliis. At Ipswich, Thursday next after the feast of St Botulph, 14 Edward II.

18 June 1321

TNA, E40/3885. 237 × 158mm, this 158mm including a 17mm turnup which has been folded out; 82mm tag. Vesica seal of natural wax, 33 × 38mm, of unusual design; device difficult to interpret, but may represent a cup and cover. The legend cannot be made out. Endorsed: Canonici huius domus communi assensu concesserunt quod tota terra infra ?continens remaneat in manu domini Prioris ut in dominico imperpetuum. Ita quod dicti canonici habeant et ?percipiant de ecclesia Sancte Marie de Cayo [*St Mary at the Quay, Ipswich*] annuatim dimidiam marcam ad pictanciam eorum imperpetuum die anniversarii infra ?continente.

473. Notification by John, son of Thomas de la Dale, that he has granted, remitted and utterly and in perpetuity quitclaimed, for himself and his heirs, to the canons, all right and claim which he had, or in any way could have had, or might in future have, in a piece of land containing four acres more or less, with the grazing of a certain way extending from Thurleston church towards Ipswich (*Gyppewycum*), as the land lies lengthways on the north [*sic*] and lies lengthways between the way and the prior's land, one headland abutting on the way from Whitton (*Whytenton'*) church towards Thurleston church on the west, of which piece of land John son of Baldwin of Peasenhall (*Pesenhale*) by his charter enfeoffed the prior and canons, towards their pittance; so that neither John the grantor nor his heirs, nor anyone in their name, may henceforth claim any right in the piece of land or the grazing of the way. Warranty is granted against all people in perpetuity. Sealed in testimony.

Hiis testibus: Thoma de Westerfeld, Baldewyno de Westerfeld, Nicholao Bonde, Normanno le Ry, Rogero Iustous, Willelmo de Holewey, Iohanne Iustous et aliis. At Thurleston, Sunday next after the feast of the Purification of the Blessed Mary, 17 Edward II.   5 February 1324

TNA, E40/3886. 245 × 111mm, 21mm turnup, 89mm tag. Seal in natural wax, 27mm round, but the face has been lost. No endorsements.

474. Grant in perpetuity by John le Kyng of Westerfield (*Westerfeld*) and Emma his wife to Prior Henry and the canons, of a piece of land lying in the township of Thurleston (*Thurlestun*) between the land which was of Michael of the Well (*de Fonte*) and the land of Geoffrey Pekok', one headland abutting south on the way called 'le Podderes Payt', the other abutting north on 'le Merelond'; to have and to hold to the prior and canons and their successors, freely, wholly, rightly and in peace, in fee and in perpetuity, of the capital lords of the fee, performing [*missing*] services. Warranty by the grantor and his heirs against all people in perpetuity. Sealed in testimony.

Hiis testibus: Roberto Martyn, Normanno [*illegible*], Willelmo de Wode, Rogero Iustuse, Waltero de Hereway, Nicholao de Fonte et aliis. At Thurleston on Tuesday next before the feast of the Nativity of St John the Baptist, 2 Edward III.

21 June 1328

TNA, E40/3696. 250 × 85mm, 14mm turnup. Left tag 65mm, seal missing; right tag 105mm, nothing left of design of seal. Endorsed: H' prior ii (14c.); two other endorsements illegible due to rubbing and dirt.

475. Notification by John Howard, knight, that whereas Prior Henry and the canons have and hold two pieces of land containing 6 acres by the gift of Nicholas Bonde, which were of Thomas, son of John of Westerfield (*Westerfeld*) in the township of Thurleston (*Thurlistone*) in the hundred of Claydon (*Cleydone*), which are held of the grantor as of his manor of Brooks by Ipswich (*Brokes iuxta Gyppewycum*), he has confirmed the said gift, and for himself and his heirs has granted that the prior and canons may have and hold the two pieces of land of him and his heirs as of his said manor, just as Thomas held them of the lords of the same manor, notwithstanding the Statute of Mortmain. Sealed in testimony.

Hiis testibus: Iohanne Halteby, Nicholao Bonde, Iohanne Horold, Roberto de Bordishowo, Thoma de Ponte, Thoma de le Dale, Norman le Ry et aliis. At Ipswich, Friday next before the feast of St George the Martyr, 14 Edward III.   21 April 1340

TNA, E40/3874. 249 × 113mm, the 113mm including a 13mm turnup which has been folded out. There are slits at the centre but tag and seal have been lost. Endorsed: Thurleston (15c.).

WHERSTEAD

476. Grant in perpetuity by John del Welle of Wherstead (*Wehrstede*) to Prior Henry and the convent, for an unspecified sum of money as a fine, of two pieces of land in the township of Wherstead (*Whersted*), one piece in 'Langeslade' between John's lands on both sides, one headland abutting on his curtilage, and the other piece called 'Eldereges' in 'Suthdoune'; to have and to hold to the prior and convent and their successors, of the capital lord of that fee by the due and accustomed service in respect thereof, freely, quietly, rightly and in peace in perpetuity. Warranty by the grantor and his heirs against all people in perpetuity. Sealed in testimony.

Hiis testibus: Iohanne Reyner, Rogero Tyvele, Iohanne Ioy, Ricardo Reymes, Andrea ?Ayaunde et aliis. At Wherstead, Wednesday the feast of St Matthias the Apostle, 9 Edward II.   24 February 1316

JRL, CRU 751. 214 × 67mm, 12mm turnup, 107mm tag. Writing is visible on the inner side of the tag: line 1: 'Sciant presen' [*lost*]; line 2: 'Prior de Gypp' [*lost*]. Seal 23 × 24mm, white wax, much abraded, design and legend lost. Endorsed: H' ii' ixs vid. (15c.).

477. Grant in perpetuity by Olive de la Walle of Wherstead (*Wherstede*) to the prior and canons and their successors, of all her heath lying between the oak called 'le Kynggisoke' and the park of Holbrook (*Holebroke*) in the township of Wherstead, to have and to hold to them and their successors of the capital lords of that fee by the services due in respect thereof and by right accustomed. Also she has remitted to the prior and canons and their successors all right and claim which she had, has, or in any way could have, in all those tenements which they purchased of John de le Walle[1] her late husband, so that neither she nor her heirs, nor anyone on their behalf or in their name shall henceforth be able to claim any right in the tenements or in her heath in perpetuity. Warranty by the grantor and her heirs in respect of the heath against all people in perpetuity. Sealed in testimony.

Hiis testibus: Roberto de Reymes, Iohanne Ryngild, Willelmo Gernown, Rogero Reyner, Rogero Tyvele, Roberto Koket, Galfrido Russel et aliis. At Wherstead, Thursday the feast of St Gregory the Pope, 6 Edward III.   12 March 1332

JRL, CRU 754. 271 × 114mm, 17mm turnup, 118mm tag. Seal 19 × 25mm, red wax much abraded, design and legend lost. Endorsed: H' ii' iiis (15c.); Wersted (16/17c.).

    1 Del Welle in no. 476.

478. Notification by Richard de le Walle of Wherstead (*Wherstede*) that he has granted, remitted and utterly in perpetuity quitclaimed, for himself and his heirs, to the prior and canons and their successors, all right and claim which he had, has, or in any way might have had or could in future have, in all the lands, heaths and tenements which the prior and canons have by the gift and feoffment of John de le Walle his late father and Olive his mother in the township of Wherstead, so that neither he nor his heirs nor anyone on their behalf or in their name may henceforth in perpetuity be able to claim any right therein. Warranty by Richard and his heirs against all people in perpetuity. Sealed in testimony.

Hiis testibus: Roberto le Reymes, Iohanne Ryngild, Willelmo Gernown, Rogero Reyner, Roberto Koket et aliis. At Wherstead, Sunday next after the feast of St Gregory the Pope, 6 Edward III.   15 March 1332

JRL, CRU 755. 229 × 103mm, 15mm turnup, 110mm tag. Seal 21 × 24mm, red wax, design much abraded, but evidently the same as the better preserved no. 516, legend lost. Endorsed: H' ii' iiis. (15c.); Werstede (16c.).

479. Notification by John le Fre that, though the prior and canons are bound to him in 40 shillingsworth of annual rent to be paid to him for life in equal instalments at the feasts of St Michael and Easter, as is more fully set out in their bond with the seal of their chapter, he has nevertheless granted that in each year during the life of his brother Laurence, the prior and canons and their successors are to be quit of 6s 8d of the said rent, on condition nevertheless that after Laurence's death the bond concerning the annual rent of 40s is to remain in full force as to the 6s 8d abovesaid. He grants also that he will acquit the prior and canons each year during Laurence's life of 40s, while they and their successors pay to him or his assigns 33s 4d during Laurence's life out of the annual rent of 40s. Sealed in testimony.

Hiis testibus: Iohanne Haltebe, Galfrido Stace, Iohanne Horold, Rogero de Godelisford, Semano Merihel, Reginaldo de Flete, Thome le Mayster et aliis. At Ipswich (*Gyppwycum*), Wednesday after the feast of St Gregory the Pope, 14 Edward III.   15 March 1340

JRL, CRU 757. 281 × 112mm maximum (to top of indentations), parts of CIROGRAFUM visible, slit for tag, but tag and seal now lost. Endorsed: Iohannes fre (?16c.).

WHITTON

480. Notification by Wymarc the widow of Gilbert Haltebe, in her free widowhood, that she has granted, remitted and quitclaimed to William the prior and the canons, all right and claim which she had or could have had in the name of dower, in four pieces of land lying in the townships of Whitton (*Quytington'*), Thurleston and Brooks (*Brokes*), so that she shall not henceforth be able to claim any right therein againt the prior and canons. Sealed in testimony. No witnesses named. At Ipswich (*Gipewicum*), Tuesday next before the feast of St Ambrose, 9 Edward I.
                                                                  1 April 1281

TNA, E40/3676. 174 × 53mm, 8mm turnup, 80mm tag. Seal 39 × 22mm (pointed oval), design of leaves; legend: + S' WIMARCE HATEBE. No endorsements.

OUTLYING HOLDINGS

CRETINGHAM

481. Grant in perpetual alms by Robert son of Godfrey to the canons, of Cretingham church with all its appurtenances, for the salvation of his soul and those of all his ancestors.   [Probably 1160s – 1170s]

TNA, E40/3348. 166 × 68mm, 21mm turnup, 123mm tag. Words are written on the inside of the tag: 'Pater creator' written large. Endorsed: Rob' fil' Godef' (13c.).

Sciant presentes et futuri quod ego Robbertus filius Godefrido do et concedo in perpetuam elemosinam Deo et ecclesie apostolorum Petri et Pauli de Gipeswico et canonicis ibidem Deo servientibus, ecclesiam de Gretingeham cum omnibus pertinenciis suis, pro salute anime mee et omnium antecessorum meorum. Et ut hec mea concessio rata et inconcussa permaneat, eandem predictis canonicis hac presenti carta mea confirmavi. Hiis testibus: Wimero capellano, Magistro Samuele, Magistro Simone Angodo de Gipeswico, Manserio, Robberto de Wulagesham, Adam de Lond', Gileberto de Ri, Robberto preposito.

Date: Wimer the chaplain occurs from 1165–66 to at least 1198 (*Dodnash Charters*, pp. 1–6; and no. 484 in this edition). Master Simon attests a Dodnash Priory charter (no. 6), late 1188 x late 1189. A date early rather than later in Wimer's career seems likely, since by the 1180s no. 481 would have been a legally troublesome document, since by then technically only a bishop should have been able to grant a church, and no canon law court would have recognised such a grant (Dr Nicholas Karn, *pers. comm.*).

482. Grant in pure and perpetual alms by Ernald of Colevill' and Agnes his wife to the canons, of a benefice of six marks *per annum* from Cretingham church, saving to the donors and their heirs for ever the right of presentation to the living; the priest when instituted to give security for payment of the benefice.

[*c.* 18 October 1198]

TNA, E40/3347. 173 × 83mm, 25mm turnup, 76mm tag, seal missing. No endorsements.

Sciant presentes et futuri quod ego Ernaldus de Colevill' et Agnes uxor mea concessimus et dedimus et hac presenti carta confirmavimus quantum ad nos pertinet, Deo et ecclesie apostolorum Petri et Pauli de Gipeswico et canonicis ibidem Deo servientibus, in puram et perpetuam elemosinam, beneficium vi marcarum argenti per annum in ecclesia de Gretingham, salva nobis et heredibus nostris in perpetuum presentationem et electionem clerici qui in eadem ecclesia de Gretingheham instituetur, qui cum domino episcopo per nos vel heredes nostros presentatus fuerit, et admissus, securitatem prestabit quod iamdictum beneficium vi marcarum fideliter prefatis canonicis persolvet ad duos synodos de Suffolchia. His testibus: Ricardo Elyensi archidiacono, Galfrido archidiacono Suffolchie, Godefrido del Ysle, Roberto filio Rogeri, Willelmo de Warenne, Osberto filio Hervei, Michaeli Belet, Eustachio de Braham, Ricardo de Seinghes, Milone

Lenveise, Elya filio Turstani, Willelmo de Manet', Roberto de Colevill', Ranuffo [*sic*] de Ludham, Adam le Danais, Willelmo Angod, Edmundo filio Edmundi Goldhavec, Ricardo de Tivile, et multis aliis.

Date: Made in accordance with the terms of the final concord made at Thetford on 18 October 1198 (no. 308). Since six of the justices before whom the concord was levied attest this charter, it was clearly made while the court was still sitting at Thetford.

483. Confirmation by John, bishop of Norwich, to the canons, on the petition of Ernald of Coleville and Agnes his wife, of an annual benefice of six marks to be received in perpetuity from the church of Cretingham, saving to Ernald, Agnes and their heirs the presentation to the church in perpetuity; the parson so instituted is to give security for payment of the benefice to the canons.   [*c.* 18 October 1198]

TNA, E40/14020. 156 × 92mm, seal missing from tag. Printed in *EEA*, vi, no. 247.

Omnibus Christi fidelibus ad quos presens scriptum pervenerit, Iohannes Dei gratia Norwicensis episcopus salutem in Domino. Ad universorum volumus pervenire notitiam nos pietatis intuitu et favore religionis ad petitionem et presentationem Ernaldi de Colvil' et Agnetis uxoris sue, ad quos pertinet advocatio ecclesie de Cretingham, concessisse et confirmasse ecclesie apostolorum Petri et Pauli de Gipeswico et canonicis ibi Deo servientibus perpetuum beneficium sex marcarum percipiendarum in eadem ecclesia ad duos synodos Suffolchie, salva omnino predictis Ernaldo et Agneti uxori sue et heredibus suis in perpetuum presentatione et electione clerici qui in eadem ecclesia persona instituetur, qui etiam cum per nos vel successores nostros ad ipsorum presentationem in eadem fuerit ecclesia institutus persona securitatem prestabit quod iam dictum beneficium sex marcarum predictis canonicis ad prescriptos duos terminos integre et fideliter persolvet. Et ut hec confirmatio nostra stabilis et illibata perseveret, eam scripto presenti et sigilli nostri appositione communimus. Testibus: Gaufrido archidiacono, Thoma Britone, Eustachio capellano, Magistro Lamberto, Magistro Waltero de Calna, Vincentio clerico.

Date: See no. 482, which grant, made in compliance with the final concord of 18 October 1198 (no. 308), is here confirmed.

484. Grant in pure and perpetual alms by Arnold of Coleville, who has the heir of William of Cretingham, to the canons, of Cretingham church with all its appurtenances, for the soul of William of Cretingham who assigned it to them and for the souls of all Arnold's ancestors. Warranty is granted.   [?October 1198 – 1200]

TNA, E40/3349. 150 × 65mm, 12mm turnup, 112mm tag. Seal 36mm round, natural wax varnished brown, device a mounted knight; legend: SIG ... LDI DE COLEVILL' Endorsed: Arnoldi de Col' (13c.).

Universis sancte matris ecclesie filiis Arnaldus de Colevill' qui habet heredem Willelmi de Gretingham salutem in Domino. Noverit universitas vestra me dedisse et concessisse et hac presenti carta mea confirmasse Deo et ecclesie beatorum apostolorum Petri et Pauli de Gipewico et canonicis ibidem Deo servientibus, ecclesiam de Gretingham cum omnibus pertinentiis que ad eam pertinent, in puram et perpetuam elemosinam, pro anima Willelmi de Gretingham qui eis prefatam ecclesiam assignavit, et pro animabus omnium antecessorum meorum. Et ego et heredes mei debemus warantizare hanc donationem et concessionem et confirmacionem Deo et predictis canonicis. His testibus: Wimaro capellano, Roberto decano, Magistro Simone de Ressemere, Stephano de Ludham, Roberto de Coleville, Roberto persona de Rendlesham, Ricardo de Brumford, Willelmo filio eius, Willelmo filio Alani, Brthenno [*sic*] de Netlestede, Gaufrido filio Alani decani de Clopetun, Magistro Waltero de Gipewico.

Date: Arnold de Coleville is named as a pledge to prosecute in a writ of the sheriff of Suffolk of 27 July 1199 (*PBKJ*, I, no. 3528). Robert the dean attests four charters, 1188 – early thirteenth century (*Dodnash Charters*, nos. 4, 6, 9, 87). The final concord of 18 October 1198 (no. 308) by which the prior and canons agree to quitclaim their rights in Cretingham church to Arnold and his wife Agnes in return for six marks a year out of the church, was carried out, probably on the same day, by no. 482. Arnold's grant of the church to the priory must therefore postdate nos. 482 and 483. Though Wimer the chaplain is not otherwise known to occur after November 1196 (*Dodnash Charters*, p. 4), it seems that he was still alive in 1198, though probably not beyond 1200.

485. Confirmation in free, pure and perpetual alms by William son of Alan to the church and canons, of 6d annual rent which Alan son of Robert the chaplain and his heirs are to pay to the aforesaid church from the land of Thisteldene called Balle.

[Late twelfth – early thirteenth century]

TNA, E40/3954. 192 × 98mm, 26mm turnup, 101mm tag, seal missing. Endorsed: de Thistiden' (14c.); de Thistilden; vi d'; Gretingham (15c.).

Sciant presentes et futuri quod ego Willelmus filius Alani dedi et concessi et hac presenti carta mea confirmavi Deo et ecclesie beatorum apostolorum Petri et Pauli de Gypeswico et canonicis ibidem Deo servientibus, in liberam et puram et perpetuam elemosinam, redditum annuum sex denariorum quos Alanus filius Roberti capellani et heredes sui reddent singulis annis prefate ecclesie de terra de Thisteldene que vocatur Balle, integre et plenarie, ad festum Sancti Michaelis. His testibus: Hamfredo decano, Iohanne de Pleiford, Roberto filio Alani, Alano filio Alani, Willelmo de Dalingeho, Waltero de Westthorp et multis aliis.

Date: William son of Alan attests Arnold of Colevill's charter (no. 484) dated ?October 1198 – 1200, and is sued by Roger [le Bigod, second] earl of Norfolk before the king's justices in 1200 [*PBKJ*, I, no. 3221].

486. Confirmation by Thomas [Blundeville] bishop of Norwich to the prior and canons, by the will and consent of Alexander the parson and at the presentation of the true patron, the lady Agnes of Cretingham, of Cretingham church with its appurtenances after Alexander's death. They are to receive of Alexander from the church an annual pension of six marks, reserving to him for his lifetime the remaining portions of the benefice; after his death they are to provide a sufficient vicarage. 16 September 1235

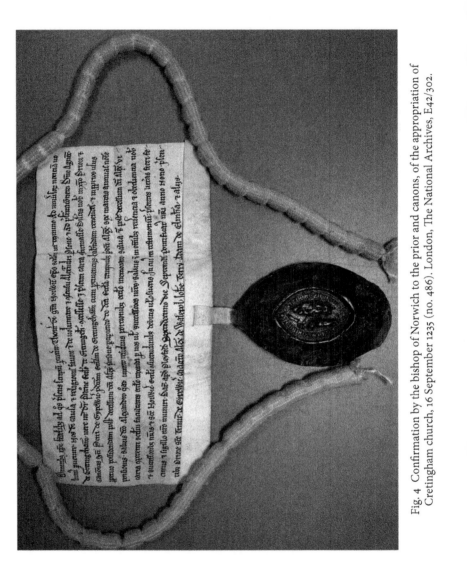

Fig. 4 Confirmation by the bishop of Norwich to the prior and canons, of the appropriation of Cretingham church, 16 September 1235 (no. 486). London, The National Archives, E42/302.

TNA, E42/302. 172 × 87mm, 14mm turnup, 12mm of tag to top of seal. Vesica seal and counter-seal. Seal legend: ... HOM ... S DEI GRACIA ... N ... CENSIS EPISCOPUS. Endorsed: Appropriatio ecclesie de Gretingham' Priori Gipwici. Norw'h dioc' (17c.); 16 Sept 1235 (18c.).

Omnibus Christi fidelibus ad quos presens scriptum pervenerit, Thomas Dei gratia Norwicensis episcopus salutem in Domino. Ad universorum notitiam volumus pervenire, nos Dei causa et religionis favore, et de voluntate et consensu Alexandri persone et ad presentationem Domine Agnetis de Gretingeham', vere ut dicitur patrone ecclesie de Gretingeham', concessisse et presenti carta confirmasse dilectis nobis in Christo priori et canonicis Sancti Petri de Gypewico, predictam ecclesiam de Gretingeham' cum pertinentiis, habendam, tenendam, et in proprios usus perpetuo possidendam post decessum dicti Alexandri persone, percipiendo de dicta ecclesia temporibus predicti Alexandri sex marcas annuas nomine pensionis, salvis dicto Alexandro quoad vixerit residuis portionibus ecclesie memorate, salva etiam post decessum dicti Alexandri vicaria competenti secundum facultates ecclesie taxanda per nos vel successores nostros, salvis etiam in omnibus reverentia et obedientia nobis et successoribus nostris et sancte Norwicensis ecclesie consue-tudinibus debitis vel consuetis. In cuius rei testimonium presentes litteras fieri fecimus et sigillo nostro muniri. Dat' apud Pleyford' sextodecimo die Septembris, pontificatus nostri anno nono, presentibus priore Sancte Trinitatis de Gyppewico, Magistro Alexandro de Walepol, Iohanne Terry, Adam de Elmham et aliis.

487. Grant by the prior and convent to Sir Alexander, chaplain of Cretingham, of 100s annually for life, towards his maintenance.[1]

[Probably 1235; not later than May 1248]

TNA, E40/3861. 160 × 72mm, 18mm turnup, two tags, that at left 175mm, that at right 125mm. Left has seal, right seal missing. Priory seal showing cruciform church, with counterseal. Endorsed: Gretingham (16c.).

Omnibus Christi fidelibus ad quos presens scriptum pervenerit, Gilebertus prior Sancti Petri de Gipewico et eiusdem loci conventus salutem. Noverit universitas vestra nos caritatis et pietatis intuiti concessisse et presenti carta nostra confirmasse dilecto in Christo fratri nostro Domino Alexandro de Gretingeham capellano, singulis annis quoad vixerit, centum solidos sterlingorum ad sustentacionem suam, ad duos terminos anni recipiendos, scilicet ad Pascha et ad festum Sancti Michaelis. Et in huius rei testimonium presens scriptum sigillo capitali nostro et sigillo ecclesie de Letheringham consignatum eidem Alexandro duximus confer-endum. Hiis testibus: Domino Willelmo priore Sancte Trinitatis, Domino Ricardo decano Codenham', Domino Radulfo decano Cleidun', Rogero de Cranesford, Simone Suilard, Roberto de Ribo et multis aliis.

1 Though this is a grant *by* the priory, it is included in this section as obviously part of the sequence of charters relating to the priory's acquisition of Cretingham church.

Date: Probably contemporary with no. 486. Prior Gilbert was elected in 1225; the licence to elect his successor was issued on 23 May 1248. Richard, dean of Coddenham attests a Dodnash Priory charter, 28 October 1223 x 27 October 1224

(*Dodnash Charters*, no. 16), and at the eyre of 1240 was accused, with Prior Gilbert, of unjustly disseising Master Robert of Coddenham of his free tenement in Ipswich (*CPSE*, no. 640).

488. Quitclaim by William of 'Thistelden' to the canons and their successors in perpetuity, in free, pure and perpetual alms, towards the maintenance of the light before the altar of the Blessed Virgin Mary in the priory church, of an annual rent of 6d to be taken at two terms, 3d at the feast of St Michael and 3d at Easter, which they used to pay for two pieces of land in Cretingham (*Gretingham*), one in the field called 'Stubbing' between the land of William Calopin and that of Thomas Colli, the other between the lands of Thomas Sturbvil; to have and to hold of the grantor and his heirs in perpetuity. Warranty by the grantor and his heirs against all men and women. Sealed in testimony.

Hiis testibus: Domino Willelmo de Swinesford tunc vicecomite Suffolchie, Domino Arnulfo de Ottel', Baldewino de Pesehale, Willelmo filio eius, Augustino de Westerfeud, Iohanne filio eius, Nicholao Suillard, Willelmo Bastard, Sturstan [*sic, for Thurstano*] del Clay, Hugone Lyu, Iohanne filio Luce de Ottel', Iohanne Bertelmeu de Tudeham, Ricardo Curle, Willelmo le Deneys et aliis.

[5 November 1255 x 25 October 1258]

TNA, E40/3953. 170 × 79mm, 13mm turnup, 126mm tag. Seal in dark green wax, 26 × 33mm, mostly perished but WILL legible; nothing of central design now intelligible.

Date: Sir William de Swyneford sheriff.

489. Quitclaim by Christiana the widow of William of Thisteldene to the canons and their successors in perpetuity, of all her right of dower in all the lands and rents which William at any time had in Cretingham (*Gretingham*); to have and to hold freely and quietly, without any demand by Christiana or her family, according to William's charter. For this quitclaim the prior and convent have given her ten shillings of sterlings. Sealed in testimony.

Hiis testibus: Domino Roberto de Aygneus milite, Arnaldo de Colevile, Nicholao Sulhard, Radulfo Halydai, Willelmo de Thisteldene, Willelmo Deneys, Rogero filio eius, Willelmo Bastard et aliis.   [After November 1255 – 1260s]

TNA, E40/3640. 183 × 64mm, 15mm turnup, 84mm tag. Seal 43mm round, device of a panache of heads of grain interspersed with ?swords. Endorsed: relax' (14c.).

Date: Post-dates the related no. 488: William of Thisteldene is now dead.

490. Grant by John Lene of Cretingham (*Gretingham*) to the prior and canons, of all the tenements which he held of their fee in Cretingham, with no reservation, to have and to hold of the capital lords of that fee, to them and their successors, freely, quietly, in fee and by inheritance, by the services which pertain to the same tenements, in perpetuity. Warranty by the grantor against all people in perpetuity. Sealed in testimony.

Hiis testibus: Ranulfo Halyday, Roberto fratre eius, Iohanne Horold, Willelmo Bastard, Iohanne Dayneus, Thoma de Rougham et aliis. At Cretingham, 20 March 13 Edward II. [20 March 1320]

TNA, E40/3629. 214 × 78mm, 14mm turnup, 96mm tag. Seal 23mm round, device of crossed gloves holding a branch. Endorsed: Cart Ioh'is Lene de ten' in Gretyngh' per h' p^i ii iiiis' (14/15c.), Gretyngham (17c.).

ORFORD

491. Grant and confirmation by Oger son of Oger to the canons, of the house with the whole messuage which Oger his father built upon the causeway of Orford, of the fee of Robert son of Ralph Brito and Philippa, daughter of William Gulaffre; rendering to the grantor 2s annually at the feast of St Michael for all service, for the soul of his father who granted the house and messuage to the canons for the love of God; for the salvation of him and of all his ancestors. [1188 x 1199]

BL Stowe Charter 407. 208 × 86mm, including a folded-out turnup of 9mm. Two slits but no tags. Shape rather irregular. Endorsed: Ogerus filius Ogeri (13c.); Orfford (15c.).

Ogerus filius Ogeri omnibus amicis suis et omnibus sancte matris ecclesie filiis tam presentibus quam futuris salutem. Sciatis me concessisse et presenti carta confirmasse ecclesie apostolorum Petri et Pauli de Gipeswico et canonicis ibidem Deo servientibus, domum cum toto masuagio quam Ogerus pater meus fecit super calcetam de Oreford' quod est de feodo Roberti filii Radulfi Britonis et Philippe filie Willelmi Gulaffre, reddendo inde mihi singulis annis ad festum Sancti Michaelis duos solidos pro omni servitio, pro anima patris mei qui predictam domum et predictum masuagium pro Dei amore eis concessit et pro salute mea et omnium parentum meorum. His testibus: Edmundo filio Eilwy, Iohanne filio suo, Willelmo magistro domni [*sic*] Ogeri, Oseberto Berte, Edmundo Goldhavec, David Undiep, Iona decano.

Date: The donor Oger was a royal justice on the south-western circuit during the visitation of 1194–95 (Crook, *Records of the General Eyre*, p. 59), and again in November 1196 (*Dodnash Charters*, no. 12). Edmund Goldhavec attests no. 43, *c.* 1180, and no. 482 dated October 1198. These dates suggest that this charter dates after the recovery by Robert, son of Ralf Brito (and husband of Philippa Gulaffre) of his forfeited lands in 1188 (*Eye Cartularies*, II, p. 59). Robert confirmed the grants of his predecessors William Gulaffre, William his son, and William son of Roger Gulaffre between 1189 and 1191 (*ibid.*), but was dead before Michaelmas 1199, when Geoffrey Maudit brought a plea of land against his widow and her son William at Westminster (*PBKJ*, I, no. 2472).

Grants and Leases by the Prior and Canons, Together with Exchanges and Agreements

(The arrangement follows that for the grants to the priory: first the core estates in Ipswich and its environs (mostly in Samford hundred), followed by the outlying holdings.)

Grants by the Prior and Canons

(Deeds which take the form of a lease for an indeterminate term to a lessee and the heirs of his body have been treated here as grants.)

CORE ESTATES

GREAT BELSTEAD

492. Indenture dated Sunday after the feast of St Edmund, King and Martyr, 16 Edward III, between Brother Henry the prior and the convent, and John Wytebrede of Great Belstead (*Belstede Magna*), Nichola his wife and John their son, whereby the prior and convent have granted to John, Nichola and John one curtilage in Great Belstead containing half a rood, to have and to hold to them and the lawfully begotten heirs of the body of John the son, of the prior and convent and their successors, rendering annually to the prior and convent and their successors 6d of silver, at the four usual terms of the year by equal portions. If it shall happen that John, Nichola, John or the heirs of the body of John the son default in payment of the rent, either in whole or in part, at any term, John, Nichola and John will by these presents and grant that it may be lawful for the prior and convent and their successors to re-enter both all the other lands and tenements of John, Nichola and John, and also the said curtilage, and to distrain and retain those things distrained until they are fully satisfied concerning both rent and arrears. Warranty is granted by the prior and canons and their successors against all people. John, Nichola and John [*several words illegible*] the whole of the said curtilage [*several words illegible*] shall wholly and fully revert and remain to the prior and convent and their successors in perpetuity. In testimony whereof the parties have sealed each other's copy of this indenture.

Hiis testibus: Roberto de Coppedok, Roberto de Predis, Iohanne ? Acras, Iohanne Belewhed' et aliis.   24 November 1342

TNA, E40/3860. Parts of the document are faded and badly stained. Chirograph; 268 × 216mm to top of indentation, 21mm turnup. Three tags, all 120mm, no seals. Endorsed: a. Ioh's Wytbred' ad t[*lost due to small hole*] (15c.); vi d' in Belsted (16c.).

IPSWICH, PARISH UNKNOWN

493. Grant in perpetuity by Prior Michael and the convent to the church and convent of St Mary of Wix, of the land which Roger of Dib'a held of them in Ipswich, free of all services pertaining to the grantors; rendering to them annually 3d, in two instalments. [After May 1196 – c. 1202]

TNA, E40/3704. 163 × 58mm, 12mm turnup, 98mm tag now attached to turnup by stitching rather than being passed through slits in the charter. Endorsed: De terr' in Gypewic' (14c.).

Universis sancte matris ecclesie fidelibus, Michael dictus prior et conventus ecclesie apostolorum Petri et Pauli de Gypeswico salutem in Domino. Universitati vestre notum sit, nos de voluntate et consensu communi tocius capituli nostri concessisse et dedisse et hac presenti carta confirmasse ecclesie Sancte Marie de Wica et eiusdem loci conventui, terram quam Rogerus de Dib'a tenuit de nobis in Gypewico in perpetuum. Tenendam libere et quiete ab omnibus serviciis que ad nos pertinent, reddendo inde nobis annuatim tres denarios, scilicet ad Pascha tres obolos et ad festum Sancti Michaelis tres obolos. Hiis testibus: Eustacio de Braham, Ricardo de Gosfeld', Mile [*sic*] Lemveise, Clarebaldo de Alno, Helia filio Turstani, Walkelino filio Normanni, Iohanne fratre eius, Eustacio de Densewell', Pani, Willelmo filio Radulfi de Wica et pluribus aliis.

Date: Prior Michael's predecessor William occurs up to 12 May 1196 (no. 309). Michael occurs between 18 October 1198 and 1208. Eustace of Brantham was active between 1165 and 1202 (*Dodnash Charters*, no. 31).

IPSWICH, ST AUGUSTINE IN STOKE

494. Grant and surrender in perpetuity in the form of a chirograph, 9 March 8 Edward II, by Prior Henry of Kersey and the canons, by unanimous consent, to Thomas le Rente of Ipswich (*Gyppewico*), of all that messuage called 'Bolnesved' in the parish of St Augustine in the suburb of Ipswich, to have and to hold of the prior and convent and their successors, to Thomas, his heirs and assigns, freely, quietly, rightly and in peace, in fee and by inheritance in perpetuity, rendering yearly to the prior and convent and their successors 6d of silver at the feast of St Michael for all services and demands. Thomas has granted for himself, his heirs and assigns, that it may be lawful for the prior and convent and their successors, by themselves or through bailiffs, to distrain upon the tenement for the 6d annual rent and for arrears of the same, and to carry off and retain the distraint until full satisfaction has been made. In testimony whereof the parties have sealed each other's copy of this chirograph. No witnesses are named. 9 March 1315

TNA, E40/3516. 219 × 106mm, the 106mm to the top of the indentations; parts of CYROGRAFUM legible, 20mm turnup, 107mm tag, seal missing. Endorsed: paroch' sancti Augustini vi ?; Ipswyth (16c.).

IPSWICH, ST MILDRED

495. Indenture made on Thursday in the week of Pentecost, 5 Edward III, between the prior and convent and Roger Deyse of Ipswich (*Gippewyco*), namely that the prior and convent have unanimously granted and demised to Roger all their void piece of ground which at some time they recovered in the king's court against John dil Halk' by the judgment of the court, in the parish of St Mildred in Ipswich, between the tenements of Christopher dil Wode and Robert Skiet on the south and a piece of land of John dil Halk' on the north, abutting east on Christopher's tenement and west upon the highway at the wool market ('le Wllemarket') and upon the messuage of Robert Skiet. To have and to hold to Roger and the heirs of his body lawfully begotten, at farm, of the prior and convent and their successors, paying in respect thereof 30d annually at two terms, namely Easter and the feast of St Michael, in equal instalments, and performing each year for the prior and convent as much house-rent (*hadgabulum*) as pertains to the said land. In case of rent arrears of fifteen days while however the piece of land lies void, the prior and convent may immediately re-enter the land, re-take seisin and retain it in perpetuity without opposition of Roger or his heirs. When the time shall come that the land may be built upon by Roger, and it shall happen that the rent be fifteen days in arrears, then the prior and convent and their successors and attorneys may immediately enter the houses built upon the land, distrain and carry off, lead away, impound and retain the things distrained, wherever they wish within the liberties of Ipswich, until they are fully satisfied and paid the rent and arrears. If it happen, which God forbid, that Roger die without lawful heirs of his body, then the piece of land, whether void or built upon, shall revert to the prior and convent and their successors in perpetuity. In testimony whereof the parties have sealed each other's copy of this indenture.

Hiis testibus: Galfrido Costyn et Thoma Whatefeld tunc ballivis ville Gippewyci, Iohanne Cobat, Thoma Randolf, Galfrido Bullok', Roberto Skiet, Cristophoro del Wode, Iohanne Coleman, Ricardo Maynard, Iohanne de Hadleye, Thoma de Stoke, Iohanne de Belcham, Iohanne Heved, Iohanne Pyk et aliis. At Ipswich.

23 May 1331

TNA, E40/3740. 245 × 213mm, 13mm turnup, 100mm tag. Seal 30mm round, with a design of two long-necked birds in profile, facing towards each other. Legend gone. Endorsed: paroch' Mildrede xxx d' per annum; Nich' Sky'ner; Rog' Deise; Rog' Deise (various hands, both 15c.).

THURLESTON

496. Notification by Prior William and the convent that they have granted and given to Martin Justuse of Thurleston (*Thurlestun'*), for his homage and service, and for a fine of 100s of silver, a messuage and a piece of land in Thurleston with all its buildings, which messuage William of Thurleston, chaplain, sometime held of them, between the courtyard of Robert Duelle on the south and Thurleston churchyard on the north, abutting on Martin's land called 'le Lintone' and on the way from Thurleston church to Ipswich (*Gypuycum*); and the piece of land lies between the messuage of John Baldewyn and Martin's land 'le Lintone', abutting west on Martin's pasture and east on the churchyard; to have and to hold of the prior and convent and their successors, to him and his heirs or assigns in perpetuity, and to whomsoever he may wish to give, sell, bequeath or assign them, freely and in peace and inheritance; rendering annually in respect thereof to the prior and convent and their successors 4d at two terms in the year, namely 2d at the feasts of St Michael and Easter, for all services, customs and demands. Sealed in testimony.

Hiis testibus: Domino Willelmo de Henleye, Baldewyno de Valle, Roberto de Cleydun', Iohanne filio Augustini de Westerfeld, Adam [*sic*] de Cleydune, Augustino Chelvig, Alano Iustuse, Martino de Akeham, Willelmo de Ri, Ricardo Algor, Roberto Lubeki', Iohanne Ade, Roberto Duelle et aliis.

[14 October 1267 x early 1289]

TNA, E40/3549. 240 × 80mm, 14mm turnup, 98mm tag, seal missing. Writing on inner face of tag, apparently from another deed, ends of lines legible:
Universis Cristi fidelibus P ...   ... in vero salutari.
Noverit universitas vestra ...   ... bone et legal'
monete sponte ...
Endorsed: Thurleston (17c.).

Date: Prior William of Seckford's election received the royal assent on 14 October 1267; he resigned early in 1289. The messuage of William of Thurleston, chaplain was leased from Prior Gilbert (1225–48), and surrendered not later than the 1240s (no. 205). Sir William of Henley held one knight's fee in Henley in 1242–43 (*Bk Fees*, Pt II, p. 915), and attests no. 138 in 1260–61 or 1264–65. A date in the earlier part of Prior William's tenure therefore seems likely, even though Martin Justuse was still alive on 8 September 1290 (no. 536).

WHERSTEAD

497. Grant by Prior Gilbert and the convent to Gilbert son of Robert de Reymes and his heirs, for homage and service and for 20s which he has given them, of the land of Perecroft and all the marsh where the mill sits and the land which Edadiva the widow held of the fee of Pannington; to be held of the prior and convent in perpetuity, rendering annually 5s at four terms of the year for all services, customs and demands, saving the king's service of 12d in 20s scutage, and the other services which pertain to the tenement.   [?1230s – early 1248]

BL Stowe Charter 410. 224 × 50mm, 10mm turnup, 44mm tag, seal missing. Endorsed: Carta Gilb'ti prioris sancti Petri (13c.).

Omnibus Cristi fidelibus ad quos presens scriptum pervenerit, Gilebertus prior Sancti Petri de Gypewico et eiusdem loci conventus humilis salutem in Domino. Noverit universitas vestra nos concessisse et presenti carta nostra confirmasse Gileberti filio Roberti de Reymes et heredibus suis pro homagio et servitio suo et pro viginti solidis quos nobis dedit, terram de Perecroft cum pertinentiis et totum mariscum ubi molendinum sedet et terram quam Edadiva vidua tenuit de feodo de Paniton'; tenend' et habend' libere, quiete, bene et in pace illi et heredibus suis de nobis in perpetuum, reddendo inde nobis annuatim quinque solidos ad quatuor terminos anni, scilicet ad festum Sancti Andree quindecim denarios, ad Pascha quindecim denarios, ad festum Sancti Iohannis Baptiste quindecim denarios, ad festum Sancti Michaelis quindecim denarios, pro omnibus servitiis, consuetudinibus et demandis, salvo servicio domini regis, scilicet ad scutagium viginti solidorum, duodecim denariis, et ad plus, plus, et ad minus, minus, et salvis aliis servitiis que ad dictum tenementum pertinent. Hiis testibus: Domino Hugone de Gosebec, Ricardo de Braham, Iohanne de Braham, Egidio de Wachesham, Earnoldo de Otteley, Waltero de Braham militibus, Philippo de Frest', Willelmo de Holebro', Teobaldo de Leyston', Iuliano de Braham, Michaelo de Frest', Willelmo Goldhavec, et aliis.

Date: The royal assent to the election of Prior Gilbert was issued on 13 April 1225, and the licence to elect his successor on 23 May 1248. Gilbert I de Reymes of Wherstead, son of Robert, was admitted a forinsec burgess of Ipswich in 1203–04 ('Black Domesday', fol. 82r.). Gilbert II, a presumed descendant of Gilbert I, and who is perhaps a more likely candidate for the recipient of this charter, was active in 1239–40 ('Reymes of Wherstead', pedigree, p. 101). Sir Hugh of Gosbeck (*CPSE*, nos. 151, 159), Sir John of Brantham and Sir Giles of Wattisham (*ibid.*, nos. 145, 147, etc.) were all jurors at the 1240 eyre, where Sir Richard of Brantham was defendant in two cases (*ibid.*, nos. 370, 500). Theobald of Leiston attests a Dodnash Priory charter (no. 83) dating to the mid-thirteenth century. These dates suggest that this charter dates from the 1230s onwards.

498. Notification by Prior William and the convent that they have granted to Hugh son of Gilbert de Reymes of Wherstead (*Qwerstede*) and his heirs [*the right*] to sing in his oratory built within his court at Wherstead, saving in all things the indemnity of the mother parish church of St Mary of Wherstead. Sealed in testimony with the common seal of their chapter. At Ipswich, in their chapter house.   1 March 1282

BL Stowe Charter 409. 150 × 63mm, 18mm turnup, 96mm tag. Seal of priory, 48mm round, damaged at left. Image of church is visible, and figure in roundel at right. Legend: SIGILLUM ECCL'S ... No early endorsements.

OUTLYING HOLDINGS

BARNINGHAM AND HEPWORTH

499. Grant by Prior William and the convent to Henry son of Henry and his heirs, of 30 acres of land in Barningham which Richard Panescene held of the fee of Humfrey Lecunte. Henry is to pay to the convent 32d annually for all services and customs saving the king's service of 4d in the mark scutage when it is levied. Further grant by the prior and convent of their land recently brought under cultivation called Susterdole in Hepworth which Humfrey Lecunte gave them, and four acres of heath, by the service of 8d annually, saving the king's service of 4d towards Danegeld.   [After Easter 1180 – before 18 October 1198]

TNA, E40/3273. 140 × 70mm, 10mm turnup folded out and included in overall measurement. Two small square holes at left and centre left. Endorsed: Ber'ingham, Berningham, Berningham (all 16c., different hands).

Sciant presentes et futuri quod ego Willelmus prior Sancti Petri de Gipwico et conventus eiusdem loci dedimus et concessimus et hac carta nostra confirmavimus Henrico filio Henrici et heredibus suis xxxᵃ acras terre cum pertinenciis in Beringham quas Ricardus Panescene tenuit de feudo Humfridi Lecunte. Et sciendum quod predictus Henricus reddet nobis annuatim xxxᵃ et duos denarios pro omnibus serviciis et consuetudinibus, scilicet ad duos terminos, xvi denarios ad Pascha, et xvi denarios ad festum Sancti Mikaelis. Salvo servicio domini regis cum scutagium venerit, scilicet ad marcam iiiiᵒʳ denarios, et ad plus, plus, et ad minus, minus. Et preterea dedimus et concessimus predicto Henrico incrementi terram nostram que vocatur Susterdole in villa de Heppwrth quam terram Humfridus Lecunte nobis dedit in bosco et in plano et in omnibus aliis rebus, et quatuor acras de bruero per servicium viii denarios ad duos terminos, scilicet iiiid' ad Pascha et iiii ad festum Sancti Michaelis, salvo servicio domini regis, scilicet ad denegeldum iiiid'. Hiis testibus: Rogero celerario, Willelmo sacrista, Waltero de Sancto Osyda, Hoseberto de Glanvilla, Humfredo de Beringham, Bartholomeo de Culwerhiston', Waltero de Heppworth, Herveo de Heppworth', Gileberto Lecunte, et multis aliis.

Date: Prior William's predecessor Hubert occurs in Easter Term 1180; William occurs 20 October 1192 and 12 May 1196; his successor Michael occurs from 18 October 1198. Roger the cellarer occurs 20 October 1192 (no. 305). Slightly later than no. 6. (The reference to Danegeld is an archaism).

CRETINGHAM

500. Grant by Prior J[*ohn of St Nicholas*] and the convent to Thomas Wylot of Cretingham (*Gretingham*), tailor, for his homage and service, of a piece of land called 'Clerkesete' in Cretingham, lying between the land formerly of Roger le Deneys on the east and the way called 'le Chercheweye' on the west; saving to the grantors the chase there as often as there shall be work,[1] with all manner of animals, for twelve feet to the east of the land; to have and to hold of the grantors and their successors, to Thomas and the heirs of his body lawfully begotten, or if he should have no lawful heirs of his body, to him and his son [*sic*] Ranulf and Ranulf's lawful heirs of his body, to give, sell or assign to whomsoever they wish, in fee and inheritance; rendering annually to the grantors and their successors fifty pence at four terms, that is, 12½d at the feasts of St John the Baptist, St Michael, St Andrew and Easter, for all services, customs and secular demands. Warranty by the grantors against all people in perpetuity.

Hiis testibus: Domino Iohanne de Todeham, Domino Iohanne de Ketleburge militibus, Iohanne de Aigneus, Thoma Roges, Willelmo Overhe, Symone le Lord, Willelmo Turpyn, Ada Leverich, et aliis. Given in the grantors' chapter house, Kal. June A.D. 1290   1 June 1290

TNA, E42/424. 187 × 111mm, 24mm turnup, 158mm tag. Seal 47 × 50mm but once round, great seal of priory in green wax, legend SIGILLUM EC … … SWIC. Counterseal: legend + IOHANNES EST NOMEN EIUS around a possible classical gem showing a standing figure in a helmet looking to the left. Endorsed: ii s' ii d' in Wetsted (15c.); Gretingham (16c.)

1 Or use (*opus*).

501. Confirmation by Prior John and the convent to Andrew Howelin of Cretingham (*Gretingham*), for his homage and service, of a piece of land in Cretingham, lying between the land of Nicholas Suylard and the common way from Cretingham, abutting on the common way from Brandeston (*Branteston'*) and on the land formerly of William le Deneys; to have and to hold to him and his heirs or assigns, of the grantors and their successors, quietly, well and in peace, in fee and by inheritance in perpetuity; rendering annually to the grantors and their successors twenty-eight pence at four terms, that is, seven pence at the feasts of St Michael, the Purification of the Blessed Mary, Easter and St John the Baptist, for all services, customs and secular demands. Warranty by the grantor against all people in perpetuity. Sealed in testimony.

Hiis testibus: Hugone filio Hugonis, Hugone Harand, Iohanne de Agneys, Thoma Rogges, Willelmo Overhe, Willelmo de Bosco, Willelmo Bastard, Willelmo Suylard, Willelmo Turpin, et aliis. At Ipswich (*Gipp'*), Tuesday after the feast of St James the Apostle, 23 Edward I.   26 July 1295

TNA, E40/3630. 260 × 97mm, 22mm turnup, 84mm tag, seal missing. No endorsements.

Leases by the Prior and Canons

GREAT BELSTEAD AND COPDOCK

502. Agreement (*ita convenit*), Anno Domini 1378, between Prior William and the convent on the one part and William Gelyn of Copdock (*Coppidoc*) and Isabella his wife on the other, whereby the prior and convent have conceded and leased at farm to William and Isabella 28 acres of arable land with an adjoining messuage in Great Belstead (*Belstede Magna*), and one acre of meadow in Copdock, to have and to hold of the prior and convent and their successors, to William and Isabella, their heirs and assigns, for a term of ten years beginning on the feast of St Michael next following, rendering annually 21s in equal instalments at the feasts of the Lord's Nativity, Easter, the Nativity of St John the Baptist and St Michael, for all secular demands. In case of arrears, in whole or in part, the prior and convent and their successors may distrain on the lands and tenements, and also on all the other lands and tenements of William and Isabella, and retain those things distrained until full satisfaction shall have been made for the rent and arrears. In testimony whereof the parties have sealed each other's copy of this indenture.

Hiis testibus: Willelmo Andrea, Willelmo de Cappidoc, Roberto de Godlisford, Iohanne Blanchevile, Thome [*sic*] de Fredis, et multis aliis.   1378

TNA, E40/3727. 225 × 120mm maximum, to top of indentation, 17mm turnup, parts of CIROGRAFUM visible at top edge; left tag 100mm, seal 25 × 20mm showing two heads facing each other; right tag 65mm, seal missing. Endorsed: Belstede (16c.).

BURSTALL

503. Indenture whereby Prior William and the convent have granted, demised and leased at farm to Godfrey Sper of Burstall (*Burstalle*) a croft in Burstall called 'the Schalledehel', 'Copehoodgrene', 'Margery Duyci' with 'Brokslade Pytel'; to have and to hold to Godfrey and his heirs from the next feast of the Purification of the Blessed Mary for the term of 16 years; rendering annually to the prior and convent and their successors 12s in four equal instalments at the feasts of Easter, the Nativity of St John the Baptist, St Michael and the Lord's Nativity, without delay. In case of rent arrears, in whole or in part, at any term, the prior and convent and their successors may distrain on the croft and pightle and retain those things distrained until they are fully satisfied of the rent and arrears. In case of arrears of more than three months, or if waste has been committed, the prior and convent may re-enter and retain the croft and pightle in their former estate, notwithstanding these indentures. Warranty is granted for the term on the above condition. In testimony whereof the parties have sealed each other's copy of the indenture. At Ipswich (*Gippewicum*), Tuesday next after the feast of the Conversion of St Paul, 4 Henry V.   26 January 1417

TNA, E40/3655. 217 × 122mm maximum, 22mm turnup, chirograph indented at top edge, 98mm tag. Seal 25mm round, much damaged and unintelligible. Endorsed: Godefrid Spear xii s' (15c.); Spear' de Burstall (16c.).

IPSWICH, GREENWICH

504. Indenture whereby Prior William Blome and the convent have leased to Robert Bryd of Ipswich (*Gipp'ci*) a close called 'Grenwychclos' in Greenwich (*Grenwych*) in the suburb of Ipswich, just as enclosed, to have and to hold to him, his heirs and assigns, from the feast of St Michael next after the date of these presents for five years, rendering annually to the prior and convent and their successors 35s of legal money, in equal instalments of 8s 9d at the feasts of the Lord's Nativity, Easter, the Nativity of St John the Baptist and St Michael, and so from year to year during the term. If the rent shall fall into arrears in whole or in part, distraint may be made until full satisfaction is made both for rent and arrears. If the rent shall be three months in arrears at any feast, the prior and convent may re-enter and repossess the close in its original estate, notwithstanding these indentures. Warranty is granted for the duration of the term on the above condition, against all people. In testimony whereof the parties have sealed each other's copy of the indenture. At Ipswich, Monday next after the feast of the Nativity of the Blessed Mary, 7 Henry V.   11 September 1419

SROI, HA 93/3/24. 254 × 140mm maximum, to top of indentation, turnup 15–18mm, slit for tag; tag and seal missing. Endorsed: Rob' Bryd de clauso in Grenewych (16c.). Ipswich (17c.). A deed of Henry 5ths time (17c., different hand). Antiq. Ipswich H. V. 7th, Wm Blome Prior of the Ch & Convt of St Peters Ips to Rob Bryd land in Granwich (19c.).

IPSWICH, ST NICHOLAS

505.[1] Demise for life by Prior Nicholas and the convent to William of Heys, chaplain, for the whole of his life, of a messuage with its buildings in the parish of St Nicholas, Ipswich (*Gipewico*), between the messuages formerly of John le Mikele and Adam Cobiten, the heads abutting on the highway and upon the land of Roysia Horold; to have and to hold of the prior and convent and their successors, to him and his assigns for his whole life, rendering to them and their successors in respect thereof 2s [*annually*] in two instalments at the feast of St Michael and Easter. Warranty is granted against all people for William's life. Sealed in testimony.

Hiis testibus: Silvestro filio Wakelini, Thurstano del Cley tunc ballivis de Gipewico, Radulfo de Thorp, Galfrido Ballard, Alano Horold, Iohanne le Cuntesse, Andrea fratre suo, Bonde [?le Tanur[2]], et aliis.

[8 January 1253 x September 1267; probably 1254–55]

TNA, E40/3637. 163 × 93mm, 18mm turnup, 77mm tag. Fragment of seal 36mm round, apparently showing part of a church building (?the priory seal). Fragment of counter-seal, perhaps a heraldic design, for it seems to be shaped as a shield; details lost. Endorsed: par' sancti Nicholai (16c.).

   1 For the earlier history of this property, see nos. 390 and 391.
   2 As in nos. 390 and 391.

Date: Prior Nicholas of Ipswich: royal assent to his election given 8 January 1253; licence to elect his successor granted 20 September 1267. Silvester son of Wakelin and Thurstan del Cley are known to have served together as bailiffs September 1254 – September 1255; they could also have done so somewhat earlier or later in the date-span.

506. Indenture whereby the prior and convent have granted to William of Letheringham their cook and Margery his wife, for the whole of their lives, a messuage with buildings which was formerly Robert Harding's in the parish of St Nicholas, Ipswich (*Gipewico*), lying between the messuage of Adam the carpenter on the east and the highway extending from the gate of the Friors Minor to the messuage which was of Ralph Blumvile sometime archdeacon of Suffolk on the other side; to have and to hold of the prior and convent for their lives, freely, well and in peace, paying 2s annually in two instalments for all service, custom and demand saving house-rent (*hadgabulo*). After their deaths the messuage is to revert to the prior and convent without anyone's objection. William and Margery are to maintain the buildings and carry out repairs at their own charge, otherwise the prior and convent will seize the messuage into their own hands. So that this grant may be observed without objection, the parties have sealed each other's copy of the chirograph.

Hiis testibus: Hugone Langestun, Matheo de Porta tunc ballivis, Roberto Wlfun, Ricardo Fader, Iohanne Lorenz, Nicholao Godeschalc, Iohanne Pulleg[os], Roberto Police, Ada Colellme, Ada Carpentar', Iohanne David.   [1250s – 1270s]

TNA, E40/3645. 236 × 100mm, 19mm turnup, part of CYROGRAFUM visible at top edge. Left tag 106mm, seal 38mm round, legend … LL DE L … . Device of sunburst/panache of heads of grain and swords. Right tag 110mm, seal 28 × 20mm, … GAR … legible of legend. Device unintelligible. Endorsed: refectorii (14c.); indenture de chamine sancti Nicholai (15c.).

Date: Ralph de Blumvile was archdeacon of Norfolk by 1236, and resigned for pluralism in 1237 (*Fasti*, ii, 66). He seems to have been archdeacon of Suffolk for all or part of the period *c.* 1219–1236, for which no names are given in the *Fasti*. Matthew de Porta is known to have served as bailiff of Ipswich at intervals between 1255 and 1279, and may have done so earlier. Hugh Langestun is not known, otherwise than in this charter, to have served with him. They must have served together at some time for which the borough court rolls are missing, between the 1250s and 1270s.

507. Quitclaim by Margaret[1] the former wife of William Cook (*coci*)[2] of Ipswich (*Gypewyco*) to the prior and convent, of all right and claim which she had or in any way could have had in a messuage lying in the parish of St Nicholas, Ipswich, between the messuage of Adam the carpenter on the east and the highway extending to the gate of the Friars Minor on the west, and surrounded by the highway (*et circuitur undique via regis*); so that neither she nor anyone in her name, nor her contingent heirs may henceforth have any claim in the messuage. For this remission and quitclaim the prior and convent have given her 2s of silver in cash. Sealed in testimony.

Hiis testibus: Laurentio Horold, Thoma Aylred tunc ballivis Gyppewyci, Iohanne Clement, Roberto de Oreford, Philippo Harneys, Hugone Lu, Rogero le Meyster, Hugone Goldyng, Rogero Fot, et aliis. Sunday next after the feast of St Hillary, 12 Edward I.   16 January 1284

TNA, E40/3644. 217 × 78mm, 11mm turnup, 118mm tag, seal missing. Endorsed: De chamino sancti Nicholai (15c.); par' sancti Nicolai (16/17c.).

1 'Margery' in no. 506.
2 Also known as William of Letheringham, cook in no. 506.

508. Indenture by which Prior Henry and the canons demise to Sir Thomas Chauntebien of Ipswich (Gippewyco), chaplain, the altarage of their church of St Nicholas of Ipswich with all its rights and appurtenances, to have and to hold from the next feast of St Michael for seven years, for 38½ marks of sterlings, of which Thomas is to pay them each year during the term 5½ marks at three annual terms, namely 24s 6d at the feast of the Nativity, 24s 5d at Easter and 24s 5d at the feast of St Peter *ad vincula*. Warranty by the grantors until completion of the term. Also they will acquit and pay the appointment to the church during the term. Sealed in testimony by Sir Thomas. At Ipswich, Monday next after the feast of St Peter *ad vincula*, 1327.   2 August 1327

TNA, E40/3556. 237 × 76mm maximum, indented at top with CYROGRAPHUM. Tongue at bottom, folded into a double thickness, 4mm fold. Fragment of seal, apparently monogram H. Endorsed: (*illegible*) de ecclesia sancti Nicholai (16c.).

IPSWICH, ST PETER

509. Indenture whereby Prior John of Monewden (*Moneweden*') and the canons, by unanimous consent of their chapter, have conceded to Margery Hakoun a chamber with a curtilage annexed thereto, built with other chambers under one roof, upon the causeway on the south side of the priory, the chamber being next to the cemetery of St Peter's church, beside a chamber in which Matilda Plomezer presently dwells; to be held for the whole of Margery's life, rendering annually to the prior and canons and their successors 3s in equal portions at the feasts of Easter and St Michael; on condition that should the rent be partly or wholly in arrears at any term, then it may be lawful for the prior and canons and their successors to distrain, and remove the things distrained and retain them until they are fully satisfied concerning all arrears; and also for default in payment for half a year after any term, to re-enter and repossess the same chamber and curtilage and hold them peaceably, notwithstanding the present indenture. The prior and canons and their successors shall well and sufficiently maintain the chamber for the whole of Margery's life. In testimony whereof the parties have sealed each other's copy of this indenture. At Ipswich, Monday next after the feast of St John before the Latin Gate, 7 Henry IV.   10 May 1406

TNA, E40/3921. 278 × 84mm, 18mm turnup, 125mm tag. Seal in red wax, 25mm round, much abraded; design shows a shield in a round cusped setting; legend lost. Endorsed: Margeria iii s' super calcetu' (15c.); in parochial [*sic*] sancti Petri (?16c.).

NACTON

510. Certified copy of indenture whereby Prior Thomas Goodwin and the convent have leased to William Mancer and Thomas Mancer his son and their assigns, their tenement with all the lands, pastures and appurtenances, parcel of 'Hundredlande', lately Denis Cole's and before that William Cole's, and the cottage, curtilage and croft annexed, parcel of 'Hundredlande', lately Denis's and formerly Simon Busdon's, in Nacton; to have and to hold to them and their assigns from the next feast of the Purification of the Blessed Virgin Mary for the full term of ninety-nine years, rendering annually to the prior and convent and their successors 13s 4d of legal money of England in equal instalments at Easter and the feast of St Michael. William, Thomas and their assigns are not to cut timber, except for carrying out repairs. If it should happen that the rent should be in arrears, either in whole or in part, by one month after any feast, the prior and convent or their successors may distrain, and retain those things distrained until full satisfaction is made for both rent and arrears. If the rent should be in arrears, either in whole or in part, by one year after any feast, the prior and convent or their successors may re-enter the property in its original estate, notwithstanding the present indenture. In witness whereof the parties have sealed each other's copy of the indenture. Given in the chapter house, 8 July 17 Henry VII.   8 July 1502

SROI, HA 93/3/52. Sixteenth-century copy. 880 × 150mm, including opened-out turnup 20mm. No seal, tag or slits. Inscribed on face: vera copia indentur' Thome Manc' exaiat' J. Smthe (16c.). Endorsed: At Candelmas in Anno Dni 1565 there was expired of [*illegible*] lease lxiii and there remayned [*illegible*] yeres qd [*illegible*] (16c.). 17 H. 7. Tho' Goodwyn Prior of St Peter's Convt Ipsh Nacton (18c.). 136. 31 July 17 Hen. VII (19c.). Copy lease from the Prior of St Peters Ipswich to Wm Manc' (19c.).

SPROUGHTON

511. Indenture whereby Prior William and the canons have leased to William Andreu of Sproughton (*Sproithone*) all their lands and tenements which Richard of 'Borwardiflech' lately held of them in Sproughton; to have [?*and to hold*] to William and his assigns from the feast of St Michael in the twenty [*missing*] year of King Edward III for a full term of two years, rendering annually four marks of silver in equal instalments at the Lord's Nativity and Pentecost, and performing for the prior and canons to the capital lords of the fee the due and accustomed services, and also paying the king's taxes [*missing*] common or all other charges for the said term. William and his assigns are to keep all the lands and tenements in good [?*repair missing*] during the term, without waste or devastation. Warranty is granted by the prior and canons and their successors against all people until the end of the two years, and at the end of the term William [*missing*] is to hold fifteen acres of the warranted land for his expenses, and nothing [*missing*] year. Also the prior and canons grant free right of entry and exit to and from the lands and tenements, and the right to pursue and take his own [*beasts*] without distraint or impediment until the Easter following the end of the term. All of which William binds himself and his executors by these presents faithfully to perform and observe. In testimony whereof the parties have sealed each other's copy of this indenture. At Ipswich on the day of the Exaltation of the Holy Cross in the year abovesaid.

[14 September [between 1349 and 1355]]

TNA, E40/3937. Poor condition; words missing at damaged left and right edges; badly scuffed and faded; parts only legible under ultra-violet light. 309 × 132mm, top indented and measured to top of indentation, the latter dimension including a turnup of 11mm which has been folded out; slits for one tag, which is lost. Endorsed: Sprouton (15c.).

Date: Part of the regnal year is missing, but the date must be 14 September in a year between 1349 (in which William of Ipswich succeeded Clement of Ipswich as prior) and 1355 (the 29th year of Edward III).

THURLESTON

512. Notification by Prior Gilbert and the convent that they have demised from year to year, for as long as they please, to William the chaplain of Thurleston, a messuage with buildings in Thurleston which lies between the cemetery of Thurleston church and a messuage of Robert Dwelle, for 2s of sterlings *per annum*. William is to repair any damage which may occur. [?1230s – 1248]

TNA, E40/3413. Text rubbed and faded, and some words illegible. 117 × 94mm maximum, indented at top with part of CYROGRAPHUM visible, 15mm turnup, 100mm tag, seal missing. Endorsed: Thorleston (17c.).

Omnibus Christi fidelibus hoc presens scriptum visuris vel audituris, Gilbertus prior et conventus Sancti Petri de Gipewico salutem in Domino. Noveritis nos dimisisse ab anno in annum quamdiu nobis placuerit Willelmo capellano de Thurlestun' unum mesuagium cum edificiis et cum omnibus pertinentiis in villa de Thurlestun', scilicet illud mesuagium quod iacet inter cimiterium ecclesie de Thurlestun' et quoddam mesuagium Roberti Dwelle. Reddendo inde annuatim nobis quamdiu predictum mesuagium tenuerit duos solidos sterlingorum. Et si ita contigerit quod predictum mesuagium cum edeficiis et pertinentiis dum in custodia sua fuerit aliquo modo [*illegible*], dictus Willelmus capellanus secundum quod custum' fuerit expensis suis propriis emendabit et in [?*dicto*] statu reservabit. Et ad hoc firmiter tenend' sine aliqua contradictione fide [*illegible*] se obligavit, et ad maiorem securitatem [*illegible*] predictus prior et predictus Willelmus capellanus presentibus scriptis cirografatis sigilla nostra apposuimus. Hiis testibus: Willelmo de Holebroc, Galfrido de Bercham, Baldewino de Pesehal, Ada' filio de sen', Willelmo de Aula, Roberto de Ri, Alano fratre suo, Galfrido Carbunel, Hugone Puppin, et aliis.

Date: Prior Gilbert was elected in 1225, and the licence to elect his successor was issued on 23 May 1248. Baldwin of Peasenhall attests in the 1230s (no. 458) and at least up to 23 April 1270 (no. 520). Robert Dwelle, or Duelle, occurs in the 1230s (no. 216) and at least to 1267 (no. 496), and is not likely to have been an adult much before 1230.

513. Indenture recording that Prior Henry and the canons have granted and demised to William of Holewey of Thurleston and Hugh his son, a piece of pasture called 'Lymmedwe' which they lately purchased of Margaret dil Walle in Thurleston, to have and to hold of the canons and their successors to William and Hugh for the term of both their lives; rendering annually to the canons and their successors 5s of silver, namely 2s 6d at the feasts of Easter and the Exaltation of the Holy Cross,[1] for all services. Warranty by the lessors against all people, for the lives of William and Hugh. After their decease, the pasture is to revert to the canons and their successors. In testimony whereof the parties have sealed each other's copy of the indenture, the prior and canons with their seal *ad causas*.

Hiis testibus: Roberto Martyn, Philippo Iustous, Willelmo le Ry, Normanno le Ry, Willelmo dil Wode, et aliis. At Thurleston, Sunday next after the feast of All Saints, 4 Edward III. 4 November 1330

TNA, E40/3650. 247 × 95mm, 18mm turnup, 92mm tag, part of CYROGRAFUM visible between indents. Seal fragment (priory seal *ad causas*) 30 × 20mm, badly damaged. Endorsed: [*two illegible words*] Lymedu (?15c.).

1 14 September.

514. Counterpart[1] of 513.   4 November 1330

TNA, E40/3651. 247 × 118mm, 21mm turnup, 97mm tags, part of CYROGRAFUM visible between indents. Seal at left 24mm round with very crude image of a horseman. Seal on right is a cross within a border, legend illegible. Endorsed: Thurleston ad [*one illegible word*] (15c.); Limedwe par' Thurleston (15/16c.).

1 The witnesses' names are given in a slightly different order than in no. 513: in no. 514 William le Ry follows William dil Wode and is the last-named.

515. Agreement (*convenit*) made on Monday next after the feast of St Michael, 34 Edward III, between the prior and canons on the one part and John Frett of Thurleston on the other, whereby the prior and canons have granted and leased at farm to John, a messuage with an adjoining croft, which messuage was formerly Richard le Webber's, and a pasture called 'le Lymmedwe',[1] to have and to hold to John, Christina his wife and John's heirs and assigns, of the prior and canons and their successors, from the same feast of St Michael for a term of one hundred years; rendering annually to the prior and canons and their successors 5s of silver, namely 15d at the feasts of St Andrew, Easter, the Nativity of St John the Baptist and St Michael, and paying suit of the prior's court every three weeks. If the farm happen to be in arrear at the terms, either partly or wholly, the prior and canons and their successors may distrain upon the tenements and the goods and chattels found thereon, and may retain those things distrained until full satisfaction shall be made concerning the farm and arrears. In testimony whereof the parties have sealed each other's copy of this indenture.

Hiis testibus: Willelmo de Pyntun', capellano, Philippo Iustus, Willelmo le Smyth, Willelmo Bele, Willelmo le Holdere et aliis. At Thurleston'.

5 October 1360

TNA, E40/3649. 247 × 173mm maximum, 31mm turnup; chirograph, indented at top margin, parts of CYROGRAFUM visible between the indents. Left tag 90mm, right tag 119mm, both seals missing. Endorsed: Limedw in Thurliston (15c.).

1 In Thurleston: see endorsement and nos. 513 and 514.

WHERSTEAD

516. Indenture whereby Prior Henry and the canons have granted and leased at fee farm to Richard de le Walle of Wherstead (*Wherstede*) for the term of his life, a curtilage which was formerly Robert Alisoun's, extending east upon the lane called 'Welle Lane' at one headland, the other headland abutting west on the land of the prior and canons; to have and to hold for the term of his life, rendering annually 20d at four terms, namely the feasts of St Michael, St Andrew, Easter and the

Nativity of St John the Baptist, in equal instalments, for all exactions and secular demands. In case of default in payment at any term, the prior and canons and their successors by their bailiffs may distrain on all Richard's goods and chattels, moveable and immoveable, and retain those things distrained until the arrears are fully paid. Warranty by the lessors for the term of Richard's life. In testimony whereof the parties have sealed each other's copy of this indenture.

Hiis testibus: Nicholao Bonde, Iohanne Ryngild, Roberto de Reymes, Rogero Reyner, Roberto Koket et aliis. At Wherstead, Sunday next after the feast of the Annunciation, 6 Edward III.   29 March 1332

JRL, CRU 756. 183 × 159mm to top of indentations, parts of CYROGRAFUM visible between indents, turnup 23mm, tag 107mm. Seal 19 × 23mm, red wax, design of a male head in profile, legend lost. Endorsed: Ad terminum vite Ricard' de le Welle de Werstede (14c.); Wersted (15c.); Wersted (16c.).

Exchanges and Other Agreements

GREAT BELSTEAD ETC.

517. Notification by the abbot and convent of Aumale (*Albemarlie*) that they have granted and given licence, for themselves and their successors, to the prior and canons of St Peter's to acquire all those tenements which were Laurence le Fre's in the townships of Great Belstead (*Belsted Magna*), Little Belstead (*Belstead Parva*), Chattisham (*Chatisham*), Sproughton (*Sproutone*), Copdock (*Copedock'*) and Washbrook (*Wassebrock'*), which are held of the grantors as of their manor of Belstead in Samford (*Sannfford*) hundred; to hold to them and their successors in perpetuity notwithstanding the Statute of Mortmain, performing annually in respect thereof to the abbot and convent and their successors all the services by right due and accustomed, namely 25s of silver at the four usual terms of the year in equal instalments, and also paying to them and their successors at the election of each new prior of St Peter's 25s of silver as a relief, for all services, customs, exactions, suits of court and secular demands. In testimony whereof the parties have sealed each other's copy of this indenture. At Great Belstead, Monday next before the feast of the Nativity of the Blessed Mary, A.D. 1332.   7 September 1332

TNA, E40/3428. 258 × 137mm maximum, 22mm turnup, 140mm tag. Part of CYROGRAPHUM visible at indented top edge. Fragment of vesica seal, brown wax, 35 × 52mm, showing a figure holding a book, head missing, on cross-hatched background; legend lost. Endorsed: abbas de Albemarle; Wasborke [*sic*] (both 16/17c.).

518. Indenture whereby, since the prior of St Peter's has purchased, to himself and his successors in perpetuity, from Thomas of Rougham, all the lands and tenements which Laurence le Free held of the abbot of Aumale in Great Belstead (*Magna Belstede*), as of the abbot's manor in the same township, the abbot has granted, for himself and his successors, that the prior and his successors may hold all the lands and tenements of the abbot and his successors by fealty and the service of 25s *per annum* for all service and exaction pertaining to the abbot and his successors in respect thereof, just as of him himself who is capital lord of the fee of the tenement, notwithstanding the suit of the prior against the form of the statute provided in respect thereof. For that agreement made between the abbot and the prior, the prior has granted, for himself and his successors in perpetuity, to be bound to the abbot and his successors in 25s in the name of a relief due from the tenement to the abbot and his successors, to be rendered within fifteen days next following the death, cession, or deposition of any prior of the said house; and that it shall be lawful for any abbot and his successors in perpetuity, for the aforesaid 25s due in the said form, to enter into all the lands and tenements and to distrain upon whomsoever it is into whose hands the tenements shall have come, and to retain those things distrained until the abbot and his successors shall be fully satisfied concerning the said 25s. In testimony whereof the parties have sealed each other's copy of this indenture with their respective common seals. At Great Belstead, Monday next before the feast of the Nativity of the Blessed Mary, A.D. 1332.   7 September 1332

TNA, E40/3429. 248 × 172mm maximum, 20mm turnup, 112mm tag, part of CYROGRAFUM visible. Seal fragment 40mm round, showing upper body and head of a churchman in vestments, facing outwards; abraded, brown wax. Endorsed: H. de Kersey xli pro fine (14c.); abbas de Albemarlia (16c.).

519. Agreement (*convenit*) dated Tuesday the feast of St Edmund, King and Martyr, 15 Edward III, between the prior and canons on the one part and Thomas of Langton' on the other, namely that the prior and canons by unanimous assent have granted and demised at fee-farm to Thomas a piece of their land in Great Belstead (*Belsted Magna*), that is, between the highway on the west and the land pertaining to the abbot and convent of Aumale (*Aumarle*) on the east, one headland abutting south on the messuage formerly of le ?Tereche, and the other abutting north on the lands formerly of Thomas Tedery; to have and to hold to Thomas, his heirs and assigns in perpetuity at fee farm, of the prior and canons and their successors, rendering annually to them at farm 6s of silver in equal instalments at the feasts of Easter, the Nativity of St John the Baptist and St Michael. However, as often soever or whenever the rent or any part of it in any year at any term shall happen to be in arrears, the prior and convent and their successors and attorneys may distrain and retain those things distrained until they are fully satisfied concerning all the arrears. In exchange, Thomas has granted and demised at fee-farm to the prior and canons a piece of land in Great Belstead, that is, between the wood and land of Alexander of Freston on one side and the land of Peter Seman on the other, both headlands abutting on the land of the prior and canons; to have and to hold to the prior and canons and their successors, in exchange at fee-farm, performing to the capital lords of the fee the services by right pertaining to that land, and rendering annually at farm to Thomas, his heirs and assigns, one red rose on the feast of the Nativity of St John the Baptist in perpetuity. If it happen that Margaret, now wife of Thomas, survives him and brings a plea against the prior and canons or their successors for her dower in the piece of land a short time ago in Thomas's hands, then the prior and canons and their successors may repossess the piece of land granted by them to Thomas in exchange, until Margaret in her widowhood releases to them all her right in perpetuity by her deed. Warranty is granted by each party regarding the lands exchanged, against all people. In testimony whereof the parties have sealed each other's copy of this indenture.

Hiis testibus: Iohanne Haltebe, Nicholao Bonde, Rogero de Godelesford, Iohanne Norman iuniore, Iohanne le Vineter et aliis. At Ipswich.   20 November 1341

TNA, E40/3745. 260 × 195mm, 10mm turnup, 88mm tag. Seal in red-brown wax, showing ?a figure on horseback; legend cannot be made out. Three endorsements, all rubbed and illegible.

BROOKS

520. Agreement (*hec est conventio*) made on St George's Day, 54 Henry III, between the prior and convent on the one part and William of Thornhegg' on the other, that whereas by a feoffment and charters made between the parties William is bound and charged with the payment of 3s annual rent to the prior and convent and their successors, and to Agatha the widow of John Costin for 6s *per annum* for a piece of meadow which she sometime held of them and paid them in full chapter in the presence of upright men of good faith, and to Alan le Schocher for a certain floor (*area*) next to William's messuage, together with the adjoining messuage which Alan holds for life, in one seam of rye *per annum*, and for the finding for the same Alan for life pasture for one cow, as is more fully contained in the charter of feoffment made concerning these things between the prior and convent and William: the prior and convent have remised and quitclaimed, for them and their successors, to William and his heirs, 12d out of the 3s annual rent for as long as Alan and Agatha shall live; that is to say that while they live, William and his heirs shall be quit every year against the prior and convent and their successors of 2s [*sic*], half at Easter and half at the feast of St Michael; and after the death of either Alan or Agatha, William and his heirs shall pay to the prior and convent 30d in all. And after the death of both of them, William and his heirs are to pay to the prior and convent 3s *per annum*, half at Easter and half at the feast of St Michael, for all the lands and tenements which he held of them in Brooks on St George's Day in the above year, and also for the messuage which Alan holds of William for life. After the death of Alan and Agatha, William and his heirs shall be quit against the prior and convent and their successors by the said service of 3s *per annum*, for all service, suits of court, secular exaction and demand, for all the lands and tenements which William held in Brooks of the prior and convent on the day and in the year abovesaid, in perpetuity. For this grant and confirmation, William and his heirs shall successively pay homage to the prior and convent and their successors in perpetuity. In testimony whereof the parties have sealed each other's copy of the chirograph.

Hiis testibus: Domino Galfrido de Badele, Domino Iohanne de Luvetot, Baldewyno de Pesehal', Roberto de Cleydon', Laurentio Rodlond, Mansero de Bordeshowe,

Roberto de Crakeford, Roberto de Orford, Ricardo Fader, Iohanne Clement et
multis aliis.   23 April 1270

TNA, E40/3773. 257 × 124mm, 21mm turnup, 115mm tag. Seal of natural wax, 26mm
diameter in a blob of wax 35mm round. Legend: + S' WILL'I DE THORNHEGGE.
Endorsed: Brok'; Thornheg (both 16c.).

521. Inspeximus and confirmation (*cartam ... inspexisse in hec verba*) by Muriella de
Luveyn of William of Thornhegg's grant by way of exchange to the canons. William
has granted in free alms to the canons, a piece of land in Brooks (*Brokes*) which
lies between the canons' land on the east and the land of Baldwin of Peasenhall
(*Pesehale*) on the west, and abuts on Baldwin's garden on one side and on the land
of John Ade of Thurleston on the other; one part of the said land lying between the
canons' land on the north and Baldwin's pasture on the other side, abutting east
on Baldwin's land; to hold and to have of William and his heirs to them and their
successors freely, quietly, well and in peace in perpetuity, for 1d annual rent at the
feast of St Michael for all secular demands. In exchange the prior and convent have
given to William a piece of land in Brooks which they used to hold by feoffment
of Agatha the widow of John Costin, of which one headland abuts on the highway
of 'Wyvelesdone' and the other on 'Aldegate Weye'; and a messuage which Alan
called Schocher held of them for life; and a meadow which Agatha held of them
and has resigned to them; to hold to William and his heirs by the service of 12d
annual rent payable at the feast of St Michael and Easter. Warranty by the grantor
against all people in perpetuity. William also quitclaims all right and claim against
the prior and convent and their successors in lands or rents wheresoever they
may be. Sealed in testimony on 23 April 1270. Muriella confirms in perpetuity all
the aforesaid gifts, concessions and confirmations as more fully contained in the
charter of feoffment in respect thereof. Sealed in testimony.

Hiis testibus: Domino Galfrido de Badel', Domino Iohanne de Luvetot, Baldewyno
de Pesehal', Roberto de Crakeford, Roberto de Cleydon', Laurentio Rodlond,
Mansero de Bordeshowe, Ricardo Fader, Roberto de Orford, Iohanne Clement,
Iohanne Martin, Willelmo de Burstall', Roberto de Bordeshowe, et multis aliis.

[23 April 1270]

TNA, E40/3735. 219 × 123mm, 9mm turnup, 120mm tag. Writing on inner side of
tag: *upper side*: Sciant presentes et futuri quod nos prior ... et heredibus suis unam
peciam prati nostri ...; *lower side*: ... a confirmavimus Will'mo de Thornhegg' ...
et pasturam domini Galfridi de Badel' ex parte ... . Endorsed: Thornhegg; Brok;
Broke (various hands, 16/17c.).

Date: Contemporary with William's grant here confirmed, and with his agreement
of the same date with the prior and convent (no. 520).

522. Agreement (*ita convenit*) made on Friday the feast of St Luke the Evangelist,
25 Edward I, between the prior and convent on the one part and Adam of Holbrook
(*Holebrok*) of Ipswich (*Gyp'*) and Alice his wife on the other. The parties have
exchanged two pieces of their land, of which that piece granted by the religious
lies between the lands of John son of John Laur' on either side in the hamlet of

Brooks (*Brokes*), one headland abutting on the highway from Ipswich to Bramford bridge, and the other abutting on 'Brademere'; and that piece granted by Adam and Alice lies similarly in Brooks, of the land which was sometime W'lfric of Brademere's which he held of the religious, of which the eastern headland abuts upon 'Brademere' and the western headland abuts against Bramford; to have and to hold the said pieces of land to the said parties for the whole of Alice's lifetime; after her decease, that piece granted to the religious is to revert to John her son and the heir of John Laur' or his heirs or assigns, and that piece granted to Adam and Alice is to revert to the religious; saving to both parties the fruits being in the same, sown by the same parties, at the time of Alice's death. Warranty is granted against all people for the whole of Alice's lifetime. In testimony whereof the parties have sealed each other's copy of the chirograph.   18 October 1297

TNA, E40/3683. 185 × 80mm, 11mm turnup. Left tag 56mm, seal 28 × 20mm, pointed oval, enthroned figure under a canopy, with praying figure in niche beneath. Right tag 54mm, seal 27 × 21mm, … IE LAVI … legible. Endorsed: Excamb' in Brok (16c.).

IPSWICH, ST AUGUSTINE IN STOKE

523. Agreement (*ita convenit*) made on St Ambrose's day in April, 23 Edward I, between Prior J[ohn of St Nicholas] and the convent on the one part and William of Holton (*Holeton'*), shepherd and Matilda his wife, their tenants in Stoke in the suburb of Ipswich (*Gypewici*) on the other. Whereas William and Matilda had and held one messuage and one piece of arable land of the prior and convent's fee by the annual service of 12d, three hens and one cock, one day's work in autumn and suit of court, and it seemed to them that this service for a tenement of such a size was unjustly onerous, William and Matilda in the full court of the prior and convent on 6 April (*octavo Idus Aprilis*)[1] surrendered into the hands of the prior and convent one piece of their land which they held of them, lying between their heath at Brooks (*Brokes*) and the messuage of William and Matilda, of which the southern headland abuts upon the highway which leads from the west gate of the town of Ipswich towards 'Wyvelesdune', and quitclaimed it for them and their heirs to the prior and convent, so that from henceforth in perpetuity they could have no right or claim in the said piece of land. For this reason the prior and convent have remitted to them in perpetuity that service of one day's work for which they were bound annually in autumn. In testimony the prior and convent and William and Matilda have sealed each other's copy of this writing made in the manner of a chirograph.

Hiis testibus: Viviano filio Silvestri et Laurentio Horold tunc ballivis de Gypewico, Iohanne de la Dale, Willelmo Suyllard, Thoma del Hel, Willelmo del Wente, Roberto Eustace, Willelmo Nicole de Gretingham, Iohanne Suyllard, Iohanne de Stok' clerico.   4 April 1295

TNA, E40/3533. 187 × 102mm maximum, indented at top edge, 15mm turnup, 80mm tag. Vesica seal, 50 × 37mm; legend: + SIGILL' … PETRI. Two saints, in an architectural setting. No endorsements, but backed with modern parchment, so perhaps hidden.

1 The dates given show that the agreement was made two days before the quitclaim.

524. Indenture between Prior Clement of the church of St Peter on the one part and Christian Merihel of Ipswich (*Gyppeswys*) on the other, to the effect that whereas Christian is bound and obliged to the prior and his successors for an annual rent of 20s in sterlings, to be paid from year to year at the feasts of St Michael and Easter in equal instalments, out of a piece of enclosed land, a barn, and a chamber built upon the piece of land, in the suburb of Ipswich in the parish of St Augustine (*Austyn*) in Stoke: Prior Clement has granted, for him and his successors, that if Christian, her heirs and assigns, or anyone in their name, pay or cause to be paid, £3 in the church of St Peter in the town of Ipswich, on the [*illegible*] feast of St Michael next after the date of the indenture in equal instalments, then the 20s annuity in St Augustine's shall be void, but otherwise shall remain in force. At Ipswich, Monday next after the feast of St Valentine, 23 Edward III.   16 February 1349

TNA, E40/3406. Anglo-Norman French. Rubbed, faded and discoloured; some words illegible. 239 × 102mm maximum, indented at top edge with part of CYROGRAPHUM visible between the indentations, 22mm turnup, 97mm tag. Writing is visible inside the ends of the tag:

At one side:	At the other side:
et hugild de	icnia est
fuit post mortem	pres? et c
omnium terrarum	et Rob'ti de W

Seal 24mm round, square visible in middle, but much lost. Endorsed: Et le dyt de Thom' del Scon' (14c.); par' sancti Petri[1] (17c.).

  1 The endorsement for the parish of St Peter is correct. By this time the medieval parish of St Augustine had long been absorbed into that of St Peter, of which it formed a detached portion on the other side of the river.

525. Indenture between the prior and convent on the one hand and John Pypho of Ipswich (*Gippewici*), fuller, on the other, whereby John has given, granted, and by his charter confirmed, to Gilbert Debenham, William Bury, Thomas Denys, Edmund Wynter and William Wynter, a piece of land in the parish of St Augustine of the same town, between the land of the prior and convent and the highway, as more fully contained in a charter made in respect thereof; the prior and convent have similarly granted and by this indenture confirmed to John Pypho and Juliana his wife for the said piece of land, three bushels of corn, to be paid annually to John and Juliana and to whichever of them lives the longer, for the whole term of their lives, at the feast of the Lord's Nativity. In testimony whereof the parties have sealed each other's copy of this indenture. At Ipswich, 20 November 38 Henry VI.
                    20 November 1459

TNA, E40/3717. 286mm wide, full height 105mm, 100mm without the wrapping tie, 85mm without the stub of the tongue. Seal missing. Endorsed: par' sancti Augustini (16c.).

IPSWICH, GREENWICH

526. Indenture between Prior John York on the one part and Richard Felawe of Ipswich (*Gippewico*) on the other, agreeing that, whereas the prior and convent had and held to themselves and their successors in right of their church a close in the hamlet of Greenwich (*Grenewych*) next Ipswich, and Richard had and held to himself and his heirs another close in the said hamlet abutting east on the prior's close, the two closes lying together between a certain way called 'le Woodweye' on the south and a stream called 'Grenewichbrook' on the north, and the prior's close abutting east on the heath and Richard's close abutting west on 'Grenewich Grene' and upon a way leading from Greenwich towards Alnesbourn; and whereas various differences, discords and prosecutions have arisen between the parties because the prior laid claim to certain pieces of land in Richard's close, and Richard laid claim to various pieces of land in the prior's close, and the boundaries of the parcels are not known, nor is any final concord between them known; after mediation and advice, the prior and convent are to have, hold and possess to themselves and their successors their close entire, with all the pieces therein as enclosed with hedges and ditches, and Richard is to have, hold and possess to himself and his heirs his close entire, with all the pieces therein as similarly enclosed, as if in exchange. In testimony whereof the parties have sealed these indentures. 16 January 18 Edward IV.   16 January 1479

SROI, HA 93/2/159. 313 × 185mm maximum, 20mm turnup, slit for tag, but seal and tag missing; top edge indented, part of CYROGRAFUM visible between indentations. Endorsed: 119. 18 Ed. 4. 16th Jany. John York Prior of the Ch. of St Peters Ips. to Rich. Felawe. Land in the hamlet of Greenwich nr Ips. (19c.).

IPSWICH, ST NICHOLAS

527. Agreement (*ita convenit*) by indenture made 5 Id. April 1296 between Prior J[ohn of St Nicholas] and the convent on the one part and Laurence Horold of Ipswich (*Gypewico*) on the other, whereby Laurence has granted, given and by his charter confirmed to the religious 2s annual rent in exchange for another 2s annual rent which the religious have granted and given and by their charter confirmed to Laurence, namely that Laurence and his heirs or assigns may take 2s annually from a certain tenement which was formerly Jordan the Carter's in the parish of St Nicholas, Ipswich, which the religious used to take annually from that tenement. Laurence, for him and his heirs, has granted, given, assigned and by his charter confirmed to the religious and their successors in perpetuity, to be taken from a certain messuage formerly Simon Beneroche's opposite the gaol of Ipswich, 2s annual rent from whomsoever shall hold the messuage in future, which is of the fee of the religious, whence they were accustomed to take 3s annual rent, on condition that from henceforth they take from the hands of the possessor of the same, 5s, 15d at the feasts of St Michael, the Nativity, Easter and the Nativity of St John the Baptist. It shall be lawful for the religious to distrain on the tenement for rent arrears as often as it shall seem expedient, just as the capital lords of that tenement, without challenge or objection of anyone. Both the religious and their successors and Laurence and his heirs will alternately warrant the rent thus exchanged against all men in perpetuity. In testimony, both parties have sealed each other's copy of this indenture.

Hiis testibus: Thoma Stace et Thoma le Mayster tunc ballivis de Gypewico, Philippo Harneys, Iohanne filio suo, Thoma Aylred, Hugone Horold, Roberto Davy, Arnaldo le Skinnere, Ricardo Godescalk', Iohanne fratre suo, Ada de Holebrok', Iohanne de Stok' clerico, et aliis.   9 April 1296

TNA, E40/3527. 175 × 53mm maximum, indented at top with part of CYROGRAFUM visible between indentations, 16mm turnup, 80mm tag. Heart-shaped seal, 26 × 31mm, with device of two birds either side of a flower on a stem; legend gone. Endorsed: par' sancti Nicolai (17c.).

528. Agreement (*ita convenit*) made on Monday the feast of St Matthias the Apostle, 13 Edward II, between the prior and convent on the one part and Thomas Stace of Ipswich (*Gippewyco*) on the other, that whereas Thomas, who holds of the prior and convent a messuage formerly Roger le Neve's in the parish of St Nicholas, Ipswich, between the messuage of Walter Stampard on the north and the messuage formerly of William le Perchemyner on the south, paying annually to them 9d at the usual terms of the year, and at the feast of the Nativity one cock and one hen, for which service of a cock and hen at the Nativity Thomas, his heirs and assigns, ought to receive at the cellar door of the priory one white conventual loaf of the greater weight and one gallon of conventual beer, and at the kitchen door one dish of conventual meat: the prior and convent, for them and their successors, have granted, remitted and quitclaimed in perpetuity to Thomas, his heirs and assigns, all right and claim which they had, have, or in any manner could have in the service of the cock and hen; and Thomas on his part has granted, remitted and quitclaimed, for him, his heirs and assigns in perpetuity, to the prior and convent and all their successors, all right or claim which he has or had or in any manner could have in the annual profit of bread, beer and kitchen dish as aforesaid. In testimony whereof the parties have sealed each other's copy of this indenture. At Ipswich.

25 February 1320

TNA, E40/3751. 258 × 128mm maximum, indented top edge, with part of CYROGRAFUM legible between indentations, 18mm turnup, 96mm tag. Seal 30 × 25mm. The device appears to be a cup and cover, legend unclear. Endorsed: paroch' Nich'i (15c.); T. Stace (15c.); pro parte tenementi Walt'i Stan … (?15c.).

IPSWICH, ST PETER

529. Acknowledgement by Vivian son of Silvester Wakelin that he is bound to pay to the church of SS Peter and Paul and the canons, 12d *per annum* in two annual instalments, 6d at the feast of St Michael and 6d at Easter, for a messuage which Seman of the Cross (*de Cruce*) sometime held of Vivian's father Silvester in the parish of St Peter, Ipswich (*Gypewico*), namely that messuage which Vivian's grandfather Wakelin held of the church, as his charter attests. Because the service due to them in respect thereof has not been paid to them for some time, as it should have been, the prior and convent, for the sake of peace, have remitted both part of the service and the arrears; so that from henceforth in perpetuity the said 12d annual rent may be paid to them without any annoyance; whereupon Vivian has granted, for him and his heirs, that the prior and convent or their attorney may freely distrain upon the messuage for the rent without force or objection until full payment and satisfaction have been made. Sealed in testimony.

Hiis testibus: Matheo de Porta, Roberto de Orford tunc ballivis de Gypewico, Roberto Wlfun, Ricardo Fader, Hugone Liu, Semanno Tophole, Iohanne Clement, Galfrido Horold, Roberto de Dinheweton, Hugone Golding, et aliis.

[1250s – 1279]

TNA, E40/3548. 128 × 158mm, 18mm turnup, 110mm tag. Seal 26mm round, legend + … II SILVESTRIS. Device a sunburst. Endorsed: paroch' Petri (16c.); xii d' (16/17c.).

Date: Vivian son of Silvester is present at the inquiry into the status of St Clement's church, Ipswich on 24 October 1251 (no. 315). He served as bailiff in 1270–71 and again at intervals until 1295. Matthew de Porta is first known to have served as bailiff (with Hugh Leu) in 1255–56. He was bailiff for the last time in 1278–79, making 1279 the terminal date for this charter. Robert of Orford served as bailiff in 1271–72, and again at intervals until 1282 (the date of his joint service with Matthew de Porta is unknown).

RAYDON

530. Notification that, whereas lately matter of contention has been stirred up between the prior and convent of St Peter of Ipswich (*Gipewico*) of the order of St Augustine and the prior and convent of St Botulph of Colchester (*Colecestria*) of the same order, concerning the annual rent of 20d, three hens and one cock which the prior and convent of Ipswich exacted from the prior and convent of St Botulph for a tenement of about 4½ acres which Osbert Mori sometime held in the township of Raydon (*Reydone*), the priors and some of the brothers of both places and some other common friends came together in the parish church of Raydon on Friday next before the feast of the Nativity of the Blessed Mary, A.D. 1298 and in the 26th year of the reign of King Edward, and resolved the contention between the parties in this manner: that the prior of St Peter, for himself, his convent and their successors and his monastery, has granted the said tenement to the prior of St Botulph, his convent, their successors and his monastery, to have and to hold freely, quietly and peacefully, paying to them annually 2s in two equal instalments at Easter and the feast of St Michael for all services and demands; and the prior of St Botulph has bound himself, his convent, their successors and monastery for the annual payment of the same 2s in the form above-written, binding himself and his successors and the tenement for distraint by the prior and convent of St Peter and their attorney if henceforth at any term or in perpetuity they default in payment.

In testimony whereof the parties have sealed each other's copy of this chirograph with the common seals of their chapters.   5 September 1298

TNA, E42/408. 244 × 115mm to top of indentations, 16mm turnup, 100mm tag. Parts of CYROGRAPHUM visible across the indentations. Seal: a vesica, 43 × 65mm, brown wax, enthroned Christ in centre, figure with mitre and staff at left, figure with staff at right; legend: SIGILL' ECCLESIE SA ... ... OTULFI DE COLECESTR'. Endorsed: Reydon' iis' de priori sancti Botulph (14c.); de priore sancti Botulphi (16c.).

SPROUGHTON

531. Agreement (*convenit*) for exchange, A.D. 1271, between the prior and convent on the one part and William, son of Osbert of Sproughton (*Sproutone*) on the other, namely that the prior and convent have granted and demised to William and his heirs two pieces of land in Sproughton, whereof one lies between the land of the prior and convent and William's land, one headland abutting on the highway extending to Ipswich (*Gypeswicum*), the other abutting towards the south on William's land; and the other piece lies between William's land and the land of the prior and convent, one headland abutting towards the east on William's land, the other abutting towards the west on the land of the prior and convent; to hold and to have to William and his heirs, freely and quit of all secular service in perpetuity. For this demise, William has given to the prior and convent in exchange one piece of land in Sproughton, between his land and the messuage of Seihiva of 'Stanbregge', one headland abutting on the highway extending to Ipswich and containing in width at that headland 21 feet, the other abutting towards the south on the land of the prior and convent and containing in width at that headland 28 feet; to hold and to have to the prior and convent and their successors in free, pure and perpetual alms in perpetuity. In testimony whereof the parties have sealed each other's copy of this chirograph.

Hiis testibus: Domino Nicholao de Hasting', Rogero Warin, Symone Vinetario, Willelmo de Northwude, Roberto Andreu, Mansero de Bordeshoh', Roberto de Coppedhoc, Oseberto Godefrei, Warino Coket, et aliis.   1271

TNA, E40/3463. 200 × 125mm maximum, to top of indentations, 12mm turnup, 90mm tag, seal missing. Part of CYROGRAPHUM visible. Endorsed: Sprouton (17c.).

532. Agreement (*conventio*) by way of exchange between Prior J[ohn of St Nicholas] and the convent on the one part and John le Ger and Christina his wife on the other, on St Michael's day 19 Edward I, namely that John and Christina have given, granted and confirmed to the prior and convent and their successors in perpetuity a piece of land 1½ roods by reckoning, lying in Sproughton (*Sprouton'*), lengthwise next to the alder grove of the prior and convent, with one headland abutting on it, in exchange for a piece of land similarly lying in Sproughton between the land of the prior and convent and the land of John and Christina, which is of equal proportion and measurement, which the prior and convent have given, granted and confirmed to John and Christina and their heirs and assigns in perpetuity; so that each party by the tenor of the present writing will warrant the other's land in perpetuity. In testimony whereof the parties have sealed each other's copy of this chirograph.

Testibus: Domino Iohanne de Aungervile milite, Willelmo del Haye, Roberto de Bordeshowe, Reginaldo Rodland, Iohanne fratre eius, Willelmo Waryn, Ricardo de Clynk, Iohanne le Viner et aliis.   29 September 1291

TNA, E40/3840. 176 × 95mm maximum to top of indentations, 16mm turnup, seal and tag missing. Endorsed: Sprouton (16c.).

533. Notification that, whereas a dispute had arisen between the prior and convent on the one part and Robert of Boss Hall (*Bordeshowe'*) on the other, upon various rents demanded from various tenements, namely that the religious had demanded from Robert 6s 6d annual rent for a piece of land in Brooks (*Brok'*) called 'Provencatresi' and 18d for another piece which Robert holds in the township of Sproughton (*Sprouton'*) called 'Gumboldeslond', and Robert had demanded from the religious 8s annual rent for a piece of land in Sproughton called 'Liketonelond': finally by the intervention of friends hereupon they have agreed in this manner, namely that the prior and convent have granted for themselves and their successors to Robert, Nichola his wife and Robert's heirs the said two pieces of land in perpetuity, to have and to hold of the religious and their successors, rendering annually to the religious in respect thereof 3s 6d, namely for 'Gumboldeslond' 18d in three instalments at the feasts of St Michael, Easter and the Nativity of St John the Baptist, and for 'Provencatresi' 2s in four instalments at the feasts of St Michael, St Andrew, Easter and the Nativity of St John the Baptist, for all services, customs, aids, exactions and demands. For this concession and for the salvation of the souls of his ancestors, Robert, for himself and his heirs, has utterly remitted and quitclaimed the said 8s annual rent to the prior and convent in perpetuity, so that neither he nor his heirs may henceforth be able to make any claim to the 8s rent. In testimony whereof the parties have sealed each other's copy of this chirograph. At Ipswich, on the Vigil of the Apostles Peter and Paul, 30 Edward I.   28 June 1302

TNA, E40/3842. 228 × 118mm, 18mm turnup, slit for tag but none survives. Parts of CYROGRAFUM visible written across the indentations at the top. Endorsed: redditus resolutus priori sancti Petri. vi d' iii s' vi d' [*sic*]. (The hand of this endorsement is very similar to that of the charter text and is presumably of similar date.) Brok' (late medieval).

534. Notification of an agreement between the prior and convent on the one part and Ralph of Tendring (*Tendryngg'*)[1] on the other, that whereas a dispute had arisen between them, namely that the religious had demanded from Ralph 7s 3d annual rent out of certain lands and tenements in Sproughton (*Sprouton'*) called 'Lyketonelond', at length by the intervention of mutual friends they are thus agreed, namely that Ralph has granted, for himself and his heirs, that they will pay the 7s 3d annual rent to the prior and convent and their successors in perpetuity at three terms, that is to say, at the feasts of St Michael, Easter and the Nativity of St John the Baptist. For faithful performance and observation, the parties have sealed each other's copy of this chirograph. At Ipswich, Monday next after the feast of St Hilary, 22 Edward III. 19 January 1349

TNA, E40/3401. 244 × 121mm maximum, to top of indentations, 30mm turnup, 100mm tag, with a second tag, 45mm, sewn to the tag bearing Ralph's seal; the seal in dark wax with the device of a stag's head with a cross between the antlers; legend illegible. CYROGRAPHUM partly visible between indentations. Endorsed: Sprowton. De Rad'lpho Te'dring viis. iiid.; then a second line, now rubbed and illegible (*c.* 14/15c.).

1 Probably the manor of Tendring [Hall] in Stoke-by-Nayland; possibly Tendring in the hundred of that name in Essex.

THURLESTON

535. Notification by Prior William and the convent that they have granted in exchange, given, and by this charter confirmed to Martin Justus (*Iustuse*) of Thurleston (*Thurlestone*), five pieces of land in Thurleston, of which one lies at the headlands of the crofts formerly of Alan Justus and John Cayman, and adjoins 'Estmedwe' on the west side and abuts north on Martin's land called 'Berenaker'; another piece lies between the land of Robert Blakeman and the land of Robert Ovebon, and abuts west on the land formerly of Alice of the Well (*de Fonte*); the third piece lies between the land formerly of Seful of Thurleston and the wood called 'Wlpet' on one side and Martin's land on the other; the fourth piece abuts south on the same piece, and lies lengthways next to the land of John Algor on the east; and the fifth piece called 'le Lothemere' lies next to Martin's land on the north; in exchange for three pieces of land in Thurleston, of which one lies next to the land called 'Androsdeleyre', another abuts north on 'Osmedwe', and the third lies between the land of the prior and convent on one side and the land of Roger May on the other; to have and to hold the said five pieces to him and his heirs, or to whomsoever they may wish to give, sell, bequeath or assign them, freely, quietly, rightly, in peace, in fee and by inheritance, in exchange for the said three pieces, of them and their successors. Notification moreover that they have granted and confirmed to Martin Justus, for his homage and service and for 2s of silver which he has given them for a fine, six pieces of land in Thurleston, of which one lies next to 'Medewytoft' and abuts east on 'le Norhtmedwe'; another lies above the pasture of the rector of Akenham church, at the headland of 'Medewytoft' on the east; the third piece lies in the field called 'Bereht' between the land of Richard de Breuse on one side and the land of John Baldewin on the other, and abuts south on Martin's land; the fourth lies similarly upon 'Bereht', between the land of Roger May and the land of Margaret Lolt, and abuts on the land called 'le Brocesslade'; the fifth piece lies similarly in 'Bereht' next to 'Wansiesmere', and abuts similarly on 'le Brocsclade'; and the sixth piece lies at 'le Kyzeres', between the lands 'Ovebon'; to have and to hold of them and their successors to him and his heirs, or to whomsoever they may wish to give, sell, bequeath or assign them, freely, quietly, rightly and in peace, in fee and by inheritance; rendering annually to them and their successors one clove of garlic at Christmas for all services, customs, suits of court and demands; doing however homage and the due service for two pieces of land which they [*the prior and convent*] held of the fee of Adam of Claydon, according to the tenor of the charter of feoffment which Adam sometime made to Margery of Rede, formerly anchoress of Thurleston.[1] Warranty by the prior and convent of the said five and six pieces of land to Martin and his heirs or assigns against all people in perpetuity. Notification moreover that they have granted and utterly quitclaimed, for themselves and their successors, to the aforenamed Martin, two pieces of land which they sometime held of the fee of the late Aylmer Pigel in Thurleston, to have and to hold to him and his heirs or assigns, or to whomsoever they may wish to give, sell, bequeath or assign them, freely, quietly, rightly, in peace, in fee and by inheritance. Sealed with their common seal for perpetual validity.

Hiis testibus: Baldewino de Walle, Ada de Cleydone, Roberto de Crakeford, Willelmo de Ey', Ricardo Algor, Willelmo de Blanchevil', Martino de Akenham, Alano Iustuse, Iohanne Ade, Augustino Brid, Iordano Ialle et aliis.

[14 October 1267 x January 1289; probably before 1280]

TNA, E40/3323. 204 × 175mm, 21mm turnup, 57mm tag, seal missing. The tag is made from re-used parchment, but so rubbed as to be illegible. Endorsed: Thurleston (16/17c.).

1 See no. 291, which is however incomplete.

Date: Prior William III (of Seckford)'s election received the royal assent on 14 October 1267; he resigned early in 1289, and the royal licence to elect was issued on 7 February. Alan Justus attests other charters from the 1230s (no. 460), and is unlikely to have been active after the 1270s.

WHERSTEAD

536. Agreement (*hec est convencio*) between Prior J[ohn of St Nicholas] and the convent on the one part and Hugh son of Gilbert de Reymes of Wherstead [*Whersted*] on the other, made on the day of the Nativity of the Blessed Virgin Mary, 18 Edward I, namely that whereas Hugh was bound to the prior and convent in 5s rent for certain tenements which he holds of them in Wherstead, and also in 12d rent for a piece of meadow formerly of William, vicar of Wherstead, in the same place, Hugh has remitted, for himself and his heirs, to the prior and convent and their successors in allowance of part of the rent, 18d which the prior and convent ought to pay to him for a tenement formerly Edmund Guthlok's in Wherstead, to have and to hold the said tenements [*sic*] to the prior and convent and their successors of Hugh and his heirs, by homage and the service of one clove annually at the Nativity of the Blessed John the Baptist for all services, customs, suits of court and demands. Also Hugh has given and granted to the prior and convent and their successors 4s 6d rent in allowance of the remaining rent, to be taken annually from his houses in Ipswich (*Gippewyco*) which were formerly of Hugh de Reymes of Ipswich, next to the fish market on the west, in two instalments, 2s 3d at Easter and the feast of St Michael; on condition that the prior and convent may distrain on the houses for the rent as often as it shall be in arrears, according to the custom of the town. For this gift, grant and remission the prior and convent by unanimous consent have remitted to Hugh and his heirs 6s rent which they used to take from the lands which Hugh holds of them in Wherstead; to have and to hold to Hugh, his heirs and assigns, of the prior and convent, by homage and the service of one rose annually at the Nativity of St John the Baptist, for all services, customs, suits of court and demands. In testimony whereof the parties have sealed each other's copy of this chirograph.

Testibus: Domino Roberto de Offord,[1] Domino Ricardo de Holebrok', Domino Gerardo de Wachesham, Thoma de Frestone, Hamone de Wolferstone, Iohanne de Pesehal', Willelmo de Cleydone, Martino Iustus, Iohanne Oliver, Iohanne Aunsys, Roberto Hasting', Willelmo Coco de Wherstede. At Ipswich, the year and day abovesaid.   8 September 1290

SROI, HD 1538/271/3. 270 × 162mm maximum (top edge indented, parts of CYROGRAFUM visible), 21mm turnup, 126mm tag, lettered 'd' on front. Seal round, in dark brown wax, 55mm diameter. Device a cruciform church, with full-face busts [SS Peter and Paul] on either side of central tower. Legend: + SIGILLUM ECCLE SCOR' PETRI ET PAULI DE GIPESWIC (the + appears to form the finial of the central tower). Reverse plain, no counterseal. Endorsed: Ipswich 18 E. I. A.D. 1290 (19c.); Whersted (?15c.); tempe Edw. filii Henrici (16c.); Phillipps MS 27820 (19/20c.).

   1 Roberto de Hufford (i.e. Ufford, not Orford) in the counterpart (no. 537).

537. Counterpart of 536.   8 September 1290

BL Stowe charter 411. 257 × 149mm to top of indentation (parts of CYROGRAFUM visible). Height includes a folded-out turnup of 9mm. No medieval endorsements, but Whersted (17c.).

538. Agreement (*convenit*) made on St James's day, 21 Edward I between Sir John the prior and the convent on the one part and Adam son of William le Keu of Wherstead (*Wersted'*) on the other, whereby, since the prior and convent used to demand against Adam 4s 5d annual rent and suit of their court of Bourne [*Hall*] (*Brunne*) or Pannington [*Hall*] (*Paniton'*),[1] every three weeks, they have granted for themselves and their successors to Adam the whole tenement which he holds or held of them in Wherstead, to have and to hold to him and his heirs or assigns in perpetuity by the said service of 4s 5d at the accustomed terms; so that the prior and convent may not henceforth demand of him, his heirs or assigns, suit of their court of Bourne or Pannington for the tenement except twice a year, namely the next courts after the feast of St Michael and Easter. Saving to the prior and convent all other things rightly pertaining to the tenement. In testimony whereof the parties have sealed each other's copy of this chirograph, the prior and convent with the common seal of their chapter.

Hiis testibus: Dominis Iohanne de Holebroc et Girardo de Wachesham militibus, Hugone de Reymes, Roberto Hasting', Thoma de Freston', Hamone de Wlfferston', Iohanne de Fonte, Willelmo Tyvile, Andrea Arinde, Gregorio de Holemedwe et aliis. 25 July 1293

JRL, CRU 748. 254 × 116mm to top of indentations, parts of CYROGRAPHUM visible. Turnup 22mm, 96mm tag. Seal 31 × 44mm, natural wax, design of ears of grain; legend: + S' ADE: … OCII. Endorsed: Werstede (?15/16c.); Wersted (17c.).

> 1 According to Copinger (*Manors*, VI, 121), the manor of Pannington Hall in Wherstead belonged in 1202 to Gerard of Wattisham (de Wachesham), who gave the advowson of Wherstead to the priory. See, however, no. 309 in this edition, which shows that the lands of Pannington were quitclaimed to the prior and canons in 1196.

CRETINGHAM

539. Grant by way of exchange by William Bastard of Cretingham to Prior Gilbert and the canons, of a piece of meadow in Cretingham abutting north on the mill pond of Master Ralph de Ainneus, in exchange for a piece of meadow of the free land of Cretingham church called 'le Harwe', between the water conduit from Cretingham bridge to 'Osewen' and the meadow of Ranulf Haliday, in perpetuity.
[16 September 1235 x 23 May 1248]

TNA, E40/3935. 174 × 69mm, 21mm turnup, 155mm tag, seal missing. Endorsed: pratum ex [*illegible*] (15/16c.).

Sciant presentes et futuri quod ego Willelmus Bastard de Gretingham concessi et in excambiis dedi Gileberto priori Sancti Petri de Gipwico et canonicis ibidem Deo servientibus, unam peciam prati mei in Gretingham, unde unum capud buttat [*sic*] super liberam terram ecclesie de Gretingham versus austrum, et aliud capud buttat super stagnum molendini magistri Radulfi de Ainneus versus aquilonem, pro una pecia prati libere terre ecclesie de Gretingham que iacet inter aque ductum qui se extendit a ponte de Gretingham versus Osewen et pratum Ranulfi Haliday, et vocatur le Harwe, quam predicti prior et canonici mihi dederunt et heredibus meis in excambiis pro alia pecia prenominata inperpetuum. Testibus Willelmo de Holebroc, Willelmo le Deneys, Adam [*sic*] Wylot, Adam filio Roges, Galfrido filio Warin, Adam filio Nicholai, Simone Bastard, Simone Turpin, Rogero Overhe, Willelmo capellano qui istam cartam confecit, et aliis.

Date: After the bishop of Norwich's confirmation of the appropriation of the church to the priory (no. 486), and before the licence to elect Prior Gilbert's successor was issued on 23 May 1248.

540. Indenture between John de Mounteaux and the prior and canons of St Peter of Ipswich (*Gippewyco*), whereby John has quitclaimed to them 2s of the annual rent of 2s 3d by which service they hold one and a half acres of land and half an acre of meadow of his fee in Cretingham (*Gretyngham*), whereof three roods of land lie between the land of John Gynour and the land of William Pylte, the other three roods of land lie among the lands formerly of William Lene, and the half-acre of meadow abuts on 'Oswanne bregge'; so that the prior and canons and their successors may have and hold the said tenement of John and his heirs by the annual service of 3d, payable at the feasts of St Michael and Easter, for all service in perpetuity. The prior and canons grant, for them and their successors, that John and his heirs may distrain upon the tenement for the rent and arrears, and retain the distrained goods until full satisfaction shall be made. In testimony whereof the parties have sealed each other's copy of this indenture. At Ipswich, Thursday the feast of St Margaret the Virgin, 9 Edward III.   20 July 1335

TNA, E40/3703. 232 × 103mm maximum, to top of indentations, parts of CYROGRAPHUM visible, 20mm turnup, 95mm tag. Seal 37mm round, heraldic design, legend gone. Endorsed: Gr'tyngham (17c.), and one illegible endorsement.

APPENDIX 1: CONCORDANCE OF ORIGINAL CHARTERS IN THE EDITION

This concordance lists all the original charters, including those which are substituted for their cartulary copies in Part I of the edition. It consists of two parts, the first arranged in order of the running numbers allocated to the charters solely for the edition, the second in order of their archival references in the various record repositories where they are held. Where no repository is named, charters are among the Ancient Deeds series in the National Archives (TNA). The remainder (a small minority) are held at the Bodleian Library, Oxford, the British Library (BL), the John Rylands University Library, Manchester (JRUL), and the Ipswich Branch of the Suffolk Record Office (SROI). The arrangement of those charters in TNA seems entirely random, and this concordance should facilitate cross-referencing.

ORIGINAL CHARTERS IN RUNNING-NUMBER ORDER, AS IN THE EDITION

1	BL Stowe charter 408	170	E40/3432
6	E40/3523	193	E40/3862
7	E40/3522	195	E40/3854
31	E42/229	209	E40/3503
34	Bodleian Suffolk charter 204	210	E40/3907
40	E40/3441	214	E40/3679
42	E40/3377	216	E40/3855
43	E40/3852	219	E40/3772
44	E40/3284	228	E40/3931
45	E40/3426	235	E40/3914
46	E40/3309	286	E40/3438
48	E40/3425	287	E40/3319
49	E40/3417	339A,B	Patent roll inspeximus,
50	E40/3305		C66/190, mem. 17
75	E40/3916	340	E40/3405
76	E40/3902	341	E40/3291
77	E40/3901	342A,B	E40/3819A,B
82	E40/3796	343	E40/3633
83	E40/3899	344	E40/3763
93	E40/3872	345	E40/3534
120	E40/3443	346	E40/3945
138	E40/3837	347	E40/3826
159	SROI, HA93/2/293	348	E40/3967
168	E40/3317	349	E40/3851

350	E40/3458	397	E40/3495
351	E40/3398	398	E40/3531
352	E40/3397	399	E40/3857
353	E40/3278	400	E40/3674
354	E40/3442	401	E40/3732
355	E40/3410	402	E40/3712
356	E40/3925	403	E40/3540
357	E40/3276	404	E40/3414
358	E40/3639	405	E40/3391
359	E40/5484	406	E40/3697
360	E40/3446	407	E40/3587
361	E40/3634	408	E40/3586
362	E40/3839	409	E40/3589
363	E40/3838	410	E40/3588
364	E40/3394	411	E40/3638
365	E40/3880	412	E40/3618
366	E40/3877	413	E40/3871
367	E40/3875	414	E40/3268
368	E40/3900	415	E40/3392
369	E40/3535	416	E40/3390
370	E40/3536	417	E40/3290
371	E40/3321	418	E40/3863
372	E40/3301	419	E40/3868
373	E40/3407	420	E40/3479
374	E40/3600	421	E40/3730
375	Bodleian Suffolk charter 214	422	E40/3731
376	E40/3949	423	E40/3424
377	E40/3707	424	E40/3558
378	E40/3293	425	E40/3940
379	E40/3292	426	E40/3332
380	E40/3294	427	E40/3333
381	E40/3793	428	*Collectanea Topographica,*
382	E40/3782		etc. 242–43
383	E40/3664	429	E40/3404
384	E40/3858	430	E40/3853
385	E40/3502	431	E40/3525
386	E40/3665	432	*Collectanea Topographica,*
387	E40/3393		etc. 243
388	E40/3688	433	E40/3524
389	E40/3909	434	E40/3419
390	E40/3635	435	E40/3551
391	E40/3636	436	E40/3841
392	Bodleian Suffolk charter 207	437	E40/3846
393A–C	E40/3776	438	E40/3844
394	E40/3960	439	E40/3845
395	E40/3512	440	E40/3277
396	E40/3848	441	E40/3412

442	E40/3418		489	E40/3640
443	E40/3435		490	E40/3629
444	E40/3272		491	BL Stowe charter 407
445	E40/3847		492	E40/3860
446	E40/3648		493	E40/3704
447	E40/3646		494	E40/3516
448	E40/3434		495	E40/3740
449	E40/3843		496	E40/3549
450	E40/3400		497	BL Stowe charter 410
451	E40/3592		498	BL Stowe charter 409
452	E40/3579		499	E40/3273
453	E40/3267		500	E42/424
454	E40/3578		501	E40/3630
455	E40/3318		502	E40/3727
456	E40/3715		503	E40/3655
457	E40/3759		504	SROI, HA93/3/24
458	E40/3280		505	E40/3637
459	E40/3281		506	E40/3645
460	E40/3310		507	E40/3644
461	E40/3684		508	E40/3556
462	E40/3677		509	E40/3921
463	E40/3415		510	SROI, HA93/3/52
464	E40/3598		511	E40/3937
465	E40/3395		512	E40/3413
466	E40/3728		513	E40/3650
467	E40/3396		514	E40/3651
468	E40/3934		515	E40/3649
469	E40/3948		516	JRUL CRU 756
470	E40/3771		517	E40/3428
471	E40/3888		518	E40/3429
472	E40/3885		519	E40/3745
473	E40/3886		520	E40/3773
474	E40/3696		521	E40/3735
475	E40/3874		522	E40/3683
476	JRUL CRU 751		523	E40/3533
477	JRUL CRU 754		524	E40/3406
478	JRUL CRU 755		525	E40/3717
479	JRUL CRU 757		526	SROI, HA93/2/159
480	E40/3676		527	E40/3527
481	E40/3348		528	E40/3751
482	E40/3347		529	E40/3548
483	E40/14020		530	E42/408
484	E40/3349		531	E40/3463
485	E40/3954		532	E40/3840
486	E42/302		533	E40/3842
487	E40/3861		534	E40/3401
488	E40/3953		535	E40/3323

536	SROI, Iveagh, HD1538/271/3
537	BL Stowe charter 411
538	JRUL CRU 748

539	E40/3935
540	E40/3703

ORIGINAL CHARTERS IN DOCUMENT REFERENCE NUMBER ORDER

E40/3267	453	E40/3398	351
E40/3268	414	E40/3400	450
E40/3272	444	E40/3401	534
E40/3273	499	E40/3404	429
E40/3276	357	E40/3405	340
E40/3277	440	E40/3406	524
E40/3278	353	E40/3407	373
E40/3280	458	E40/3410	355
E40/3281	459	E40/3412	441
E40/3284	44	E40/3413	512
E40/3290	417	E40/3414	404
E40/3291	341	E40/3415	463
E40/3292	379	E40/3417	49
E40/3293	378	E40/3418	442
E40/3294	380	E40/3419	434
E40/3301	372	E40/3424	423
E40/3305	50	E40/3425	48
E40/3309	46	E40/3426	45
E40/3310	460	E40/3428	517
E40/3317	168	E40/3429	518
E40/3318	455	E40/3432	170
E40/3319	287	E40/3434	448
E40/3321	371	E40/3435	443
E40/3323	535	E40/3438	286
E40/3332	426	E40/3441	40
E40/3333	427	E40/3442	354
E40/3347	482	E40/3443	120
E40/3348	481	E40/3446	360
E40/3349	484	E40/3458	350
E40/3377	42	E40/3463	531
E40/3390	416	E40/3479	420
E40/3391	405	E40/3495	397
E40/3392	415	E40/3502	385
E40/3393	387	E40/3503	209
E40/3394	364	E40/3512	395
E40/3395	465	E40/3516	494
E40/3396	467	E40/3522	7
E40/3397	352	E40/3523	6

E40/3524	433	E40/3679	214
E40/3525	431	E40/3683	522
E40/3527	527	E40/3684	461
E40/3531	398	E40/3688	388
E40/3533	523	E40/3696	474
E40/3534	345	E40/3697	406
E40/3535	369	E40/3703	540
E40/3536	370	E40/3704	493
E40/3540	403	E40/3707	377
E40/3548	529	E40/3712	402
E40/3549	496	E40/3715	456
E40/3551	435	E40/3717	525
E40/3556	508	E40/3727	502
E40/3558	424	E40/3728	466
E40/3578	454	E40/3730	421
E40/3579	452	E40/3731	422
E40/3586	408	E40/3732	401
E40/3587	407	E40/3735	521
E40/3588	410	E40/3740	495
E40/3589	409	E40/3745	519
E40/3592	451	E40/3751	528
E40/3598	464	E40/3759	457
E40/3600	374	E40/3763	344
E40/3618	412	E40/3771	470
E40/3629	490	E40/3772	219
E40/3630	501	E40/3773	520
E40/3633	343	E40/3776	393A–C
E40/3634	361	E40/3782	382
E40/3635	390	E40/3793	381
E40/3636	391	E40/3796	82
E40/3637	505	E40/3819A,B	342A,B
E40/3638	411	E40/3826	347
E40/3639	358	E40/3837	138
E40/3640	489	E40/3838	363
E40/3644	507	E40/3839	362
E40/3645	506	E40/3840	532
E40/3646	447	E40/3841	436
E40/3648	446	E40/3842	533
E40/3649	515	E40/3843	449
E40/3650	513	E40/3844	438
E40/3651	514	E40/3845	439
E40/3655	503	E40/3846	437
E40/3664	383	E40/3847	445
E40/3665	386	E40/3848	396
E40/3674	400	E40/3851	349
E40/3676	480	E40/3852	43
E40/3677	462	E40/3853	430

E40/3854	195	E40/3953	488
E40/3855	216	E40/3954	485
E40/3857	399	E40/3960	394
E40/3858	384	E40/3967	348
E40/3860	492	E40/5484	359
E40/3861	487	E40/14020	483
E40/3862	193	E42/229	31
E40/3863	418	E42/302	486
E40/3868	419	E42/408	530
E40/3871	413	E42/424	500
E40/3872	93	C66/190, mem. 17,	
E40/3874	475	Patent Roll Edward III	339A,B
E40/3875	367		
E40/3877	366	BL Stowe charter 407	491
E40/3880	365	BL Stowe charter 408	1
E40/3885	472	BL Stowe charter 409	498
E40/3886	473	BL Stowe charter 410	497
E40/3888	471	BL Stowe charter 411	537
E40/3899	83	Bodleian Suffolk charter 204	34
E40/3900	368	Bodleian Suffolk charter 207	392
E40/3901	77	Bodleian Suffolk charter 214	375
E40/3902	76		
E40/3907	210	JRUL CRU 748	538
E40/3909	389	JRUL CRU 751	476
E40/3914	235	JRUL CRU 754	477
E40/3916	75	JRUL CRU 755	478
E40/3921	509	JRUL CRU 756	516
E40/3925	356	JRUL CRU 757	479
E40/3931	228		
E40/3934	468	SROI Iveagh, HD1538/271/3	536
E40/3935	539	SROI Saumarez, HA93/2/159	526
E40/3937	511	SROI Saumarez, HA93/2/293	159
E40/3940	425	SROI Saumarez, HA93/3/24	504
E40/3945	346	SROI Saumarez, HA93/3/52	510
E40/3948	469	*Collectanea Topographica*, etc. IV	
E40/3949	376	pp. 242–43	428
		p. 243	432

APPENDIX 2: CORRIGENDA TO PART I

p. xv, line 16:   Prior William (I), *for* occurs 20 October 1292, *read* occurs 20 October 1192
p. 12, paragraph 2, line 7:   *for* duravit, *read* duraverit
p. 59, paragraph 4, line 6:   *for* in respect of the mill (318), *read* in respect of the mill (313)
p. 76, paragraph 1, line 6:   *for* HA93/2/193, *read* HA93/2/293
p. 90 (no. 15), line 11:   *for* solidatus, *read* solidatas
p. 99 (no. 30), line 7:   *for* qui, *read* que
p. 101 (no. 33), line 13:   *for* donam, *read* donum
p. 106 (no. 40), line 14:   *for* Hagneford, *read* Hageneford
p. 109 (no. 44), line 2:   *for* 24s-worth, *read* 24s ¾d-worth
p. 138 (no. 92), line 16:   *for* guaranteed, *read* granted
p. 164 (no. 140), line 1:   *for* terra Osberti, *read* terram Osberti
p. 179 (no. 163), lines 2 and 6: *for* Agnes, *read* Alice
p. 185 (no. 172), line 11:   *for* solidos, *read* solidis
p. 186 (no. 173), line 11:   *for* tenentum, *read* tenementum
p. 206 (no. 207), line 9:   *for* clerico, *read* clerici
p. 235 (no. 253), line 5:   *for* (no. 254), *read* (no. 252)
p. 255 (no. 290), line 10:   *for* darios, *read* denarios
p. 262 (no. 296), line 3:   *for* St George, *read* St Gregory
p. 290 (no. 331), line 23:   *for* May 1244, *read* May 1344

INDEX OF PERSONS AND PLACES

Numerals given first, in *italic* type, refer to page numbers in the introduction. There follow, in Roman type, the document numbers in the volumes. Consecutive numbers are compressed to save space. A 'W' after a reference to a personal name indicates a witness to a charter. The names of parishes, where not embedded in surnames, are given in capital letters; all are in Suffolk, unless otherwise indicated.

Aci, Alexander, son of Geoffrey, 386W
Acras, John, 492W
Ada, wife of Baldwin Tirepeil, 43–4
Adam,
    the carpenter, 506W, 507
    the merchant, 195W and n., 196 and n.,
        209W–10W, 214W, 216W, 219W,
        225n., 235W, 287W, 459W, 461W,
        463W
    ?son of, 512W
    son of Humfrey, 6W
    son of Nicholas, 539W
    son of Osbert, 435
    son of Roges, 539W
    son of dean of Westerfield, 286W
        and n., 290 and n., 460W, 464W,
        465W and n.
    son of, *see* John
Ade, John, of Thurleston, 464W, 466W,
    467W, 496W, 521
Agatha,
    sister of Gratian son of John the
        chaplain, 380
    sister of Sara, daughter of Roger of
        Carlton, *see* Agatha, wife of
        William Other (Oter)
    widow of John Constantine (Costin),
        15, 31–2, 393A, 520–1
    wife of Geoffrey Bunban, *30*, 163
    wife of William Other (Oter), *35, 64*,
        146 and n., 155–7n.
Agnes, *2*, 305
    daughter of Baldwin Lolt of Thurleston,
        see Agnes wife of Robert
        Blakeman
    daughter of Cecilia of Freston, *40*, 30
    daughter of Roger (of) Bramford,
        44–5, 63, 138, 143n., 436n., 444n.,
        448n., 450, 451 and n., 453–4
    mother of Adam de Blancheville, *62*,
        170–1W, 172 and n., 179n., 210n.

    mother of John son of Baldwin of
        Peasenhall, 471–2
    widow of Roger of Badley, *24, 59–60*,
        30
    widow of Roger (of) Bramford, *44, 63*,
        449
    widow of William the clerk, 387
    wife of Arnold de Colville, *19*, 308, 482,
        484n.
    wife of Edmund Plumbe, *30*, 163
    wife of Ralph son of Walter, 313
    wife of Robert Blakeman, *27*, 278
    wife of William de Ceresi, *29*, 4, 5
Aguilun, Robert, 150n.
    wife of, *see* Margaret
Aigneus (Agneys, Ainneus),
    John de, 490W, 500W, 501W
    Ralf de (mr), 539
    Robert de (knight), 489W
Airmyn, William, bishop of Norwich, *3,
    14, 56*
AKENHAM, *29*, 185n.
    charters, 234, 320
    court of, *62*, 337
    court of Sir Richard de Brewse, 291n.
    court of Sir William Ruffus, 197
    expansion of canons' holdings in, *28–9*
    highway from, 246
    inhabitants of, *see* Bosco, Robert de; Ry,
        Robert de; Wood, Robert of the
    land of rector of, in Thurleston, 291
    lord of, *see* Breuse, Sir Richard de
    mill of, 180
    parson of, 337
        land of, 223, 271
        pasture of, 535
    places in, Nexerstowe, *23*, 337
    priory holdings in, *45, 65*
    priory rents in, *29, 45–6*
    tithe of, *23*, 291, 337

INDEX OF SUBJECTS

Numerals given first, in *italic* type, refer to page numbers in the introduction. There follow, in Roman type, the document numbers in the volumes. Consecutive numbers are compressed to save space.

Henry of; Cornhill, Reginald of;
Creping', Walter de; FitzNeal,
Richard; Garland, John de (mr);
Gernun, Rudulf; Glaner, John;
Heriard, Richard de; Insula,
Godfrey de; Insula, Simon de;
Insula, William de; Lexinton,
Robert of; London, William of;
Mantel, Robert; Mileton, Thomas
de; Muschet, William; Oger, son
of Oger; Osbert, son of Hervey;
Otho, son of William; Oxford, John
of, bishop of Norwich; Pattishall,
Simon of; Prestone, Gilbert of; R.,
archdeacon of Hereford; Ralegh,
William de; Richard, archdeacon
of Ely; Ridel, Geoffrey, bishop of
Ely; Robert, son of Roger; Roger,
son of Remfr'; Ruffus, William;
Saukevill, Jordan de; Segrave,
Stephen of; Seyng', Richard de;
Shardelowe (Sherdelawe), John de;
Sherdelawe, Robert de; Usseborne,
Thomas de; Verdun, Walter; Walter,
Hubert; Walter, son of Robert;
Warenne, William de; Wautone,
Simon of (mr); Weyland, Thomas;
Wurthested, John de

King, *see* Charles I; Edward I;
Edward II; Edward III; Henry I;
Henry II; Henry III; Henry VIII;
John; Richard I; Richard II; Stephen
King's service, *see also* House-rent
(*Hadgabulum*); Scutage
defence from, 438

Lamp, *see also* Light
grant for maintenance of
in St Matthew's church, Ipswich,
307n.
before altar of BVM in priory
church, 11, 12, 32–3, 397, 465
before cross in priory church, 51,
407–8
Land, *passim, see also* Ware land
acquitted from indebtedness to Jews,
138
alienated, 292n., 295, 298–9
for building, 495
leased to canons, 241
of canons, protected, 339A, B
of increment, 6, 468, 499
title to, proved by king's precept, 428

Lane (*venella*), 436
Lawsuit, 16, 19, 53, 245, 250n., 321, 325–6,
328, 332
Lease, 54–6
as security for loan, 66, 241
consideration for, 55, 463
covenant against,
committing waste, 55, 503, 511
cutting timber, except for repairs,
55, 510
for distraint, 55
for maintenance and repair by
lessee, 55, 506, 511–12
for maintenance and repair by
lessor, 55, 509
for service to capital lords, 55, 511
for duration of life, 505, 509, 516
for duration of lives, 55, 506
surrender of, 55, 420, 507, 513
for 2 years, 55, 511
for 5 years, 55, 504
for 7 years, 55, 508
for 9 years, 55, 463
for 10 years, 55, 502
for 16 years, 55, 503
for 99 years, 55, 510
for 100 years, 55, 515
from year to year at lessors' pleasure,
54–5, 512
in association with
brother, 463
mother, 463
son, 510
wife, 502, 515
to lessee and heirs, 503, 515
and assigns, 504
to priory servants, 14, 506
Letters patent,
of prior, 334
royal, 72, 339, 367
Library of Congress, 73
Librate, 135n.
Licence,
to dispense with Statute of Mortmain,
52, 366
to purchase tenements of abbot of
Aumale, 517
Light, maintenance of, before altar of BVM
in priory church, 48, 51, 375, 377,
488, *see also* Lamp
'Little Domesday' of Ipswich, 5
Loaf, conventual, 17, 528